Black Philosopher,
White Academy

Black Philosopher, White Academy

The Career of William Fontaine

Bruce Kuklick

PENN

UNIVERSITY OF PENNSYLVANIA PRESS

PHILADELPHIA

Published by
University of Pennsylvania Press
Philadelphia, Pennsylvania 19104–4112

Printed in the United States of America on acid-free paper

10   9   8   7   6   5   4   3   2   1

A Cataloging-in-Publication record is available from the Library of Congress.
ISBN 978-0-8122-4098-6

For Deborah Broadnax and Barbara Savage,
teachers and friends

CONTENTS

PREFACE ix

INTRODUCTION 1

CHAPTER ONE
A Cultured Education 5

CHAPTER TWO
A Student of Philosophy 20

CHAPTER THREE
Ambition Constrained 41

CHAPTER FOUR
The Sociology of Knowledge 53

CHAPTER FIVE
Social Change and World War II 64

CHAPTER SIX
The Ambiguity of Success 82

CHAPTER SEVEN
Social Philosophy and Civil Rights 95

CHAPTER EIGHT
Conservative Pan-Africanism 107

CHAPTER NINE
White Racism and Black Power 116

CONCLUSION 135

NOTES 137
BIBLIOGRAPHY OF THE WRITINGS OF WILLIAM
    FONTAINE 161
SOURCES AND ACKNOWLEDGMENTS 165
INDEX 167

PREFACE

IN THE MIDDLE of 2001 the American Academy of Arts and Sciences commissioned me to write an essay about philosophy in the United States after World War II and about the way the university system housed this scholarly discipline. The academy did not want a study of great American thinkers in philosophy but an appraisal of how the field served undergraduates and of what connection the area of inquiry had to other subjects and to the outside world. In working on the project, whenever I traveled, I went to university libraries to explore the records institutions might have kept. I was interested in student enrollments, courses taught, interdisciplinary cooperation, and other peculiar aspects of campus life. The pickings were slim. In many cases schools do not keep files from academic departments at all. In other instances relevant documents show up in the collections of deans and provosts and presidents. Where records survive, they look erratic—material for one span of years gets saved, while for another span everything disappears. Sometimes librarians have saved enormous quantities of the personal papers of individual philosophers, and sometimes the material in them pertains to the practices of the discipline at a given time. Sometimes, however, someone seems to have performed triage on these collections of philosophers, or pertinent material does not get preserved. I could never predict what I would find, and I never stumbled on extensive information applicable to my topic.

For well over a year, I neglected to search at my own school, the University of Pennsylvania. I had gone to Penn in the early 1960s as an undergraduate philosophy major, and I supposed that I knew the place well. In late December 2002, nonetheless, I decided to visit the University Archives, located in the bowels of Penn's football stadium, Franklin Field. The existing records paralleled those at other colleges. I located some departmental information in the cartons of mail, publications, typescripts, and lecture notes of long-dead professors of philosophy. Penn had no documentation for some stretches of time, but the staff did come across a substantial amount of material from the period when I studied there. In addition, the archivist asked me if I wanted to see the personal manuscripts of William Fontaine, a black man who had taught in Penn's Philosophy Department for some twenty years. Fontaine had lectured to me. I had vaguely positive memories of his classes, but I could barely recall him or them.

It was the mid-afternoon of a gray day shortly before Christmas, and I wanted to get home. Yet I knew in the end I would have to examine everything in the Penn depository, and I was told the Fontaine papers were limited. I would check them. In fact the collection was minute: two pieces of African sculpture, a plaque for a teaching award, and one small box of correspondence. Most of the paper documents consisted of notes for a book Fontaine published late in his life, written on the backs of envelopes and old exams. The box also held a quarter-inch-thick file comprising mostly what I call "flimsies," onionskin duplicates of standard forms noting Fontaine's yearly appointment status and salary. A miscellany of mail about departmental affairs made up what remained. I flipped through these messages, and my eye caught one that had printed in a bold hand in the top right-hand corner KUKLICK. Over forty years before Fontaine had recommended me to graduate school. I had no recollection that I had known him well enough even to ask for a reference or that I had even applied to the school to which he had directed the letter. The mere existence of the recommendation stunned me far out of proportion to the importance of the words of praise.

I could hardly look at the carbon copy. I walked out of the small reading room and asked the assistant archivist if she would get the page with my name on it, photocopy it, and put it in an envelope. I walked home with the envelope, mind spinning, and had my wife look at the piece of paper before I was willing to scrutinize it myself.

I am not a superstitious person. But the discovery rattled my metaphysical bones. It summoned me to an era that I hardly recalled and asked me to understand events of which I had been unaware. One of the first black men to cross the color line in higher education, Fontaine, it turned out, had a distinctive historical pedigree. As the only African American philosopher at a first-rank university, he had lived uniquely between the black and white segregated worlds. He had subjected himself, and been subjected, to pressures that astounded me. How had I managed, as a young man, to meet up with such an uncommon human being? What had my relationship with him been like? Why, in Fontaine's tiny collection, had there endured a letter about me?

Why had he, dead in 2002 for almost thirty-five years, tapped me on the shoulder?

Over the next few years, sometimes obsessively, I tried to answer these questions. I began to dream about Fontaine and to refer to him as "Bill," as if he were still around. I first thought I would get a handle on the issues by writing an article on his career at Penn. Five years later I had become absorbed in his compelling life story for its own sake. I framed new questions and, almost beyond my will, composed this book-length biography.

Renown escaped Fontaine. To write about him has required detective and salvage work. The research has sent me on a series of small journeys during which I have harassed librarians and archivists and accessed many collections of documents with far less material about Fontaine than he left behind at Penn. I have, from time to time, come to tears when reading some of the primary sources. I have mercilessly pestered good-natured colleagues with an expertise in African American history. Nothing that I have written depends solely on my own memories, which kept tumbling into my head, although I have used odds and ends from a variety of secondary sources, a scrap here, a scrap there. Scholars can trace my comings and goings from a complete set of footnotes, and my "Sources and Acknowledgments" at the end of this book also indicates where I have come up short. Moreover, I have interviewed over twenty-five people who knew Fontaine. I have, however, gathered nowhere near the material I would have thought necessary to put together a coherent account. The story of Fontaine's life waxes and wanes relative to the evidence I have unearthed for any given time. The project could not have gotten off the ground except as a biography that makes extended use of published writing to track his intellectual development. Still, the overall experience resembles that of a sailor who observes on the water the wreckage of some marine craft and who tries to piece together the nature of the sunken boat from the flotsam on the waves.

I have exploited the available evidence for all that it is worth and more. But the evidence still does not do enough. Attentive readers will note that appropriate qualifying phrases intimate the constraints on the narrative, and readers may well add some qualifications of their own. The shortage of the facts and thus Fontaine's elusiveness as a historical figure have tied themselves, over the last several years, to my own perplexities in getting inside his skin. I realize, moreover, that white institutions have excessively generated the present sources. The lost and unexplained aspects of Fontaine's life and my own difficulties of historical comprehension symbolize for me the mystery of his in-betweenness. In writing the book and attempting to give the man his due, I have often found myself paying a personal debt—but incompletely.

The American philosopher William James once remarked about the pathos of death that all the intensity of a personality is reduced, after death, to a few lines of print, a mere musical note in a symphony. I have had that feeling in reconstructing this life.

Brief is the life of man, and of uncertain duration is his handiwork. . . .
But the echoes from soul to soul will go on as long as human life lasts.
　　—Morris Cohen

Introduction

IN THE SPRING of 1947 the University of Pennsylvania in Philadelphia appointed William Fontaine to a one-year visiting lectureship in its Department of Philosophy for the academic year 1947–48. The black man at once took leave of Morgan State College, an African American school in Maryland that had hired him after World War II as a professor and the chairman of its Philosophy Department. Pennsylvania repeated the arrangement for 1948–49. As part of his entrée into the white academic world, in the summer of 1948, Fontaine applied to take a place in the American Philosophical Association, a prestigious scholarly organization that one could not join merely with a check.[1] The APA traditionally held its annual conventions over the Christmas holidays of the collegiate world, and at the end of 1948 Fontaine made plans to attend the gathering of the premier Eastern Division of the association. The University of Virginia in Charlottesville, Virginia, a few hours to the south, would host the meeting where the APA would formally accept Fontaine into full membership.

Fontaine got a ride down and back with Nelson Goodman, his colleague at Pennsylvania, who was to become known as one of the most formidable professional American philosophers in the fifty years after World War II. Morton White, who was already regarded as an influential student of American thought, also traveled in the car. He taught at Pennsylvania for a few years in the late 1940s and later went to Harvard University and then to a lifetime appointment at the Institute of Advanced Study located near Princeton University. On the way back, Goodman filled his car by giving a lift to the visiting Oxford philosopher A. J. Ayer. Intellectuals knew him as the most famous thinker in the English-speaking world, the aged Bertrand Russell aside. Knowledgeable people interested in the history of British empiricism spoke of its great tradition: John Locke, David Hume, John Stuart Mill, Russell—and Ayer.

Ayer would give one of the two plenary addresses at the meeting; Glenn Morrow, another of Fontaine's colleagues from Pennsylvania, would deliver the second.

All of Fontaine's traveling companions were assimilationist Jews, demanding their acceptance in the Christian civilization in which they lived. They despised prejudice and had a vivid sense of what they saw as the chief issue of World War II, bigotry based on racial stereotypes. Personally fastidious and consistently formally clothed, the white thinkers seemed to challenge the social order to find fault with their accomplishments, intelligence, or culture. Fontaine, too, unfailingly dressed in a suit to signify that he was no ordinary black man. On their arrival in Charlottesville, however, the philosophers crossed the tracks and made their way into the "Nigra' section" of town—the South was of course segregated and Fontaine would not be staying at the official APA hotel. The group found his black lodging house, and the elegantly attired men of mind climbed out of the car and dusted off their garments. The white members of the party helped Fontaine with his luggage and clumsily assisted him on the sidewalk. They saw him into the establishment, professed that they would meet up with him later, and piled back into the automobile. What did they say to one another as they proceeded to the convention? Morton White remembered the end of the trip as "chilling."[2] In his memoirs Ayer too recalled the incident, which prompted a criticism of American racial practices.[3]

The next year, to their credit, these men and others passed a resolution not to hold APA meetings in segregated cities.[4] But I am more interested in Fontaine's response. What kind of impact did experiences of this sort have on him? How did he respond to this shaming in front of men such as Goodman, White, and Ayer? Did he talk about its significance to other African Americans? What did it mean to him, a few hours later, to wait outside the APA's hotel until some white philosopher came to the entrance and told the doorman—was he black?—that Fontaine belonged with the philosophers but of course was not staying at the headquarters?

Black Philosopher, White Academy tells Fontaine's story. Raised in a poor and segregated community in Chester, Pennsylvania in the early part of the twentieth century, Fontaine matriculated at the African American Lincoln University in 1926. Six years of advanced part-time graduate study at the University of Pennsylvania earned him a Ph.D. in philosophy in 1936. He then taught at Southern University in Louisiana and Morgan State College, two more all-black institutions. But the changing racial climate after his service in World War II led to a permanent position in the Philosophy Department at Pennsylvania, where he made a career for two decades.

I have examined Fontaine's ideas and the development of his thought, but more than anything else I have tried to get inside his head and understand his psyche. What did he make of his position? How did it feel to be in his shoes and walk his walk?

For many years one of the very few black academics in the white university world, Fontaine stood well nigh by himself at prestigious institutions as an African American. Perhaps of greatest significance, Fontaine remained alone as the only philosopher of color in the Ivy League at a time when philosophy had its place as a foundational discipline in the collegiate arts and sciences. He had entered the inner circle of what the Caucasian West conceived as its civilizing mission. An oddity in his time, Fontaine in many ways could not represent the overwhelming majority of African American scholars who never broke the racial line. He cherished his status and believed in the promise of American democracy that he personified. But his position took an enormous personal toll. The problematic evolution of his career illuminates both his exceptional nature and the common culture of one sort of "Negro intellectual." African American determination and self-doubt formed this culture. So too did white racism, genuine moral principles on both sides, and the condescending liberalism particularly prevalent after World War II.[5]

Fontaine lived out most of his life in the period just before the fulfillment of the civil rights movement in America in the mid-1960s. During this time America put most on display the discrepancy between its ideals and the reality of the treatment of its black citizens. During World War II and the following Cold War against the old Soviet Union, the United States proclaimed more than ever the "freedom and justice for all" that characterized democratic society. Everyone imbibed the slogan "All men are created equal" with his mother's milk. Yet white America, again and again, turned its collective face from the fact that, in the South, most African Americans could not even vote. In the North, where they had better lives, the white world regularly scorned and despised them. Blacks surely resented their second-class treatment; they resented even more the monumental hypocrisy, a form of invincible ignorance. Yet African Americans could scarcely influence the system and negotiated it with constricted choices.

Fontaine climbed to the heights of this system. In putting his life in context, I have emphasized both the modern American university and the role of the professional philosopher within it. Of equal importance, I have looked at Fontaine's understanding of African American history that for him and others shaped a commitment to a desegregated United States. These two frames of reference, the collegiate world and segregated America—one white, one black—molded Fontaine's lived experience.

CHAPTER ONE

A Cultured Education

Chester

FONTAINE'S FAMILY HAILED from Chester, Pennsylvania, an industrial town on the Delaware River, just southwest of Philadelphia. Europeans first settled the area in the seventeenth century. When the Quaker William Penn arrived in 1682 to oversee his "Holy Experiment" in the English colony of Penn's Woods (Pennsylvania), he had hoped to make Chester the capital. But Penn moved thirteen miles upstream to Philadelphia, and in the eighteenth and nineteenth centuries the hamlet of Chester grew very slowly. It nonetheless remained important to the Quaker farmers who spread into the Delaware Valley. The Society of Friends gave a special character to what became Delaware County, Pennsylvania, split between the town of Chester and its farming backcountry.

The Dutch had brought slaves to the area by the 1660s, but Pennsylvania had passed a gradual emancipation act in 1780. The free black population steadily increased as migrants and runaways came north from nearby Delaware and Maryland, where slavery existed. The Quakers accepted the small communities of free African Americans scattered over the large rural areas of the county. The largest nucleus of blacks was established in Bethel Court, the southeast corner of Chester. Still a small town in 1850, Chester had 417 blacks, 9 percent of its citizens, but Bethel Court soon had the reputation as Chester's vice den.[1]

African American inhabitants multiplied from the time of the Civil War, 1861–65, but stayed constant as a proportion of Chester's population. By

1900, however, the percentage of African Americans living in the city had jumped to 13 percent, just over 4,400. Black enclaves spread. Most blacks populated the West End, close to the water and some twenty blocks from Bethel Court. Although recognized for its gambling and drinking, the West End had homes and legitimate businesses. African Americans who valued respectability resided there. Black Bethel Court now had a notorious standing as the red light district, and African American families seeking to better themselves moved to the more reputable western ghetto.

Pennsylvania's southern border, the Mason-Dixon Line, had separated the old slave South from the antebellum North. After the Civil War, blacks in Chester and in other cities north of this border still usually survived in marginal circumstances. While African Americans in the North had more latitude than those in the South, segregation ordered racial affairs. White society cut itself off from the black social world of shopping, church going, schooling, leisure-time activities, and often employment. Some women in the West End had positions as domestics in sections of Chester distant from where they lived, and brought back tales of how the white folk lived. Men worked as unskilled laborers, often on the waterfront, but they had all the menial jobs and were divided from the white working class. The hierarchical African American social order itself mimicked that of the whites, and skin color played a role: the lighter did better. The black community also found Protestant religiosity a key to propriety. Finally, steady employment as a craftsman or tradesman, or as a policeman, barber, or porter, advanced one into the black middle class. Even for those of darker color—such as Fontaine—education proved the cornerstone to real improvement in life, perhaps as a minister or a teacher. But the residents of the West End also valued its gritty side. Its amusements on the social edge attracted even white people, who frequently had their only contact with black America there.

Growing Up

William Thomas Fontaine was born on December 2, 1909, at 609 Central Avenue, an important thoroughfare in the middle of the West End. William Thomas was the son of William Charles Fontaine and Mary Elizabeth Boyer, who often went by Ballard, the name of the grandparents who had raised her.[2] The first son and second child in a family of fourteen siblings, "Billy," or later "Bill," also lived with his father's mother, Cornelia Wilson Smith

Fontaine. As Fontaine wrote, "she had been a slave when Lee surrendered" at the end of the Civil War in 1865. The Fontaines, the Ballards and Boyers, and other members of his father's family all had houses within shouting distance of each other. Fontaine's father had uncertain work in the steel mills on the Delaware River and later fired the furnaces at General Chemical Company in nearby Marcus Hook. Young Billy described his father's occupation as that of a "laborer." The son said that the older man did the most "backbreaking," "dangerous" jobs for "bosses [who] were frequently Europeans who could barely speak . . . English." William Charles and Mary Fontaine tried to instill in the children the values of African American churchgoing decorum, and the family worshipped at the nearby St. Daniels Methodist Episcopal (ME) Church, later the United Methodists.[3]

Fontaine had an exclusively black and, he said, "overcrowded" elementary education at Watts Grammar School, now named after Booker T. Washington, close to his home. He recalled that his African American teachers ranged "anywhere from high school graduates to graduates of two- and four-year normal schools." The latter teacher training academies formed the lowest stratum in the system of American higher education in the early twentieth century. In the summer after his eighth grade graduation and whenever thereafter he could, he worked some of the same jobs that his father did.[4]

Under slavery blacks knew clearly that the southern master did not want them reading and writing. African Americans defying slavery and then the segregated "Jim Crow" society of the post–Civil War era thus had special reason to believe in the value of book learning. Determined that people should think well of the children, Fontaine's mother also pushed the virtue of schooling on them. The family came to see education as the basis of achievement in the black world, part of if disconnected from the dominant white pecking order. Although black Americans occasionally attended high school, the Fontaines eventually displayed an unusual drive for training beyond the primary grades.

While whites went to Chester High, a good twenty-block hike from the Fontaine home, the institution also matriculated African Americans. During this period the state of Pennsylvania admitted and graduated two classes a year from its schools, and Fontaine enrolled in ninth grade, in February 1922, at the age of age twelve. He took the "academic" course of study. It demanded four years of English, three of mathematics, three of history, three of foreign language, and two of science. Students, moreover, had the choice of carrying "five majors" as an upperclassman. Fontaine did opt for a fifth major in his senior year and wound up with four years of mathematics and four years of foreign languages, two of Latin and two of Spanish.[5] While the academic curriculum sometimes prepared students for more advanced study, it just as often culminated formal education in the United States. A substantial establishment, the high school of the time transmitted most of the culture and civic knowledge with which society would acquaint the overwhelming majority of Americans. Even confident members of the white middle class presumed that worldly prosperity and enrichment required only the "secondary" diploma.

A gawky and skinny teenager over six feet tall, Fontaine never weighed more than 130 pounds. In ninth grade he made the football team, but long legs and big feet made him an awkward athlete, and he focused more on the life of the mind. Soon after he began to learn Latin, he changed his name in many formal documents to William Thomas *Valerio* Fontaine. Derived from the Latin, the word connotes mental strength and health. He played first violin in Chester High's orchestra for three years, "the first colored boy in the annals of the school," he noted, "to obtain that distinction." He participated in the Latin Club and then the Debating Club: "the team consisted of myself and three white boys." Finally, Fontaine joined the Dunbar Literary Society, which was named after black poet Paul Lawrence Dunbar.[6] The existence of "the Dunbar" showed that Chester High sheltered a core group of African American students. Nonetheless, by eleventh grade for Fontaine the Dunbar Society had given way to the Literary Society. Apparently a step up, the Literary Society had purportedly a more ecumenical, that is white, approach to English prose and poetry.

Fontaine's grades averaged in the mid- to high 80s, a solid B. But we hardly know what to make of the transcript since we do not know the standards or his class rank. Nor do we know if blacks bumped up against a glass ceiling. The "Certificate of Recommendation" of the Association of Colleges for Negro Youth did mention that he had graduated in the top one-third of his class. And he was commended in his senior year for his ability "to speak Spanish fluently."[7]

Coming to Consciousness

If being black and having some classroom ability did not make Fontaine socially self-conscious, his experience in the Chester community itself surely

did. By the end of the nineteenth century, the little city was flourishing with
its share of industry located on the river. Then the decade between 1910 and
1920 transformed Chester and its surrounding areas. The city expanded from
39,000 to 58,000, and the black population from 4,800 to 7,100. The sleepy
center of Delaware County that mainly employed men in textile mills turned
into a manufacturing hub with far more jobs in shipyards, steel mills, loco-
motive works, and oil refining. Much of the work demanded the sweat of the
likes of Fontaine's father. Growth was stimulated by World War I, which
had begun in 1914, with Britain and France, the Western Allies, fighting
the Central Powers, Germany and Austria-Hungary. In America the overseas
conflict resulted in a booming war economy in need of a greater industrial
laboring force. Then, in 1917 and 1918, the United States associated with the
Allies to defeat the Germans. From 1916 though 1918 a flood of southern
blacks traveled north. They looked for and found employment and a mitigated system of segregation. Officials estimated that during this period
20,000 African Americans crowded into Bethel Court and the West End.
Permanently settling in Chester attracted some people, while other restless
itinerants lived in wretched temporary quarters built for the war workers.[8]

The war, which fueled the first part of "the great migration" of African
Americans from the rural South to the urban North, confirmed the arrival of
a new era of racial conflict and of change in the United States. Oblivious of
their prejudice, white Americans looked upon "the Negro" as "a problem"
and struggled to maintain supremacy and to avoid the contradiction at the
heart of the American creed of equality. When African Americans trekked
north, they upset the standing order. In occupying northern cities, they
struck dread into the hearts even of white progressives.

Blacks and white now lived together tensely in Chester, and in July 1917
a weeklong conflict broke out between the racial groups in Bethel Court and
spread to many parts of the city, including the West End. Fontaine saw
firsthand "the smashed windows, the looted showcases and shelves, the gar-
bage cans, bricks, and missiles hurled from rooftops." By the time authorities
brought the disturbances under control, seven people had died. Fontaine
understood the "bloody race riot" as a white expression of fear at the seismic
shifts taking place. Later, in 1923, the Ku Klux Klan marched through Chester. In the nineteenth century the Klan had terrorized African Americans in
the Deep South. The KKK's scary outburst in southeastern Pennsylvania in
the early 1920s briefly revived malevolent ideas that had spread north. "Nor-

dic" Americans made a last-ditch effort to uphold the existing racial state as well as to resist the spread of mores they saw as threatening.[9]

Fontaine, a young teenager, remembered these events for the rest of his life but also later interpreted them as signs of evolution in a black movement for equality. "World War One for democracy had shaken the status quo in America," he wrote. Black Americans "worked in foundries . . . and joked with fellow workers of the white race, learned to call them 'Mike' or 'Nick' instead of 'Mistah' and rode home in the front of street cars." Some African Americans even died for their country, and those who came home spoke of different racial attitudes in France. "Upon returning they brought new social philosophies." In the United States a few years later, Fontaine continued, "race friction found the Negro unafraid and willing to fight." "He fought back against the mobs of East Saint Louis [in Kansas, another center of racial animosity,] and Chester."[10]

As Fontaine declared many times, war promoted social change, and the efforts of the United States to win its wars could easily undermine segregation. World War 1 first made him viscerally experience this truth. The conflict put accepted white ways of doing things on the defensive.

From the late nineteenth century onward, the extraordinary Republican machine of the politician John McClure dominated Chester's government. His great strength lay in the black wards of Bethel Court and the West End. In these "Zero Districts," the Republican organization would tally no opposition votes. McClure and his lieutenants made their money running shady hotels and saloons. Particularly during Prohibition, which lasted from 1920 to 1933, the Republicans solidified their control by illegally selling liquor to blacks and whites alike in Chester. Through intimidation and restrictive real estate covenants, McClure's government saw to it that blacks did not leave their own precincts. But local politicians also helped and assisted their black constituents when they stayed in their segregated quarters. Indeed, loyal African Americans could work their way up in McClure's Chester. The African American sub-leadership would then secure political occupations for worthy black voters in their districts, as well as jobs in the police force or in the black schools. By the 1936 election, in which President Franklin Roosevelt swung black voters across the North into the Democratic column for the first time, African Americans in Chester had begun to register some non-Republican votes in national elections. Nonetheless, at the local and state levels Chester's black wards still went safely for the McClure candidates and Republicans until the 1990s.[11]

Fontaine's family was oddly Democratic in this Republican stronghold, and Fontaine vividly remembered the impact of city politics on his early life. Relatives labeled one of his brothers, Herman, "the family gangster" because he was caught up in a local world of petty crime.[12] Fontaine himself recalled that the white political boss, Ed Fry, one of McClure's henchmen, ran the slot machines, poolrooms, gambling, and prostitution in the area where Fontaine's family lived. Fry, said Fontaine, controlled the locality, Ward 9, "the nigger ward." Almost next door to the Fontaine home was the local boss's saloon at Seventh and Central Avenue, the main drag in the neighborhood. "Shapely caramel-colored girls," Fontaine recalled, always stood on duty "with painted cheeks and the perpetual 'Hello baby.'" Fry appointed the two black policemen stationed in the ward. They patrolled the nearby theater with a small upper section, "the buzzards' roost," reserved for African Americans. The black teachers at Watts Elementary contributed to the local Republican war chest.[13] Fontaine's later description of the neighborhood in the 1920s is worth quoting at length:

> On the "avenue" running through the heart of the Negro section, one encountered three kinds of laughter: jazz, the blues, and a kind of double-edged satire on the race question. These were heard, seen or felt in the talk, street scenes, gestures and actions taking place on the corners, in the barber shops and homes.
>
> It was the fashion for young "sharpies" of the twenties to wear jazz suits—fancy coats with pleated backs, narrow waists and bell-bottom trousers. Jazz suits were their "new look." The word "jazz" sounded everywhere. Shoeshine boys would greet a prospect with, "Hey! Git a jazz shine!" Bosomy, young, brown girls, in two's and three's, strolled the streets at sundown singing, "Um a jazz baby!" Silk-shirted pimps and loafers lolling on the corners carnivorously eying the budding brown beauties answering, "Hi, sugar. Would you like to be my jazz baby?" And from an unpaved, black dirt alley off the avenue I can still hear the sad flute-like voice of Mamie Smith:
>
> Ain't had nothing but sad news
> Now I got the crazy blues.[14]

Fontaine's Aunt Nettie and Uncle Herman Hunt lived on West Seventh Street, around the corner from their relatives. The two had ample resources for they had no children, and Herman busied himself as a real estate broker in Ward 9. Nettie provided the money for the Fontaine children to continue their education. When Fontaine's parents died in the 1930s, Nettie raised the younger children herself and may also have further subsidized Fontaine at various stages in his life.[15] In 1926 Bill went to college, to the all-black Lincoln University, some thirty miles west of Chester near the Pennsylvania-Maryland border. It cost between $300 and $400 each year. At sixteen years old, he wanted to be a teacher.[16]

Lincoln University

With almost no exceptions skin color partitioned collegiate training in the United States in Fontaine's day. Fontaine entered the oldest African American institution of higher learning in the United States, and Lincoln led in producing an educated black leadership.[17] In 1854–56, the school had come into existence as the Ashmun Institute, named after the Congregational minister Yehudi Ashmun, and instruction had begun in January 1857. An advocate of the American Colonization Society, Ashmun had served as the U.S. representative to Liberia in 1822. Hoping to get blacks in America out of the United States, he helped to establish the struggling community of African American colonists in Liberia. It was hoped that these settlers would begin the repatriation of all African Americans to their native land and ultimately cleanse the United States. In the 1850s, the Presbyterian clergyman John Miller Dickey guided the Ashmun Institute. He had received his divinity degree from the Princeton Theological Seminary, at the time closely connected to what is now Princeton University. Fiercely opposed to those who wanted to abolish slavery at once, Dickey and his like-minded friends favored a gradual manumission. As proponents of the American Colonization Society, these men continued Ashmun's quest for ways slowly to rid the United States of bondage and of blacks. In a measured process of emancipation, the ACS would export blacks to Africa, mainly Liberia. The institute had a motto: "Glorified by Africa." Dickey argued that a "special providence" of God had originally sent the slaves to the North American colonies. When Presbyterians like Dickey had seen to it that black men obtained the essentials of culture, they would, returning to their true homes, advance the whole of the Dark Continent to Christianity.

Immediately after the Civil War, in 1866, the school took a new name,

Lincoln University. At places such as the Hampton Institute in Virginia, and Tuskegee in Alabama, both of which opened slightly later, educators presumed that blacks would remain in the United States. Teachers, white and black, prepared African Americans in the manual occupations that befitted the status they would have as "freedmen." In contrast, Lincoln still supposed that African Americans would embrace their continent of origin and become African leaders. Different from Tuskegee or Hampton, Lincoln would give its charges learning in the essentials of Western civilization that would help Africa's leaders raise up their ancestral regions. Even more extraordinary, Lincoln encouraged applications from black Africans themselves. After an education in the United States, they would surely return to and elevate their homelands.

More conservative than its rival black institutions in its sense of where blacks belonged, Lincoln showed great radicalism in its view of the capabilities of African Americans. The university sustained its faith in a "classical curriculum" for its students even when Reconstruction after the Civil War made clear that the blacks would not leave the United States. Served up with a dose of Presbyterian biblical piety, the course of study imitated what occurred in white colleges such as Princeton, where students took to heart the learning of the ancient world, moral and intellectual philosophy, and mathematics. Lincoln, however, justified the curriculum differently. The white professors stressed that they were preparing missionaries and an elite who might do their work in Africa. Even during the height of anti-black feeling in the United States, from the 1890s to the 1910s, when the impulse to give only manual training to American blacks climbed to its high point, Lincoln resisted the vocational. It refused to accept the fashion in African American education that came to the fore when the black leader Booker T. Washington promoted the value of tutoring the Negro to work with his hands. While the university did nod to the pressure with some classes for the training of teachers, in many ways it led the new black schools of higher education founded in the liberal arts mold after the Civil War. Howard in Washington, D.C., and Fisk in Nashville, Tennessee, resembled Lincoln; they provided blacks (and at Lincoln native Africans) with the same core of Western learning available at white schools.

When Fontaine arrived on Lincoln's campus in the fall of 1926, Latin, ancient history, mathematics, philosophy, and the natural sciences formed the key part of instruction. Modern history and languages, and social studies did not have priority, and the school offered limited "electives." In the late nineteenth century Lincoln had put into place the basic course of study that Fontaine signed up for in the late 1920s. The curriculum indeed displayed more rigidity than that at many white schools, which in the early twentieth century had "reformed" with more choices and greater emphasis on practical knowledge. Although students and alumni complained even during Fontaine's time on campus, the faculty at Lincoln only slowly yielded in the weight it gave to the classical world.[18]

Wealthy Quakers in and around Philadelphia supported Lincoln. Their financial contributions largely explained the location of the school, on the southern edge of Pennsylvania in Chester County, which had originally contained Delaware County and the city of Chester itself. Lincoln students lived in isolation, fifty miles southwest of Philadelphia, twenty-five miles west of Wilmington, Delaware, and fifty-five miles north of Baltimore, Maryland. The closest town was Oxford, Pennsylvania, where Dickey had ministered to the Presbyterian Church. But the countryside surrounding the school encroached on the Maryland border, ten miles from the Mason-Dixon Line. The area had supplied one of the routes of the Underground Railroad from the slave state of Maryland to the North and to Canada. Sparsely populated and within a stone's throw of slavery, the area still lay near to sympathetic religious whites and non-slave blacks. The Presbyterian pastors established the school in farm country that persisted as rural into the twenty-first century. It was far from anyone who might be disturbed by an institution offering such a peculiar thing as a modification of the College of Princeton's curriculum to northern blacks and Africans.

After the Civil War, Lincoln attracted freedmen from the South, but urban growth in Chester and Philadelphia to the north, and Baltimore to the south, did little to alter the school's remoteness. To get to the institution students traveled on railroad spurs to nearby towns, but thereafter walking gave the surest form of transport. Visitors from afar would usually journey to Philadelphia and then make their way south to Lincoln by local trains.[19]

By the 1920s the federal government had improved U.S. Route 1, an important highway, so that it skirted Oxford. Only then could automobiles take paved roads to pass near the school. In the 1920s and 1930s Fontaine would sometimes go from his home in Chester, and later from the outskirts of Philadelphia, to Lincoln using this turnpike. Nonetheless, little more than a dirt track made up the last few miles of the trip. The campus of 145 acres charmed the students, but they were cut off and self-contained. Langston Hughes, already a well-known poet and literary figure when he attended

Lincoln about the same time as Fontaine, wrote that "from its dormitory window a view of farm lands for miles around is to be seen. Down the campus road a piece there is a tiny village of a dozen houses, with a general store and a railway station. Four miles away by train or road is Oxford."[20]

Lincoln's trustees and faculty usually consisted of ministers trained at the Princeton School of Theology who may also have had undergraduate degrees from Princeton University. By the 1920s some also possessed a doctoral degree in some non-theological field. The staff, however, did not exceed fifteen full-time teachers. Lincoln itself additionally possessed a divinity school. Programs in addition to the one leading to a traditional bachelor's degree chiefly designated a school as a *university* and not a *college*. But at Lincoln the "collegiate program" resulting in the baccalaureate enrolled more students than the divinity school. The professors thought it important to indoctrinate students in the theology of Presbyterianism, but they thought it more significant to expose students to the classics that embraced the broader Christian culture of white gentlefolk. Moreover, even if Lincoln functioned as a university, it did not compete with Howard and Fisk and had little training to offer beyond the bachelor's degree in the practical or liberal arts. At Lincoln, the bachelor of arts took precedence, and the school retained its detached aura of serious moral concern for the noblest realms of Western culture.

Lincoln wanted to lift what was called the Negro race to a higher calling. The institution's leadership thus long defied the alumni and students who argued that blacks might serve as trustees and faculty. The white men had similarly withstood black pressure to make the school more vocational. Because faculty inculcated ancient wisdom, administrators and trustees naturally assumed that only Caucasian professors could undertake the instruction. Lincoln self-consciously trained Negro leaders yet refused to think that even its own best graduates might teach at the school. Paradoxically, blacks could become the vessels of civilized learning only if they were to live in Africa. Students and alumni were criticizing this contradictory policy by the 1920s, but white scholars alone taught Fontaine. The school appointed its first full-time black faculty member in 1932, two years after he graduated. Nonetheless, custom allowed that select upperclassmen would teach introductory classes. Fontaine benefited from this policy when, as a junior in 1928, he instructed in elementary Latin.

Lincoln regularly drew students from Pennsylvania and the upper South. While Fontaine had an unexceptional background for the school, men from the southern states now disproportionately made up the undergraduate body.

The university's commitment also meant that over the years it attracted African students who would voyage back to their native lands. Fontaine befriended Nnamdi Azikiwe when he came from Nigeria in 1929. Their connection would contain the seed of Fontaine's interest in Africa that would flower three decades later when "Zik" become the governor-general and later the (ceremonial) president of Nigeria.

Lincoln never had large numbers of undergraduates. In the 1920s and 1930s each collegiate class would have perhaps seventy students, and in any year fewer than three hundred undergraduates would live on campus. They had talents. In the first half of the century surveys consistently showed the prominence of Lincoln alumni in the "Who's Who in Colored America." Even though the white faculty would not relinquish its prerogatives, it *was* educating a black elite. Although the school itself had little money and its graduates as a group never gained great wealth, the campus buzzed with energy and a proud tradition of achievement.[21]

College-educated black Americans almost never went to white institutions, and among black ones they could hardly do better than Lincoln. An adolescent with aspirations to the intellectual life could thrive in a heady atmosphere. In the 1920s aesthetic excitement and artistic accomplishment electrified literate African Americans. Most noteworthy were the figures of the Harlem Renaissance, who presided over cultural activities in uptown New York City. The Lincoln administrators persuaded black artists and luminaries such as Alain Locke, as well as white "race liberals" such as Carl Van Vechten and V. F. Calverton, to make the out-of-the-way trip to Lincoln for lectures and on-campus visits.

The state of the university nonetheless displayed the limitations on black life in the segregated society of the United States from 1870 to 1930. Impoverished, Lincoln could not avoid debt and physical disrepair. The prosperity of the 1920s had barely allowed the institution to get itself into some sort of reasonable financial shape and clear its liabilities when the Great Depression of the 1930s dealt it an economic blow. Aware of the extraordinary status higher education would bestow upon him in the black community *and* as a black man in the white community, Fontaine still knew of the subsidiary status of what would become his alma mater.

Undergraduate at Lincoln

Students at Lincoln could not yet select majors, and Fontaine concentrated in the standard program of languages (Latin) and (ancient) history. He excelled in his language courses, and in addition to four more years of Latin, he took further Spanish, and French and German. He added several philosophy courses to those required in religion. His grades averaged to a B—that is between 81 and 89—if we can translate Lincoln's marking system into the more recognizable one of the twenty-first century. But we lack a grasp of what this meant in terms of academic ability. Fontaine did rapidly distinguish himself within a group that included Hughes, Azikiwe, Therman O'Daniel, later a well-known scholar of African American literature, and Thurgood Marshall, who rose to a Supreme Court justiceship. Fontaine and these men usually ranked in the "second group" of "honor men" on the dean's list, although Fontaine just failed to make the debate team, which Marshall led.[22]

As an undergraduate in the late 1920s, Fontaine wrote for the school newspaper, *The Lincoln News*, later *The Lincolnian*. By his junior year, 1928–29, he had taken on the paper's assistant editorship, and *The Lincoln News* published some of Hughes's poems. Because Hughes already had a substantial stature, the publications rewarded Fontaine more than Hughes. Fontaine also contributed editorials on current student issues, as well as short stories and poetry.

The nymph Nausicaa charmed and seduced Odysseus in the Greek epic *The Odyssey*. Fontaine's very short story, "The Modern Nausica," illustrated the faintly erotic themes in his writing. Unsurprising in the voice of a nineteen-year-old, these sexual imaginings reappeared over the years. The story told how a beautiful black hostess vamped a customer at a nightclub. He bought a drink from her after she did "the shimmy" with him.[23]

Fontaine also composed juvenile poems such as "The Lover of Mankind":

If heaven's beauty were my bride
And we were wedded but an hour
To save this world I'd push aside
In sacrifice her starry dower.
Thus giving is to love the more.
He lost a throne and split his gore
Who saved this squalid world.[24]

Other contributions criticized white America. Fontaine argued that Negro "race pride" mitigated the selfishness of the so-called superior race. The goddess Fortune, "which seems so much a Caucasian divinity," would "anoint the illustrious head of Ethiope's gallant sons" if they displayed "ability, aggressiveness, and cooperation."[25]

Overall, these early literary efforts show Fontaine's interest in the African American spiritual voice, a burning topic for the black leadership in the 1920s.[26] The writing intimated Fontaine's desire, usually disguised or restrained, to participate directly in the literary arts as distinct from academic endeavors. The arts equaled scholarly production as a way to express black concerns. Fontaine would publish analytic essays, but sometimes the essays argued about how readers could obtain insight from black literature. Moreover, he occasionally made his points using poetic or novelistic devices, and he always appreciated jazz, which he saw as a distinctive aspect of black cultural expression.[27]

Like most American college students, however, Fontaine and other Lincolnians did more than discuss high culture. Langston Hughes said that, except for classes, the white faculty distanced itself from the students. It gave little oversight to extracurricular matters, and raucous dormitories often resulted. The faculty retreated to its on-campus housing, and the young black men made their own living arrangements. Azikiwe wrote about the unusually loud undergraduate get-togethers and Fontaine's contributions as a "woofer" to vociferous bull sessions.[28] In the surrounding rural community, and in Oxford, another alumnus maintained that Lincoln men had a reputation as boorish and undisciplined in their public conduct.[29] But the segregated community of Oxford may have invited bad behavior.

Fraternities existed on campus, and sophomores hazed freshmen. Fontaine survived and in 1927 joined a fraternity called Pi Gamma Psi.[30] In the 1920s Howard and Lincoln had an intense football rivalry that the half-time pageants of the competing schools enlivened and that Lincoln's abuses of the athletic system exacerbated.[31] Through the long winters "there were snowball fights, a pond in the village for skating, a barn of a gymnasium for basketball, and movies in the chapel on Saturday nights." In the spring "young ladies—often chaperoned by their mothers—would come out from Philadelphia, Baltimore, or even New York, or from nearby [black] Cheney Teachers College."[32]

The Lincoln yearbook called Fontaine "Kingfish" after the stereotyped long-winded and often unintelligible character in the popular (white) radio program about black men, *Amos 'n' Andy*. His friends also knew him as "Footney" because of the large feet attached to his gangly legs, although he danced well.

In the fall of 1928 as a junior, he taught elementary Latin to freshmen, and Azikiwe recorded that Fontaine starred in the philosophy class of George Johnson.[33] A professor of theology and philosophy, Johnson taught from 1902 to 1943. He also served for a time as dean of the faculty and mentored Fontaine. Fontaine's peers elected him president of his class as a senior, and he rose out of the second rank of honor men to graduate first among those who received the B.A. in 1930.

CHAPTER TWO

A Student of Philosophy

Teaching and Graduate Study

FONTAINE TOOK HIS DEGREE from Lincoln in the spring of 1930, just as the United States was entering the Great Depression. Over the next six years he earned his living as an instructor there, one of several part-timers. He just preceded the first black professors whom the institution hired as standing faculty. Fontaine taught Latin, and from elementary Latin—the learning of the grammar of the language and the reading of Caesar's *Gallic Wars*—he moved to classes in authors traditionally considered more advanced, Cicero, Vergil, and Livy. He shared teaching duties with Azikiwe, whom Lincoln had appointed to a similar position in history. In 1935 Azikiwe brought Kwame Nkrumah from the Gold Coast (later Ghana) to Lincoln. Nkrumah, who later emerged as the first black leader of Ghana, became perhaps Fontaine's most famous student, although he was also a friend. Robert Carter, later a civil rights lawyer and a federal judge, studied under Fontaine. Carter remembered a "virtually cadaverous" Fontaine as a vigorous and engaging young scholar and kept up with him for decades.[1]

Besides Latin, Fontaine taught history and government, and at the end of his efforts at Lincoln, in 1935–36, he contributed to the modernist inroads on the classical curriculum. He created one course on contemporary international politics.[2] This evaluation of Communism, Fascism, and democracy took up the heated international issues of the 1930s. With Communism, Fontaine examined the ideas of the new "Soviet" state in Russia, based on the theories of Karl Marx and devoted to the inevitable collapse of capitalism and the rise of a proletarian democracy. The "Bolsheviks" had seized control in Russia during World War I, and under Lenin and Stalin they codified these Communist ideas. Soon thereafter another self-consciously innovative group, the Fascists in Italy, came to power. Fascists in Germany, led by Adolph Hitler in the early 1930s, followed the Italians. Fascism and its German variant, Nazism, based their beliefs more in a nonrational notion of a *Volk* or people than in rational notions of economic exploitation. In his lectures Fontaine contrasted both Communism and Fascism to the more modest ideas associated with the growth of the "Western" and capitalist democracies in England, France, and the United States. The course began Fontaine's lifelong interest in the *theory* of politics, a concern a little removed from the hurly-burly of real political life but not indifferent to it.

Perhaps more important, Fontaine initiated instruction in "black history" at Lincoln. The "historically black colleges and universities" had begun sporadically to teach it in the second decade of the century, but lecturers still only occasionally explored the subject in the 1930s. While Lincoln lagged behind many innovating schools, Fontaine led there in devising a pathbreaking two-semester class entitled "The Negro in African and American History." Only fifteen years later would Lincoln regularly offer another version of Fontaine's teachings, which its first black president, Horace Mann Bond, would sponsor.[3]

Even though Fontaine had a heavy and varied instructional load, Lincoln did not consider him a full-time employee, and he was taking graduate courses at the University of Pennsylvania in Philadelphia as well. Black men with inclinations to scholarship would usually gain a post-baccalaureate diploma only through part-time (and summer) training at northern colleges, while they held down other jobs and prayed that they might use their advanced education. Lincoln's dean, the philosopher George Johnson, who had a B.A. and a Ph.D. from the University of Pennsylvania, may have encouraged Fontaine, not only in his part-time work at Lincoln but also in his part-time graduate education.[4]

Virtually all African Americans, even in the North, received their undergraduate degrees at black institutions such as Lincoln. By the 1930s Howard University offered a master's degree, but for true graduate instruction the hopeful scholar of color had to penetrate the higher reaches of the white academy outside the South. The University of Pennsylvania, along with the University of Chicago, Columbia University in New York City, and Cornell University in Ithaca, New York, led premier white educational centers in admitting blacks to degree programs beyond the bachelor's. In Cambridge, Massachusetts, Harvard University, not as open as the others, had produced the most famous black scholars, W. E. B. Du Bois and Alain Locke. But just *because* Harvard, Yale, and Princeton capped the top stratum of colleges, they were more discriminatory than Columbia, Chicago, Cornell, and Pennsylvania. At the same time blacks could always aspire to graduate enrollment in most northern schools that had professional or advanced offerings.

The origins of the University of Pennsylvania went back to the College of Philadelphia that Benjamin Franklin had founded in the eighteenth century, but its status as a university was associated with its more famous medical school. In the early twentieth century, the university had a more than respectable reputation, although it still rested on its professional training, not just in medicine but also in law and in its notable Wharton School of Business. Centered in "the College" at "Penn," the baccalaureate arts and sciences dominated the university far less than they did at Harvard, Yale, and Princeton. Experts ranked Penn at the bottom of the lofty group of schools informally known as the Ivy League. In part the institution's low rating among the Ivies was owing to the prominence of preparation in practical education instead of veneration for the customary academic disciplines; in part to the school's comparative friendliness to Jews. Penn occupied a niche more urban and secular and, if truth be told, more vulgar and useful than most of its Ivy League peers. The school had only begun its rise to international prominence.

Despite its professional emphases, Penn had a well-regarded tradition of graduate instruction in a number of the liberal arts that dated back to the late nineteenth century. Fontaine set foot on campus as an advanced student in philosophy, a candidate for the Master of Arts degree. This one-year graduate program could also be completed in two years of part-time study. The famed Jewish scholar Isaac Husik undertook the job as Fontaine's first white graduate-school mentor. Husik had immigrated to the United States from Russia as a boy and had himself received his higher education, including a doctorate in philosophy, from Penn. He had written on Aristotle, but the learned world mainly respected him for his work on medieval Jewish thought, and his editing and translating of this material.[5] While Husik took Fontaine under his wing and shepherded him through the program, Fontaine did not take many courses from the philosopher. Instead the advanced study of Latin at Lincoln had interested him in Roman thought.

In this work a younger professor of philosophy at Penn had a major influence on the new graduate student. Francis Clarke, a dignified scholar of medieval ideas, was a rare Roman Catholic outside the quasi-segregated Catholic system of higher education. Clarke interpreted the theology of Thomas Aquinas (1225–74), the leading schoolman of medieval Europe, and encouraged Fontaine to look at Latin philosophy from the time of the Roman Empire to the early modern period, roughly 300 B.C. to 1500 A.D.[6] In this endeavor, Fontaine would build on his extensive knowledge of the Latin authors he had read and taught at Lincoln.

Edgar A. Singer, the senior member of the Philosophy Department and a man of high local reputation, proved even more important to Fontaine at Penn.[7] Singer augmented Fontaine's knowledge of ancient and medieval thought through an admiration for the course of thinking from the time of the scientific revolution of the seventeenth century.[8] Singer introduced Fontaine to the modern philosophy of the seventeenth, eighteenth, and nineteenth centuries and stressed the German heritage of Immanuel Kant and G. F. Hegel. For early twentieth century American thinkers such as Singer, Kant stood out as the vital historical figure.

Kant argued that, in knowing, human beings did not just grasp the external world. Knowledge rather arose when they applied a framework of concepts to an otherwise unknowable sensory input. Kant identified knowledge with the structure of a universal human perspective, with what finite rational beings could obtain. He compromised "absolute" knowledge. Humanity could only approach it, Kant maintained, as an ideal that might regulate conduct. Human beings could legitimately hope that such knowledge existed, and so direct their energy to achieving it, even though they must fall short. Kant's successor Hegel examined the human perspective from which knowledge came in the context of history. The perspective could and did change. Human beings at different times had inevitably different perspectives, and their knowledge had varying shapes. At the same time, for Hegel, history progressed and somehow led to absolute knowledge in an indefinite future.

After Kant and Hegel, Singer focused on American ideas, which at Penn consisted of the pragmatism that had developed over the preceding fifty years. The writings of Charles Peirce and William James, both connected to Harvard University, founded this school of thought at the end of the nineteenth century. More recently and most famously, John Dewey, who had taught at the University of Chicago until 1904 and had retired from Columbia in 1929, brought pragmatism to fruition. Finally, George Herbert Mead, who had taken over Dewey's position at Chicago and had died in 1931, brought further nuance to pragmatic ideas.

Under Singer, Fontaine learned how pragmatists had carried forward the views of Kant and Hegel. The pragmatists called attention to science and common-sense experimentalism in the human engagement with the world. They were unlike traditional empiricists, who tended to view the mind as the passive recipient of material. The pragmatists instead focused on the way human beings interacted with their environment, and how the mind, as Kant and Hegel had stressed, molded what it knew. Ideas, for the pragmatists, did not inertly match up (or not match up) with the world; they were instruments of action. True ideas led us through experience in a perspicacious way. For James they "worked" and had "cash value." He defined truth as "only the expedient in our way of thinking." James epitomized a friendly, open, and pluralist understanding of the world and dismissed the pursuit of the unconditional, as Dewey would later attack "the quest for certainty."[9] Dewey especially advocated the use of social knowledge, the new social sciences, to approach public issues.

Finally, Singer laid out the implications of pragmatic thought for dynamic intellectual work in the United States. Although Singer had received his academic degrees at Penn, he had studied with James and brought pragmatic emphases to the university. Singer revered James, but he also talked about Mead's notion of the social nature of the human person. Selves, for Mead, developed jointly in a partially man-made cultural framework that offered an array of challenges and a repertoire of acceptable responses. Singer gravitated even more to Dewey's social activism and pointed out how human communities could bring scientific, rational understanding to bear on contemporary problems. He supported the liberal views of Franklin Roosevelt's political New Deal of the 1930s. A spirit of trial and error permeated the politics of the Democratic Party of that era, and Singer even espoused the more outré ideas associated with the coterie around the president's wife, Eleanor.

Voracious in his interests, Fontaine loved being a student. In addition to higher-level lessons in Latin at Penn, he did courses on specific thinkers in the long history of Western philosophy from the pre-Socratics to Friedrich Nietzsche; on thematic issues in aesthetics, the philosophy of religion, ethics, and political philosophy; and in contemporary problems of epistemology and logic. Later, as a post-graduate, he continued wide-ranging advanced studies in philosophy, history, international politics, and languages.[10] Many years later critics would deprecate this range of learning as being overly attentive to "dead white European males." Fontaine set his sights on mastering just this knowledge.

In 1932 he earned his M.A. from Penn. A year later, after continuing to take courses, he spent the summer studying philosophy at Harvard, easily the commanding institution of higher learning in the United States.

The Philosophic Scene

By the time Fontaine went to Harvard, he likely planned to plug away at a doctorate in philosophy, which would require several more years of effort. Penn's pragmatic ambience, which Singer exemplified, probably influenced Fontaine to go to Harvard. His journey may also have been emulating Du Bois and Locke, the two acclaimed black social philosophers of the early twentieth century. Each had a Harvard connection perhaps overvalued because of its rarity but famous among elite blacks. The connection at least showed how African American intellectuals could seek ultimate approval in the white academic world.

What did the doctorate mean in real terms for a budding philosopher? Certainly the upwardly mobile Fontaine wanted a Ph.D. as a strategic credential. He doubtless also thought of his work on this terminal degree as a quest for culture, wisdom, and answers to life's enduring problems. In reality, a Ph.D. in philosophy seldom rewarded the lonely seeker, or even the man in the cloister. It rather entailed expert schooling in the history of the subject with partiality shown for past thinkers who had "something to say" on topics fashionable in the present. Professors instructed in the details of the schemes elaborated on in learned journals—idealism, realism, naturalism, pragmatism; personal idealism, objective idealism, subjective idealism, absolute idealism; neo-realism, critical realism, representative realism; and so on. If one were fortunate, especially fortunate if one were African American, the schooling eventuated in a job in the system of higher education. Even in the 1930s preferment depended on publishing essays on these complicated topics in the latest issues of the same arcane magazines for which one's teachers wrote.

The burden of this kind of "professionalism" made itself felt even in those circles of philosophers who struggled to escape the narrow and the technical. At the end of the nineteenth century and in the first decade of the twentieth, Harvard's William James had conveyed to many, including the likes of Walter Lippmann and Gertrude Stein as well as Singer and Du Bois, that as an area of expertise, philosophy liberated people. James poked fun at "bald-headed" doctoral candidates "boring each other at seminaries, writing those direful reports on the literature" for the periodical *Philosophical Review*. James wanted philosophers to escape "the desiccating and pedantifying process" that often accompanied higher training.[11] His vision of the history of his subject and his open temperament had roused many students to take philosophy out into the world and to imbue the political and social with the practical and workable, rather than the traditional and conventional. After James's death in 1910, commentators often agreed that Dewey, who had a more sustained and grounded social and political theory, had picked up James's banner. But the days of his intellectual generalist were numbered. While James's "pragmatism" may have been a mouthful, Dewey named his version of the philosophy "instrumentalism." Dewey wrote about it and its relation to society in polysyllabic language that used the passive voice and abstract nouns. Dewey had a grand view of reformist philosophy but also professed it in the academy.

By the 1920s younger pragmatists had succeeded James at Harvard, but they redefined pragmatism to emphasize its theory of knowledge. Instead of a fundamental interest in how human action and reaction to the environment might change the world, Harvard thinkers after James wanted to know how they could justify an epistemology that underscored the efficacy of human choice. Even thinking about more abstruse questions of knowledge did not go far enough. Philosophers at Harvard argued that understanding epistemology required a grasp of a new field, "symbolic logic." Moral and social issues at Harvard receded into the distance. Learned discussion of an almost impenetrable realm of inquiry joined to the foundations of mathematics replaced such issues.

Philosophers (and historians who have written about them) have had a long and contorted conversation about the quality of the civic engagement of philosophers. Were the consequences of the professionalizing influence good or bad? Some matters remain certain. The status of the discipline in the wider American community may have reached its high point in the period between 1870 and 1930. But during this era the university world had also grown dramatically, and new areas of study had arisen. In the world of academic specialization of the later twentieth century, philosophy could not continue to thrive in "the public square." Sociologists, psychologists, and political scientists had far better equipment to speak with authority on social issues and on contemporary life. Philosophers did not just forsake the world; in part others took it from them.[12]

Through the 1930s the long-term outcome of professionalization remained unclear. Work in symbolic logic, the paradigmatic example of the novel tendency, mixed with other speculative currents, but over the next two decades academic philosophy found even Dewey's views less and less relevant. Excruciatingly careful reasoning demanded attention. The ever more constricted dialogue revolved around yet another former student of James, C. I. Lewis of Harvard. He had written his *Survey of Symbolic Logic* in 1918 and his celebrated *Mind and the World-Order* in 1929.

In 1933, when Fontaine moved to Cambridge, Massachusetts, for his summer of study, Lewis had begun a twenty-year *floruit* in his chosen profession. Making his way to Harvard, the young black man had made a challenging and sophisticated choice. But Lewis's "conceptual pragmatism" directed philosophy away from religion, culture, and politics and toward mathematics and epistemology. Lewis argued that the human community was not given frameworks of understanding but chose them to interpret experience and could change them. In part we constructed the world we knew in response to our needs and interests. Lewis, however, did not focus on civic or social life and how human effort might alter it. He rather examined the premises of the construction. He built a reputation in the 1920s on his ruminations about the element of choice in the foundations of logic. By the time he wrote *Mind and the World-Order* he was concentrating on the pragmatic assumptions of our scientific knowledge. His philosophical stance, while pragmatic, diverged from that of James and Dewey. Moreover, while Lewis reasoned that the concepts with which we approached experience came out of social needs and interests, he was also committed to natural science as our fundamental way of knowing. In the struggle of interpretative frameworks, Lewis preferred those of the hard sciences and tried to demonstrate their superiority. In 1946, when he published *The Analysis of Knowledge and Valuation*, the descendant of *Mind and the World-Order*, he laid the basis for the movement of "analytic philosophy," which was dominant in the United States in the 1950s, 1960s, and 1970s. His conceptual pragmatism exemplified "analysis."[13]

Fontaine's coursework at Harvard consisted of more studies in the history of philosophy with the junior members of the department who were willing to teach in the Harvard summer school in July and August.[14] But we can infer from the evidence that Fontaine left Cambridge with knowledge of

Lewis's work, crucial in unseating practical emphases in professional philosophy. During his career Fontaine made much of Lewis and published essays on the application of Lewis's concerns to "meta-ethics." That is, Fontaine did not write about actual moral choices (normative ethics) but about the preconditions of alternative moral decision making, usually found in the different language structures used to talk about practical problems.[15]

Race Knowledge

Less than two years after his time at Harvard and his assimilation of conceptual pragmatism, Fontaine prepared his course on the history of the Negro in Africa and America that he taught at Lincoln in 1935–36. Fontaine had two interests, poles apart. Abstract philosophy gripped him. But he also investigated the African American history and culture that demanded some kind of social commitment to fight segregated American life—"race knowledge." These two very different areas of expertise exhibited at this early point the two intellectual worlds Fontaine would inhabit and try to reconcile.

His course at Lincoln started with American black history from the Civil War of 1861–65.[16] The Reconstruction of the South had followed, with faltering attempts to erect an integrated bi-racial social order. This Reconstruction built on the Fourteenth and Fifteenth Amendments to the Constitution of the late 1860s, which guaranteed rights of citizenship to the former slaves. But Reconstruction had ended in failure in 1876, and over the next fifteen years the United States had rescinded African American attempts to achieve a modicum of equality. The South had solved its "Negro problem" by denying the vote to African Americans, by excluding them from white public life, and by maintaining a social order premised on inequality. Many white scholars in the 1930s thought this outcome acceptable. They ignored how the United States had disregarded the Civil War amendments and turned its face from the egalitarian creed of Thomas Jefferson. Mainstream academics allowed that African Americans did not have the necessaries to participate in genuine American life. The whites of South had evolved a sensible solution to the trouble of a lesser race living in their midst.

Fontaine along with other black thinkers took a different tack. They told what many years later became a common story of freedom denied. The North and the federal government had refused to implement the amendments because of growing racial antipathy. The South had been permitted to develop a social system that closely resembled slavery because racial fears prevented the country from living up to its democratic ideals.

Such was the political history. In his teaching at Lincoln, however, Fontaine called attention not to history but to a rather different genre of writing, the fiction and poetry of African Americans after slavery. If we looked at black literature, said Fontaine, we would see that a growing complexity of mental outlook signaled a kind of progress in the development of the black American mind. Racism diminished African American intellectual effort. Nonetheless, by exploring black creative expression Fontaine proposed to access the black psyche. The exploration perhaps provided a basis for comprehending how African Americans might find a path to improve. He was committed not just to the study of popular culture but also to a respect for it as an authentic revelation of consequential truths about race in the United States. And like all other individuals who wrote on these topics, Fontaine believed that written higher thought could best lead scholars to understand the unified culture of a people.

Dunbar

From what I can determine, at this point in his career Fontaine fixed on three periods of writing and a limited number of authors. For the era after the Civil War he read with care the poetry of Paul Lawrence Dunbar (1872–1906). Dunbar wrote narrative verse, often in the uneducated southern black vernacular of the late nineteenth century. For Fontaine the poet evinced the ideas of a disfranchised population puzzled about its status, disillusioned but not yet bitter and hateful. Dunbar's art functioned to sustain the black man until better times came and to mask the anguish of his position with a sort of inner contempt for the goods of this world. For example, in Dunbar, black Protestant religion, encumbered by the hereafter, positively responded to a social status that held little hope of immediate alteration. In Dunbar's *Lyrics of Lowly Life* (1896) whites widely read African American poetry for the first time.

Du Bois

Fontaine most respected the texts of the extraordinary W. E. B. Du Bois, whom Fontaine construed to represent a mental evolution subsequent to

Dunbar. Du Bois (1868–1963) had been educated first at Fisk (B.A., 1888) and then, as was often noted, at Harvard (B.A., 1890). After further study at the University of Berlin, he returned to Harvard for a Ph.D. in social studies in 1895, working along the way with William James. Of the students of James, Du Bois easily deserves to be ranked with C. I. Lewis and continues to attract more than respectful attention. Du Bois was the most gifted member of the first generations of African American scholars that included the historian Carter Woodson (1875–1950) and the social scientists E. Franklin Frazier (1894–1962) and Allison Davis (1902–1983). Du Bois was associated with Atlanta University (now Clark-Atlanta) in Atlanta, Georgia, where he taught for two stretches. But in his long career as a social critic and biting commentator on the inequities of American life, the public more usually connected him to the National Association for the Advancement of Colored People (NAACP), which he assisted in organizing, and to its magazine, *Crisis*.

Du Bois had first come to national notice in his debate with Booker T. Washington (1856–1915) over the appropriate education and social commitments of African Americans at the turn of the century. Fontaine would sympathetically expound Washington's "accommodation" of segregation, but found Du Bois more appealing in the Washington-Du Bois discussion. Among many other dimensions of this confrontation inside and outside the educated black community, Fontaine most noted that Du Bois affirmed the value of the lofty higher learning Fontaine had imbibed at Lincoln and was mastering at Pennsylvania. For Du Bois a "talented tenth" of African Americans should acquire such culture in a more equitable society.[17]

Fontaine also used Du Bois to position himself in a long debate over the autonomy of African American culture in the United States. The debate caught African American intellectuals between two impulses. On the one hand, they were convinced that white America had given the person of color the short end of the stick; one could prove this simply by looking at the resources denied to African Americans. On the other hand, black commentators did not want to confirm, with white America, that black America was of no account. How did the intellectuals such as Du Bois point out white America's ill will without acknowledging that it had fatally hurt African Americans and degraded their culture?

In an 1897 address, "The Conservation of Races," Du Bois had argued for a diversity of subcultures in the United States. American national life should recognize and permit an independently honored and honorable American black culture. For Du Bois this pluralism cashed out one meaning of

James's open-minded tolerance. Pluralism differed from a desire for black separatism, or for an African—and not African American—orientation for black folk in the United States. At the same time, Du Bois wanted to avoid assimilation of African Americans to white society. He saw such assimilation as a threat to the independent worth of black culture.

A complex dialogue about these issues occurred in the black community. In "The Conservation of Races" Du Bois had a hard time avoiding taking a position along a spectrum that ranged from a segregated black cultural life to an integrated cultural life. But over the next ten years his position developed. He had a brief appointment as a lecturer at the University of Pennsylvania in 1896–97, which more than anything else revealed how hesitantly even white urban higher learning in the North acknowledged black aspirations. No white school wanted an extended connection to any black scholar. But in his time in Philadelphia, Du Bois had researched a classic in the nascent field of sociology, *The Philadelphia Negro* (1899). Work on the volume made him reflect more deeply on the dichotomy between separatism and assimilation. In a new book, *The Souls of Black Folk* (1903), to which Fontaine returned time and again, Du Bois developed ideas that premised interaction between white and black mentalities. Commentators early recognized the observations on white American social mores in their connection to American blacks as uniquely perceptive. Fontaine directed his exegeses of *The Souls of Black Folk* to what Du Bois called the "double consciousness" of the Negro.

Du Bois explored the impact on the black man of the American ideal of equality and the mean reality of segregation. The conflict corrupted the African American sense of self. The hypocrisy tormented individuals personally and debilitated them as a group. Nonetheless, Du Bois reckoned that the tension made the African American self-conscious and aware in a far more percipient fashion than his white peers of what we might today call the social construction of worldviews, the relativity of cultures.

Du Bois's analysis reinforced Fontaine's view of an underlying belief in one cohesive African American mentality. The older man's powerful vision made it hard to see beyond a single black American consciousness. But Du Bois had also examined black identity in conjunction with a mutating white identity. As one scholar has noted, an emphasis on "hyphenation" resulted.[18] Fontaine would clarify these concerns. Both racial groups were transforming themselves as they engaged socially. The process would overwhelm both racial makeups, which were in reality always in flux. Fontaine would hold up black assimilationism as an ideal but one that would only come to fruition as white identity altered as it too assimilated to a new ideal. For Fontaine something higher and richer that simultaneously preserved and cancelled the old segregated identities would materialize.

Fontaine later argued more lucidly than Du Bois for assimilationism based on a dialectic and not a dichotomy. Fontaine was to transcend the standard debate and recast the issue. Yet his ideas had their roots in Du Bois's study of double consciousness. When he first read Du Bois in the 1920s and 1930s, however, Fontaine also saw a tension in Du Bois's position. Du Bois's feeling for the contingencies and complexities of social understanding went hand in hand with his desire to expose the deep bigotry embodied in the American way. That is, he had a relativistic sensibility about racialized knowledge of the human world at loggerheads with his absolutist idea of morality.

Du Bois's veneration for Western culture, which Fontaine shared, reflected the absolutism. With Du Bois, Fontaine believed that some African Americans, the talented tenth, could command the West's high cultural verities. Accomplished and culturally sophisticated, Du Bois judged that his intellect could vault him into a realm where color did not count, "beyond the Veil" of race. This realm of higher learning divulged the impartial wisdom of the ages. Literally with a capital T, Truth had come down through the pharaohs, Plato and the Greeks, and the schoolmen during the otherwise Dark Ages; then to Oxford, Leipzig, and Harvard; and, with some wishful thinking for Du Bois, at the turn of the twentieth century to the liberal arts at Howard, Fisk, and Atlanta. Not culture bound, this learning licensed the black man "to soar in the . . . air above the smoke." As Du Bois eloquently wrote: "I sit with Shakespeare and he winces not. Across the color line I move arm in arm with Balzac and Dumas, where smiling men and welcoming women glide in gilded halls. . . . I summon Aristotle and Aurelius and what soul I will, and they come all graciously with no scorn nor condescension. So, wed with Truth, I dwell beyond the Veil."[19]

Du Bois saw deeply into the perspectival nature of our cultural knowledge. He also needed and wanted an absolutely valued intellectual location from which to argue the evil of racism. Thus he had two inconsistent viewpoints. The thinking of many pragmatists displayed this common tension. William James in fact had suggested to Du Bois that he could not make ethics objective.[20] Who could complain about undermining the stuffy conventions of thought with James? But then one could not attach any special status to one's own convictions. Where did one stand to criticize, if all positions depended on the vague notion of their "working"? Finally, at a personal level, Du Bois's elitism and snobbery undermined his attack on the subjective nature of racial categories. He wanted the Harvards of the United States to accept him. Still, Fontaine's own study and reading in philosophy resonated with Du Bois's fusion of pragmatism, cultural superiority, and social critique. Fontaine had a similar dream of a learned humanism. He spent his life adjudicating the boundary between a social identity inevitably based in the mind of beholders and a moral appraisal that had to be incontestably grounded in reality and verifiable fact.

In the early part of the century Du Bois's assessment of American life demanded only that the United States live up to its adamantly stated ideals. Over the longer span of his career, he could not conceal his anger and lashed out at what he saw as the cruel and even unequalled prejudices of white Western civilization. But while Fontaine followed Du Bois's later thought and had a measured respect for it, he found the very early "conservative" Du Bois most attractive and continuingly relevant.

The Harlem Renaissance

So at Lincoln, Fontaine lectured first on Dunbar and next on *The Souls of Black Folk*. The Harlem Renaissance of the 1920s produced the last set of writings to which he attended in his course. This writing bore out belief in a certain coming of age for an entire younger generation of black artists, who not merely criticized the United States but asserted literary and cultural independence from it. In addition to feeling the allure of their African heritage, the African Americans of the Renaissance combined elements of this heritage with their own one-of-a-kind outlook on America. They had the secret to a culture that at least equaled and surely differed from dominant white creative endeavor.

Fontaine considered the jazz, art, and theater, which had nurtured these intellectuals in Harlem. Nonetheless, the writing gripped him. He read carefully Claude McKay (1889–1948), Countee Cullen (1903–46), and most of all his fellow Lincolnian, Langston Hughes (1902–67). Finally, Fontaine familiarized himself with Alain Locke (1886–1954) who had put the Harlem Renaissance on the map with his anthology *The New Negro: An Interpretation* (1925).[21] Raised in Philadelphia, Locke had gone to Harvard and then had become the first African American to go to Oxford as a Rhodes scholar. In 1918, he earned a Ph.D. in philosophy from Harvard. His scholarly work in

Cambridge concentrated on the area of value theory. Teaching at Howard, however, Locke did not make a professional reputation as what would be called "a moral philosopher." He did not conceive philosophy as a group of specialties but as a way of thinking about life. He focused on proclaiming the contribution of African Americans to American culture, a focus that received its most stunning expression in *The New Negro*. In this striking book Locke did not just collect the varied written creative works of black intellectuals but organized them with illustrations and illuminating essays. Locke looked to Africa for some of the sources of Negro high culture in America, but he also saw an imaginative fruition in the publications of writers located in Harlem. Fontaine used the volume in his own teaching. At this time *The New Negro* represented for him an advance over *The Souls of Black Folk*. Black culture had reached an independent maturity in the Harlem Renaissance that it had not had in Du Bois's writing.[22]

To this canon of books Fontaine later added *Native Son* (1940) by Richard Wright (1908–50) and *Invisible Man* (1952) by Ralph Ellison (1914–90), both of which he was to write about.

While preparing his black history course, Fontaine had arranged for Locke to make an appearance in the class in the spring of 1936.[23] Locke also lectured to the university as a whole. After the Lincoln engagement, the younger man respectfully maintained this important contact. He soon was asking Locke for employment references, a natural request if only because black doctorates in philosophy comprised such a tiny group. He periodically sought out Locke for advice and on at least one occasion traveled to Howard in Washington for guidance.[24]

An Insightful Course

Fontaine's lectures showed an investment in the history of black culture and its devotion to social equality. About the only group that he did not much emphasize was the "Back to Africa" movement of Marcus Garvey (1887–1940). "Back to Africa" combined a concern for black peoples around the world with a plan to colonize Liberia and other parts of Africa with African Americans. Most black intellectuals in the United States disdained the crudeness of "Garveyism" and its popularity among nonintellectuals. But even in 1935 and 1936 Fontaine did not ignore Garvey's activism, and later he sympathetically acknowledged it.

Overall, for Fontaine, race knowledge gave priority to the intellectual and cultural dimension of African American history. The deep two-facedness of American values that had special relevance to black people dominated the narrative line. He looked at the frustration of black politics in white culture but studied how black writers expressed the impact of collective insincerity on their consciousnesses. Fontaine innovated in teaching black history, but over the next half-century his views became standard and interpretatively compelling. Only the rise of social history in the 1970s challenged his literary priorities and the idea of a monolithic African American intellectual culture.[25] I also assume that Fontaine did not put out of his mind his own participation in a problematic American democracy.

Boethius and Bruno

In the mid-1930s Fontaine was still forming his grasp of the world of learning. In the early spring of 1935 he passed his written "preliminary" examinations for the Ph.D. at the University of Pennsylvania. Three days of writing covered modern philosophy, emphasizing ethics; and ancient philosophy, emphasizing Roman authors.[26] Husik examined him.[27] In yet another display of virtuoso erudition Fontaine had already begun his dissertation on the history of ancient and early modern philosophy. Instead of Husik, who would die in 1939, Fontaine worked with Clarke and Singer. He pondered Ancius Severinus Boethius (ca. 480–525), a late classical Roman thinker, but the dissertation, "Fortune, Matter and Providence," also studied the early modern thinker Giordano Bruno (1548–1600).[28]

In his thesis, Fontaine declared invalid Boethius's arguments connecting chance and purpose. But, the thesis contended, one thousand years later Bruno worked over the same problems as Boethius and showed the soundness of a position similar to Boethius's. Boethius assumed the primacy of purpose, which he called Providence, in the world. An overriding intelligence produced the universe, which we could subject to our understanding. But this assumption contradicted Boethius's belief in a brute material substrate, the realm of chance. If chance really existed, the universe could not conform to an overall purpose. If such a purpose manifested itself, the material world of chance did not possess an ultimate reality. Bruno later explicitly made this material world subservient to a world of Platonic ideas that exhibited purpose. He defined the material as only the ideas in the making. Boethius urged that man had the power to grasp chance positively, said Fontaine, but Boethius could not make the commitment coherent. Bruno rendered the position legitimate by reducing chance to a relative event. Chance existed only for finite beings who might not understand it as an aspect of a larger purpose. Centered on the logical cogency of the thinkers, Fontaine turned out a densely written and tightly reasoned thesis, fifty pages when published. Producing these pages required fluency in Latin, German, French, and Italian (in addition to his Spanish), and he later learned Portuguese.[29] Fontaine received his doctorate from Pennsylvania in the 1936 commencement, just as he finished teaching his course on African American history at Lincoln.

Philosophy and Life

The discipline of philosophy exercised the mind's highest powers. Among the theories that Fontaine had absorbed, those of the German Immanuel Kant and the American Charles Peirce were removed from daily problems, although both thinkers also promised relief from worldly cares. While standing apart from the day-to-day, philosophy simultaneously gave Fontaine a rubric to examine social troubles. From Socrates to Baruch de Spinoza, philosophers might suffer for a cause, or from Plato to Bertrand Russell, pledge themselves politically. Philosophy as a field of inquiry allowed its practitioners simultaneously to approach the world and to cut themselves off from it. For Fontaine, in addition, the journey to Harvard, the teaching at Lincoln, and the doctoral dissertation illustrated a specific form of agency that would endure throughout his life.

On the one side, Fontaine's interest in conceptual pragmatism and choice of thesis exhibited a yearning for the timeless. To understand C. I. Lewis required recondite work in symbolic logic, and Fontaine's dissertation was lodged in the fifth century A.D., fifteen hundred years distant. Philosophy could take Fontaine far away from contemporary America.

On the other side, Fontaine's dissertation had taken up Boethius's *Consolation of Philosophy*, a treatise on the nature of happiness, the problem of evil, and the connection of fate and free will. Boethius wrote it during imprisonment for treason and before his execution. As Fontaine claimed, men through the ages had "sung praises to its wisdom and beauty." While Boethius occupied center stage, we should not forget that Bruno, as Fontaine noted also, "martyr[ed]" himself and was burned at the stake in the Catholic

Inquisition.[30] Moreover, while Lewis's pragmatism had no public dimension, the earlier pragmatism of James and Dewey obviously did, as Fontaine had heard from Singer.

Closer to home Fontaine had taught his path-breaking course at Lincoln on black history. He was interested in an ideal intellectual world, but like many African American intellectuals he inevitably engaged with the racial troubles of the United States and issues of social action.

A Teaching Position

In the spring of 1936, Fontaine officially received his degree. In the preceding months, he had, in a time-honored fashion, begun to look for an academic job in the way of most humanistic students in graduate programs. Indeed, he had effectively determined at least to try to spend his life as a teacher and scholar. The twenty-six-year-old, however, began with two strikes against him. First, he sought work in the middle of the Great Depression, when colleges had limited employment. Second, because he was a black man, the small and underfunded public and private black schools offered the only realistic opportunities. These previously mentioned historically African American colleges and universities comprised the institutions of higher education open to him.

In rough outline, many of these places had similar profiles. Most had developed in the South. Religious groups, often with links to northern white Protestants, had founded the private schools after the Civil War. Black Republican governments in the defeated Confederacy had established public universities during Reconstruction. The land-grant college acts (the Morrill Act of 1862 and another such act in 1890), which specifically included the South, motivated organizers. The legislation afforded national sponsorship to higher education in the various states, at first by ceding federal land whose sale would produce revenue for education. In the South the black institutions could initially barely be equated to high schools, but they insured some federal money for African American education. Later, southern whites grudgingly supported these organizations as they evolved into teacher-training academies. White officials reasoned that, with tiny support for black education, the states might guarantee more funds for their segregated white colleges and universities from the government in Washington.

Through the last third of the nineteenth century and the first third of the twentieth all the black institutions, North and South, were launching themselves as enterprises that would offer instruction beyond that available in secondary or even primary education. Many educators wanted vocational training; some wanted distinctively academic study. Most but not all of these schools admitted only men, and many opened their doors to both whites and blacks, though whites hardly ever attended. Many of these schools had black faculty, though some (such as Lincoln) struggled with the notion that only whites could successfully teach students, even if the students were black.

White philanthropists often persuaded the schools to focus on preparation for manual occupations rather than on the less-than-practical liberal arts, and they promoted campus conservatism. African American collegiate administrators nonetheless stuck to their own path in devising curricula, realizing that a liberal education could have many benefits for black Americans. These leaders understood the cachet of non-useful higher study. The managers of black colleges also knew that the ruling white society wanted them to produce respectful and subservient African Americans. Black educators, however, needed little tutoring in making their institutions an unadventurous community presence. The leaders exhibited their own authoritarianism.[31]

Howard, Fisk, and Atlanta topped the list of African American schools. These three and Lincoln attracted the most ambitious and intellectually gifted black undergraduates. Well known, the Hampton Institute and Tuskegee were not identified with the rarified knowledge in which Fontaine had expertise. Tuskegee did not change its name from "normal school" to "institute" until 1937. The black elite widely admired Lincoln as a ranking body among African American schools, although Lincoln could not lay claim to a research agenda like Howard's, or the black scholars who were beginning to congregate there. The most valued of such scholars—people always cited Du Bois and Locke—had attended white institutions for top training, and both racial groups assumed the higher quality of such education. Somewhat independent of the white world of learning, the black centers of learning had started to make their own imprint on social thought in the United States. But African American academics overwhelmingly would have preferred to have careers at a white university. They looked at salaries, amenities, teaching loads, and the prestige of the Caucasian world. That was the reality in the white-dominated culture. When, in a tiny number of cases, black men readily accepted the call to teach in a university *not* "historically black," they reinforced this evaluation. Commentators repeatedly cited Du Bois's brief service at the University of Pennsylvania as an example. After the 1960s, when African Americans broke the color line in higher learning, schools such as Howard and Fisk quickly saw their tradition of black scholarship subverted.

The system thus restricted African Americans to an array of colleges in straitened circumstances or that were downright poor.[32] Many, especially those in the South, had little more than the curriculum of a trade high school, although they gave blacks at least the veneer of higher education. At the same time, the institutions put a little distance between themselves and the constricted ideas of white learning—the study of African American history is an outstanding example. These places upheld black culture in a nondemeaning way; and they cultivated young minds in ways that white society could not do. Finally, the colleges offered an occupational niche that might provide employment for men such as Fontaine.

Like many newly minted Ph.D.s, he had naive ideas about the academic world he was entering. He disdained Lincoln, "where no Negro has ever taught with a Ph.D.," perhaps because the school had just begun to hire full-time black faculty and because he felt that that fact would limit his rise. But he also complained that a position there "offered demotion not advancement"—he had already taught at Lincoln without a degree. Instead, while he indicated an interest in the (Pennsylvania) State Department of Education, he applied for employment at Dillard University in New Orleans, which two other schools had combined to create in 1930; Bennet College in Greensboro, North Carolina, a small women's school; and Lincoln University of Jefferson City, Missouri.[33]

In the summer of 1936 Fontaine accepted a professorship of philosophy and history at Southern University in Scotlandville, Louisiana, near Baton Rouge.[34] A state-supported college, Southern accepted men and women for study and gave a sort of higher education to people of color.

When Fontaine left Southern six years later, he had risen to head the Department of Social Sciences, but in the interim Louisiana tested the innocent ambition that he had displayed in his scorn for Lincoln. He long recognized the need to adopt a certain style when dealing with the dominant white society in the racial system of the North. But while he never forgot the impoverished environment from which he had emerged, Fontaine had already come a long way from Chester's West End. Especially at the University of Pennsylvania he had learned to mingle deference with gentility. By the time he left Penn, he no longer evidenced the bull session "woofing" that had characterized him at Lincoln. Instead, he had matured into a demure scholar who could behave himself in an upper-middle-class white environment. Still, as a northern black man, he had had some small room to maneuver, and *Dr.* Fontaine had credentials from a prominent school. Now he would be a black man in the South in the 1930s; and his situation would be far worse.

CHAPTER THREE

Ambition Constrained

Louisiana

Southern Louisiana had a French (Cajun) and Spanish heritage reflected in mixed European and African American (Creole) cultures. These cultures were centered in New Orleans, a large and thriving metropolis with a permissive flavor. Black Catholics abounded. The one Roman Catholic black college, Xavier, was located in the city. Up and down the Mississippi, on which New Orleans sat, oil refineries made Louisiana a wealthy southern state. It also had more people living in cities, although the exotic New Orleans did not represent more conventional southern towns such as Baton Rouge, Shreveport, and Alexandria.

Northern Louisiana and the eastern counties, the so-called Florida parishes, typified the South more. Commentators described them as being like Alabama and Mississippi. The "black belts" in Louisiana, also along the rivers, held most of the African Americans, although by 1930 they had fallen from 50 percent to 36 percent of the population. Outside of New Orleans, the blacks had little money. Uneducated small farmers, they had begun to move off the farms and into Louisiana's cities, or to the North.[1]

The rise of the famous or infamous Huey Long, one of the most compelling and eccentric southern politicians of the early twentieth century, complicated the social geography of the state. As governor and then senator, Long dominated politics in the late 1920s and early 1930s, and "Longism" defined public life in Louisiana even after Huey's murder in Baton Rouge in 1935, about a year before Fontaine arrived. Huey's brother Earl briefly governed the state in 1939 and 1940, and then another Democratic faction wrested power from him until the late 1940s, when Earl again took control. The Longs harnessed the support of poor "red-neck" whites, often underrepresented in voting, and constructed a machine that roughly catered to their needs but in a brutal and despotic fashion. According to one expert, Longism "built upon Louisiana's well-established traditions of political thuggery, flagrant disregard for civil liberties, and racial oppression." Nonetheless, Longism had its own idiosyncrasies, and it tilted toward the masses. Neither Huey nor Earl looked antiblack in the overall context of southern politics. Quite the contrary. The brothers inspired Louisiana's African Americans to think about what a movement based in the lower class might accomplish.[2]

Before the Longs, black striving for political rights had been limited to the tiny black educated class, which was genteel and conservative. What might happen if blacks mobilized the thousands of disadvantaged, rural, and illiterate African Americans? Faced with such a threat, the Longs accommodated blacks in their organization and garnered what black vote there was. Shortly before his murder Huey told a young NAACP official, Roy Wilkins, that he, Huey, was working "quietly for the niggers." Under Earl the percentage of black voters in the state increased as the southern prohibition on the African American franchise slowly eroded. But even Earl's racial attitudes make one's skin crawl. Campaigning before black audiences, he would regularly hold up a smoked ham and say, "I want the biggest, blackest, ugliest nigger in the crowd to come up here and get this ham." In the governor's mansion he would entertain white guests by having the black servants dance jigs or do routines imitating Stepin Fetchit, an actor widely known for his stereotypical portrayal of a lazy, shiftless black character.[3]

From this mix of forces came the culture of "The Big Easy" in New Orleans and the nastiest sorts of racism and a proclivity for lynching elsewhere in the state. Louisiana after all gave America the *Plessy v. Ferguson* Supreme Court decision of 1896 that upheld the state's railroad segregation law and the doctrine that permitted segregation under "separate but equal" public facilities. Between 1882 and 1952, with 355 lynchings, Louisiana came in second to Mississippi in proportion of killings to population. The Ku Klux Klan often relied on lynchings to maintain its version of white supremacy, and the gruesome rituals kept blacks in line. The South pursued a frightening form of social control and gave a sport to mobs. Vivid fears of interracial sex between black men and inviolate white women often motivated lynching. By convention only rape could explain such sex, and so offending blacks deserved the supreme punishment. Lynching occurred mainly in the northern black parishes. Incidents declined in the 1920s but went up in the early 1930s, just before Fontaine arrived, probably due to the economic stress of the Great Depression.[4]

Horace Mann Bond graduated from Lincoln in 1923. He later served as its first African American president and was an acquaintance of Fontaine. In 1934–35 Bond spent most of his time in Washington Parish, Louisiana, some sixty miles from Baton Rouge, as part of a northern liberal project to study and improve black southern elementary education. At the beginning of 1935 a particularly ugly lynching occurred in the parish and prompted Bond to complete his work in New Orleans. Lynching did not reach near its pre–World War I levels but formed an ever present backdrop to African American life. And as Bond's case shows, it had a particular relevance to educated blacks with ideas about Negro uplift. Might not whites perceive degreed African Americans from the North as "uppity" or threatening? "Whites expected, and usually received, abject deference from blacks," one historian has written, "and teachers were no exception."[5]

Southern University and A&M College

Historians have long recognized that the segregation and the absence of political rights—the "Jim Crow" South—did not come immediately into existence after the end of Reconstruction in 1876. Whites slowly developed their cure-all for their antipathy to social connections with African Americans. In 1879 and 1880 the black New Orleans politician Pinckney Pinchback originated the legislation that had created Southern University as a segregated institution. On the one side, whites supported the school *because* it would assist in the separation of the races. On the other side, blacks feared to press for integration. Pinchback argued that segregated training trumped what African Americans would otherwise have—none. Louisiana had originally installed Southern University in New Orleans, and in the 1880s Southern's instruction began at the primary school level.[6] In 1890 the U.S. Congress extended the land-grant college act of 1862 (the Morrill Act) in a "second" Morrill Act. It gave Louisiana the opportunity to get federal money for its segregated education, and the addition of an Agricultural and Mechanical Department changed the status of Southern to entitle it to such funds and to make it a university.[7] But at the turn of the century Du Bois described South ern as a "manual training school," and its president in 1919 described his mission as "eliminat[ing] illiteracy." Southern awarded its first B.A. in 1912, although the school had trouble maintaining a minimal curriculum in the collegiate liberal arts.[8]

Between 1912 and 1914, the state moved Southern to Scotlandville, some two hours north of New Orleans, just outside of Baton Rouge. The black private colleges in New Orleans did not want competition, and ruling urban whites wanted blacks out of a prime area of the city. The governor argued that Southern was only serving as a New Orleans high school, and the crowded city constrained it purpose to train black farmers and mechanics. The institution required a "central agricultural community in the state."[9] In Scotlandville, as at Lincoln, Fontaine inhabited a rural enclave, but now he overlooked the Mississippi in a "black belt" community of the Deep South.

In the 1920s Southern established a real four-year teacher training program and a legitimate bachelor of arts degree. But black educational bureaucrats ruled their staff and students with an iron hand, apprehensive that the disapproval of white lawmakers would destroy the university. Even in the late 1930s and early 1940s, Southern gave "annual musicales of black folk songs" to get legislative support for its budget. The occasions honored the governor and local politicians, and the African American academics invited the leading whites in the parish to attend as well.[10] In addition to such enforced deference, those who ran black colleges had their own plantation mentality and behaved autocratically. The long-serving president Josiah Clark punished and dismissed faculty members at his whim and added to their duties such chores as the mowing of Southern's lawns. In 1943 the president of Southern wrote that "the majority of . . . [black southern] schools are characterized by poor housing, over-crowded conditions, [and] very little equipment."[11] Another analyst said that at black colleges of that time one saw "a uniform picture" of "low faculty salaries, excessive teaching loads, minimal library allocations, negligible research support, and no faculty travel funds."[12]

In the early 1930s Clark hired his son Felton as dean, and a day after his father resigned in 1938 Felton took over the headship of Southern. He had a doctorate from Columbia University and governed the school intelligently and effectively. At the depth of the Depression from 1932 to 1934, the dean had advocated more manual training at Southern—more vocational study for blacks—to insure undiminished state appropriations. But by the mid-1930s Southern was getting various grants of New Deal money, and Felton Clark successfully lobbied his father to expand the liberal arts faculty and to develop real departments in the arts and sciences. After the heyday of Booker Washington, educated blacks again and again acted on the belief that cultural power would flow from an impractical higher learning akin to that of the whites. Felton thus wanted a curriculum that did not merely emphasize hands-on skills.[13]

By the late 1930s, with the collaboration of his father, Felton had appointed a group of young black academics in the sciences, social sciences, and humanities. The coterie included Fontaine and also Saunders Redding, later a noted literary figure. They became friends, even though Redding left after a couple of years.[14] Fontaine instead took over the organization of a new division of the social sciences at Southern.

With some five hundred full-time students and between sixty and seventy staff, Southern was still woefully constrained. On the quarter system, the university also had summer and night programs. The Clarks had Fontaine on a ten and a half month contract at a yearly salary of $1575. Expected evening school teaching gave him an additional $225, while he also sometimes taught at Southern's extension school (later a branch campus) in New Orleans. At around the same time, Lincoln offered Horace Mann Bond a position at $2,700, although he remained at Dillard University in New Orleans at $3,600.[15] Bond had accomplished more as an academic, but Southern still subsisted at the low end of the black colleges. Fontaine took his six-week vacation in the summer at the pleasure of the Clarks. He lectured in a wider range of disciplines and at a lower level and to more disadvantaged students than he had at Lincoln.[16]

And Fontaine lectured well. As at every institution that employed him, administrators noted that he "consistently . . . inspires student groups." Southern, moreover, recognized Fontaine as a brilliant scholarly addition, and he helped to create the first profile of its research activities.[17] Nonetheless, as head of the social sciences, he managed the offerings and oversaw the personnel in history, sociology, geography, economics, political science, and philosophy.[18]

We have a detailed accounting of Fontaine's workweek only for the spring quarter of 1938. In addition to supervisory duties and student advising, Fontaine taught five courses, on five days a week, in three different disciplines: classics (intermediate Latin); philosophy (introduction); and history (American, modern European, and political). He had a total of ninety-two students.[19]

We must also recognize, however, that many academics, white and black,

met demanding requirements in the 1930s and 1940s. The explosion of wealth
in the American university system and a more privileged lifestyle would not
come until the last one-third of the twentieth century. Moreover, the life of
a black scholar, however demarcated, exuded far more luxury than that of
most uneducated or even educated black men. Fontaine had steady employment, honor in his local community, and a long summer vacation.

Love, Marriage, and Life in Louisiana

Fontaine soon wanted to leave Louisiana and to make his way back north
toward home.[20] But he had gone to Southern with high hopes, and his personal life may have fulfilled some of them. Toward the end of his graduate
career in Philadelphia, the slender and handsome philosopher had met Willa
Belle Hawkins. She was a remarkable beauty with an intelligent and extro-
verted personality, a sensuous grace, and a taste for a social life with a little
flair. Two years younger than Bill, Belle dressed chicly and did herself up
well. She had a complexion light enough that black and white southerners at
the time would term her "high yellow." The "blue blood" that one could see
through her skin spoke to her objective of social advance. She had little
interest in permanently "passing" into the white world, but from time to
time she did so and was often mistaken for white. At least Belle saw her skin
color as an entrée into the black elite. She was also imperious and often self-
absorbed.[21]

    Belle was married, with two small girls, but she was considered separated
from her husband. She and her family were also interested in disengaging
her completely from an unsuitable match, and her mother encouraged her
socializing. One of her girlfriends belonged to a group called "the Lincolnettes," young women who dated Lincoln men. Bill made her acquaintance
through the Lincolnettes, and the two were soon keeping company. He
would regularly meet her on a corner in downtown Philadelphia near the all-
white secretarial school that she attended but that he could not enter.[22]

    Bill's family in Chester immediately suspected Belle. They may have
thought she fancied herself better than they because of her skin tone, and
they were in all likelihood correct. They may also have been jealous—and
irritated and alarmed that Belle would snag Bill as she proceeded toward a
legal break-up from her husband.

    One can conjecture that for Fontaine the romance with a married woman in this era touched the margins of propriety. When he first traveled to Southern to begin his new job, she remained in Philadelphia to obtain a formal end to her marriage. Belle then made her way down to Louisiana, and the sexually attractive divorcée and the dignified professor married on Southern's campus in 1936 at the home of Saunders Redding. For Bill the union brought with it the four- and five-year-old children from Willa Belle's first marriage, Jean and Vivian. But while Bill and Belle resided in Louisiana, the girls were left in the care of Belle's ex-husband.

Not always easy, the marriage eventually graduated to the permanently difficult, although Bill never got over being smitten by Belle. Especially while Bill and Belle lived in the South, Fontaine had firsthand experience that white men coveted good-looking women of color. He had a visceral sense of the erotic boundaries of whiteness and blackness. Nonetheless, like other black intellectuals of this period—and white ones also—Fontaine gave little thought to the dilemmas of women in a patriarchal society. He was sensitized to the plight of the black male. In the South, Fontaine noted, he participated "in a game in which personal worth and sexual prowess are at stake."[23] But except in his alertness to the reality that white men might prey on attractive African American women, he did not attend to issues of gender. Unreliable lenses refract much of our understanding of Belle.[24]

The marriage came at a time when Fontaine, at least in his writings, was rejecting the traditional Protestantism that dominated the social lives of many black Americans. Raised as an upright Methodist, he now suspected black religion's reliance on the afterlife as a cure for human ills. "Frustration of the here and now," he wrote "may be resolved by projecting a world beyond time in which eternal justice guarantees self-realization."[25] He increasingly noted that African American thinkers denigrated the evangelical style of black Protestant religiosity.[26] Belle belonged to the black Episcopal Church, the most lofty African American protestant denomination. She thought of the upper levels of the black spiritual hierarchy as the height of social respectability and dearly wanted this in her religion. Bill exchanged the Methodism that he mistrusted because of its supernaturalism for a conventional and worldly Episcopalianism. The Episcopalians with whom he associated were not interested in disturbing the status quo that placed them at the top of the ladder of African American churches. Bill knew the import of religion within the black upper class and did not disrespect it. Nonetheless, in consequence of the marriage Belle might have regularly dragged him to Sunday services about which he had misgivings. He seemed to have enjoyed more the evenings of bridge or poker, lubricated by scotch and water, that pitted him and Belle against the Clarks.[27]

Belle also could cook with style and threw a party with verve. On the Scotlandville campus Bill and Belle also owned the only large record machine, a mainstay of her entertaining. As Belle put it, they "danced to the jazz, danced close with the lights down low," and Bill along with the guests enjoyed the liquor. Through Belle's efforts, the couple additionally mingled with the upper crust of Baton Rouge Creoles.[28] For the reserved Fontaine, Belle might have been a necessary and even a happy social prod. After Bill's immersion in the world of white graduate study, Belle returned him to a bolder sensibility. In some ways more congruent with his earlier experience of Chester than with that of advanced education at Penn, the joie de vivre at Southern showed the adventurousness of the black elite.

Did this new and enriched personal life compensate for the culture shock? As a professor, Fontaine got esteem if not reverence within the Baton Rouge black order and was automatically one of its privileged folks. Yet the Deep South in the 1930s had an evil atmosphere and held particular dangers for someone such as Fontaine. He wrote about the lynchings that might comprise torture, hanging, and burning: "To live under 'lynch law' . . . was to live under threat of violent death. . . . The entire Negro community was under surveillance, and the explosive word 'rape' could ignite a pyre of human flesh at any point."[29] He later told about a "curiosity item" or "conversation piece" on display in a local white Scotlandville grocery store—the fingers of lynched African Americans.[30]

Years afterward Fontaine would also recount humiliating if less horrifying tales about living in this segregated world. In some measure designed to be entertaining, the storytelling would narrate, for example, the foolishness of having segregated places to urinate for black and white men in the middle of some rural wooded area. But these tales probably only amused him in memory. In the North, Fontaine wrote during this period of his life, black academics ordinarily carried on as "an out-group, a counter-race." But in the South, the vast majority of teachers "upon the soil of ancestral slave relations, some of whom are still alive," had an even harder row to hoe. They faced a life of "inferior status, of economic, political, and civil discrimination, of sexual repression, of insult to self and Negro womanhood and, above all, of the threat of mob murder without recourse."[31]

Fontaine regularly returned home to Chester on the Christmas and Easter college holidays and at the end of the school year in June. His loyal visits inspired large family gatherings. In the late 1930s President Josiah Clark was traveling in the North in the middle of the summer, and Fontaine had his boss to dinner at Aunt Nettie's. Living with their aunt after the death of their parents, his younger siblings called him "Billy" and his nieces and nephews called him "Uncle Billy," but they all addressed him with "Yes, sir." His two stepdaughters made friends with his little sisters. Uncle Bill would always have to put his head down when he came through the doorways at Aunt Nettie's, but the children liked to have him pick them up to touch the higher ceilings of the house. Bill would sit quietly when his relatives assembled until he unwound a bit and stretched out his long legs; then he would tell his people about the South and about the lives of the black professional class.[32] Nonetheless, Bill never trumpeted his accomplishments to his family or to guests or to strangers. "Your gifts will make you known," he would say.[33]

The Coming of World War II

By the time Fontaine got to Southern, the peace that Europe had achieved after World War I was breaking down. Under Hitler, Germany once more looked to dominate the continent. By 1937 and 1938 the United States was moving slowly to shore up its allies from World War I, the British and the French. After they declared war on Germany in September 1939, the war little by little drew America to active belligerence, again with the Allies in opposition to Germany. American competition with Japan in the Pacific complicated matters, and the dangers increased after Germany (and Italy) signed a pact with Japan. Global politics transformed Roosevelt's New Deal as the United States prepared for war. Most important, a growing military and then in October 1940 the first peacetime draft defined the nation. The draft enlisted young men in great numbers after the Japanese attack on Pearl Harbor in December 1941 and the subsequent German declaration of war on the United States. America made total war on two fronts, in the Atlantic and in the Pacific, against two bloodthirsty regimes built not just on racial ideals but on exterminationist policies toward their ultimate enemies. In particular the genocidal policies of Hitler's Nazis gleamed as an obscene thread in the struggle.

Fontaine saw war as an uncertain experiment in domestic social adjustments. He knew this from his own experience in Chester twenty years before. Now race heightened divisions in Louisiana. African Americans crowded into cities for defense work, and black soldiers from all over the country asserted themselves in Louisiana's army bases and surrounding towns. Blacks and whites had not been so cheek-by-jowl since Reconstruction. A major disruption occurred in January 1942 in Alexandria, Louisiana. Black soldiers and white MPs clashed in the town's ghetto in the "Lee Street riots." At the same time, because of deficiencies in the health and education of Southern blacks, proportionately fewer of them served than did whites. A senatorial candidate in 1942 worried that the drafting of white males would leave Louisiana "populated by Negroes incited by northerners to seek social equality." And, indeed, the absence of white men did benefit blacks, for example in employment. Nonetheless, the army also took black soldiers, many from Louisiana. In June 1943, Felton Clark noted, Southern had devolved into something close to an "all female" institution.[34]

Thousands of German prisoners of war also resided temporarily in Louisiana, and some of them did farm labor in the interior of the state. Fontaine probably did not meet any of these men. The German POWs did not arrive in Louisiana in any numbers till after July 1943, by which time Fontaine had left Southern. Moreover, while African Americans lived in areas segregated from whites, the Nazis did not.[35] For blacks, fighting a war on two fronts did not mean facing both Japan and Germany. Rather, African Americans urged, they must battle for democracy abroad *and* for democracy and an end to segregation at home.

The war, in addition to Longism, invigorated black politics in the state. In the late 1930s and early 1940s the Louisiana NAACP grew rapidly after a long period as a negligible factor among local African Americans. Reasoning with the Longs that political power could emerge from the masses, the NAACP discarded its elitist moorings. It now promoted Negro rights by pushing to overcome splits between light- and dark-skinned blacks, the urban and the rural, and especially the educated and the uneducated. The great rural African American proletariat could force change.

Americans had excoriated the "reds" or Communists from World War I, when the revolution in Russia had created the Soviet Union. But in the Depression, after Hitler came to power in 1933, the Russian state sought an alliance with Roosevelt's New Dealers in a union of all progressive forces. In public the Soviets boldly lied about their murderous domestic politics, which intimated the repressive nature of their regime. But in public Communists also denounced the Nazis and attracted Americans who were rightly worried about the capitalist response to the Depression and about the disparities of wealth and poverty in the United States. The "Soviet experiment" was concerned about economic inequity and stood up to Hitler. Moreover, the Communist Party in the United States ostentatiously accepted blacks and appealed to many "advanced" liberals among Roosevelt's Democrats and to some African Americans. The American Communist Party secretly enrolled members, and only tiny numbers of the politically active joined, but even in the South some engaged people gravitated to Soviet doctrine. The conflict between black Protestant religiosity and Communists who proclaimed their godlessness made it unlikely that Communists could draw a large African American proletariat following. More likely, some educated blacks would wind up, along with some white radicals, as followers of the policies of the Communists, "fellow travelers." Moreover, the Communists eagerly participated in any groups, "popular fronts," opposed to the Nazis.[36] Overall, the freewheeling liberalism of the New Deal generated a space in the United States for politics to flower further to the left. During the 1930s, in general, the political spectrum in America expanded on *both* the right and the left. The troubles of the decade encouraged unconventional solutions to community problems and politicized many people who might not otherwise have attended to civic life and economic affairs.

American Communists did have a very hard time from mid-1939 to mid-1941, when Russia repudiated the West and anti-Fascism. In a turnaround that indicated the degradation of ideologies in the 1930s, the Soviet Union and Germany adhered to a neutrality pact at the start of the war in 1939. Suddenly the Russians, to avoid war with Germany, made common cause with the Nazis. But then in June 1941, Hitler unilaterally abrogated his agreement with the Soviet leader, Joseph Stalin, and launched a surprise attack on the Soviet Union. The British immediately embraced Stalin, and the Communists joined the fight for freedom. For the rest of the war many Americans put aside their concerns about the barbarous Soviet state and overlooked the gullible aspect of advanced liberalism.[37]

In Louisiana local Communists benefited from the war-inspired social activism and pressed the NAACP for a more aggressive stance. As one historian has noted, the American Communist Party encouraged a paradigmatic event in this popular-front movement in Louisiana, the Southern Negro Youth Conference. It took place in New Orleans in 1940.[38]

The evidence suggests that for the first time politics beyond the Republicanism of black politics in Chester, Pennsylvania intrigued Fontaine. Circumspect, he always reflected more than he acted. Yet he had taught his course on international politics at Lincoln. He attended the Southern Negro Youth Conference. The war and black hardships in the South, of which he had firsthand experience, energized Fontaine. But more than the global conflict and the limitations of mass industrial society animated the man. Intellectual striving and a desire to get out of Scotlandville also drove him. In the summer of 1937 he taught as a visiting professor at Atlanta University in Georgia. Thereafter, in addition to speaking at various schools in the South, he delivered a lecture at the annual meeting of the Association for the Study of Negro Life and History in New Orleans in 1939.[39] In 1940 he did a first stint of postdoctoral work. During the summer he studied at the University of Chicago, a stronghold of pragmatism and a central gathering place for African American academics, especially in the social sciences. Fontaine obviously wanted to make a name for himself as a scholar. By 1941 he was looking, unsuccessfully, for positions in northern black schools, and Felton Clark supported Fontaine's attempt "to better himself."[40]

CHAPTER FOUR

The Sociology of Knowledge

EAGER TO LEAVE Southern, Fontaine still knew that Louisiana's social setting had jelled inchoate ideas about he what wanted from life. Disliking the South, he was motivated to write, to make a reputation as a thinker, and to publish his way out of Scotlandville. In any case, the period brought his most sustained intellectual success, a time in which he thought most coherently about the problems of race in America. Over these years he wrote four essays about such questions.[1] In them, of greatest significance, he explicated his intricate sense of how individuals understood their social world. He put together his knowledge of the pragmatists with his own grasp of some new European ideas. Fontaine applied his conjectures to American racial issues—but did so after sorting out his connection to Alain Locke.

Alain Locke

In early 1935 Fontaine had begun the acquaintanceship with Locke that eventuated in Locke's trip to Lincoln in the spring of 1936 and Fontaine's cultivation of the older man.[2] Although at Harvard Locke had not studied with James, who had died in 1910, Locke had oriented himself around the part of Cambridge that promoted James's pragmatism. One of James's followers, Horace Kallen, promulgated "cultural pluralism," a position Kallen took to embody James's theory of knowledge and its wider implications. Locke promoted a version of cultural pluralism. He looked on knowledge as an almost personal instrument for human growth. In the world of affairs, people had to recognize a diversity of values and ways of living as equally legitimate. Locke's philosophy developed one of the nonabsolutist accounts of ethics that were heralding tolerance in interpersonal relations.[3] Yet activity within formal academic philosophy did not restrict Locke's career. He envisioned a vibrant black life that would enrich and diversify an American society in need of mutual respect. Intellectuals celebrated his *New Negro*, and by the 1930s Locke led black leaders in the codification and extension of an indigenous tradition of high and popular black culture.

Locke encouraged Fontaine's interest in "race knowledge." He also almost certainly instigated the various incomplete literary forays Fontaine made during the late 1930s and early 1940s.[4] The young man had begun a play and mulled over a textbook on philosophy that would have a contemporary, problematic thrust, with an emphasis on aesthetics.[5] Twenty-five years later, Fontaine still often tried his hand at conveying in writing the realities and rhythms of ordinary black life and the dialect and dialogue that went with it.[6] He would have been peculiar had he not found the talented and engaging older man an admirable mentor.

Nonetheless, the arts and aesthetics did not primarily hold Fontaine's allegiance, and he may have exaggerated his interests to Locke to make a bond with the famous thinker. Fontaine had theoretical and analytic proclivities not entirely compatible with Locke's stress on aesthetic diversity. In October 1939, they got together again in Harlem, and the meeting shaped Fontaine's self-identity. The decorous and genteel Fontaine had recently married and was not ungratified that his wife had a sexually provocative dimension. Locke was a mild and respectable man but also an active homosexual. In pain because of desires that were publicly illicit, he may yet have been on the lookout for a liaison of some kind. In the early 1920s Locke had vainly approached Langston Hughes, although when the approach failed, both men were able to get along thereafter.[7] I can only make an educated guess about the psychological dynamics at work when Locke and Fontaine met.

Locke intimated a relationship to Fontaine. Was Fontaine, Locke asked, "even half as interested in my friendship as I am in yours"? Locke wanted "to borrow a little warmth and joy of life from youth." But a gap separated "youth and crabbed middle-age"—Fontaine was twenty-nine, Locke fifty-four. Locke worried about what he could offer Fontaine, "an exceptional youngster." He merited "even more than life ha[d] yet given" him. Were Fontaine committed to art and literature, Locke had "connections that really would make it worthwhile" for him. But Locke fretted about his usefulness because Fontaine had primarily other interests. Indeed, after this meeting, Locke wrote to Fontaine, it was "entirely up to [him]" whether their paths would cross again

Fontaine never received this note, but shortly after Locke wrote it, the acquaintanceship changed. Locke adopted a more formal address, calling Fontaine not by his surname as he previously had, but as "Dr. Fontaine." Fontaine deferred less. And after the middle of 1940, the correspondence broke off completely.[8] Locke lived for fifteen more years, but the meeting effectively ended the association for Fontaine, and he displayed less interest in African American arts and letters.

Between Hegel and Marx

What did command Fontaine's critical skills? He elaborated a complex view of how thought and society were joined, using John Dewey and George Herbert Mead but going beyond them. He wanted to learn how African American identity developed in the United States. Rather than rejoice in American negritude, Fontaine would examine it dispassionately.

Knowledge for Dewey never entailed that a disembodied mind met up with the external world. His theory of truth asserted that scientific knowledge integrated present experience with guided activity to deliver desired future experiences. Dewey made the argument many times but most effectively in one essay that became required reading for generations of students, "The Construction of Good," Chapter 10 of his book *The Quest for Certainty* (1929). Dewey eloquently called for the "method of intelligence" in human affairs. Earlier philosophy had abdicated responsibility. The intelligentsia articulated the "purely compensatory" to console them "for the actual and social impotency of the calling of thought to which they are devoted." Philosophers had sought "a refuge of complacency in the notion that knowledge is something too sublime to be contaminated by contact with things of change and practice." Philosophy had made knowledge "a morally irresponsible estheticism." Again and again Dewey accentuated the "active and operative" elements of knowledge. Only reorganizing the environment, scientifically removing specific troubles and perplexities, would procure human goods. Skepticism often confronted Dewey about the application of "funded experience" and "contriving intelligence" to social life. On the contrary, he contended that if philosophers disallowed his theory, they left in the public arena only "routine, the force of some personality, strong leadership or . . . the pressure of momentary circumstances."[9] The twentieth century, Dewey and his successors presumed, should apply to the human world the experimental method that had advanced understanding of the natural.

As Fontaine liked to quote Dewey, experience was "a doing and an undergoing" in which patient and thorough investigation might move human life ahead through the control of experience.[10] But especially at Chicago, after Dewey left for Columbia, his successor George Herbert Mead emphasized how human selves grew through this process. All the pragmatists agreed that they best construed *mind* not as an abstract noun—an inner entity—but as an adjective. The *mental* delimited certain forms of behavior. Fontaine described human individuals as *minded*. Mead and Fontaine assessed how social interaction formed minds, how they became what they were. They displayed organizing abilities that enabled them to control experience. Stimulus and action complexly produced selfhood, said Mead, as the human organism acted on, and reacted to, its environment. Selves grew up in contrast to an "other," a somewhat mysterious background that Mead also called *sociality*.

Unlike Dewey, Fontaine did not highlight the theoretical underpinnings of science and how it could nourish cultural knowledge, although this issue figured in his writing from time to time. Rather, like Mead, Fontaine concentrated on how various sorts of social selves might emerge in experience. Never given, the cultures of an exploited black group and a dominant white group unfolded in a distinctive social and natural world.

Many commentators and historians have rightly claimed that the origins of this sort of pragmatism go back to Hegel. He argued that diverse forms of consciousness developed temporally through a complex dialectic. In his *Phenomenology of the Spirit* (1807), Hegel famously discussed the collective journey of souls that led (in translation) to lordship and bondage, the relation between master and servant. Nonetheless, in an intricate way, for Hegel, altering forms of human consciousness did not just reveal the evolution of human natures over time. In the final analysis an absolute spirit defined the universally right in the ultimate nation-state. Karl Marx connected this evolution not to abstract stages in the development of ideas as he supposed Hegel had, but to the economic bases of various societies. For Marx systemic economic tensions led to the overthrow of exploitation in capitalist states and to the inevitable final existence of an egalitarian order. In the early twentieth century, pragmatism at Chicago and Columbia corrected Hegel in a friendly but "naturalistic" direction. Like Marx, the Americans also wanted to bring Hegel down to earth, but consciousnesses did not materialize in the brutal constellation of economic systems of Marx and his many followers. Dewey and Mead instead talked about a more benign set of ties to the environment. Consciousness percolated out of human interaction with problematic but at least semi-hospitable surroundings.

The Americans did not eschew a teleological direction to history. But they liked their present more than Marx did, although less than Hegel allowed. The Americans, too, were less certain of a final societal end than Hegel and Marx and his followers.

Fontaine did not escape the "soft" reinterpretation of Hegel that dominated American thought. But he had independently read Europeans in the tradition of Hegel and Marx who had arrived at more "materialistic" conclusions than the more "idealistic" Americans. Continuing his reading in the foundations of political life, Fontaine had by now mastered this critical literature. Chief among the Europeans, Fontaine studied Karl Mannheim, a Central European thinker in a field called the sociology of knowledge. Mannheim had written a core essay in 1929, "The Prospects of a Scientific Politics." Influenced by Marx, Mannheim announced the "relational" aspect of political and historical knowledge. The social and cultural matrix out of which the scholars came determined the knowledge. Relationalism did not make the knowledge subjective, although it made knowledge partial and perspectival rather than definitive or certain. Such partial knowledge might best be said to move forward when different perspectives were amalgamated, adjudicated in a nonmechanistic manner.[11]

Despite the kinship between Dewey and Mannheim, they disagreed. Dewey held out the hope, at least in the future, of a scientific ethics, an objective value system that empirical investigation would provide. In contrast, for Mannheim, people must fall short. Their social outlook would inevitably color their sense of justice.

Fontaine did not reject Dewey, but via Mead he sympathized more with Mannheim. The "interaction of plastic human nature with its social environment" produced thought. The "social situation," Fontaine said, entered into the constitution of the mind of any community, its attitudes, feelings, and plans of action. More important, this situation formed the profounder aspects of psychic activity—self-consciousness, the hierarchy of values, and a sense of time. "Forces existing in the . . . social environment" "stamp . . . the mentality [of a culture] in its own image." This environment "permeates experience and is the final tribune of all meaning." A passive intellect did not acquire knowledge of the human world. Groups constructed such knowledge. An "empirical foundation," or as Fontaine put it less neutrally, one's place in an unequal social order, molded the knowledge. Fontaine had a Hegelian emphasis on the efflorescence of consciousness but a "greater regard" for its structural conditions.[12]

Fontaine did not escape the hocus-pocus that appeared in the writings of many thinkers such as Mead and Mannheim. Fontaine allowed that some small minority of people might escape the vague social situation that located thought. The environment was "determinative" only for "the vast majority of individuals."[13] The imperatives of the empirical foundation created the grasp of the world, but in rare cases an originating mind might break free from the clutch of the material. A scholar, wrote Fontaine, might fulfill a "social role," "yet produce a body of knowledge uncorrupted by social purpose." "Social interest" might "quicken the attention" of a scholar but need not "'determine' the logic of his situation."[14] But despite his waffling, we can easily see where Fontaine wanted to go.

This vision that blended the pragmatists and Mannheim allowed for criticism of the existing order. Fontaine had "relativized" the moral world of the dominant groups and in some measure reduced it to a reflection of the power relations in a society, for this world and its social milieu mirrored one another. In Mannheim's terminology the dominant groups had an "ideology" that justified their place in the world. Weak groups believed in a "utopia" that gave them in ideal what they did not have in reality. Yet the position had another side. How could Fontaine claim ethical superiority for reformist or revolutionary views? Could not the dominant group profess purity for its arrangements? Dewey thought humankind might develop an objective ethics through science, and that therefore we would progress toward social justice; we might nail down the belief that the dominant group's view only reflected its power and not the general good. But, with Mannheim, Fontaine would not close with Dewey. Fontaine hesitated and worried, always, that he had no standard against which to measure the supposed evil of American race relations.

Another aspect of post-Hegelian thought finally came to the fore. Alternative consciousnesses developed, according to Hegel and such quasi-followers as Mannheim, as they clashed with one another. No one had all the truth in a syndrome of challenge and response. Winners and losers, women and men, diplomats and warriors, radicals and reactionaries, each depended on the other for the exposition of social commitment.

Over and over, for the next twenty-five years, Fontaine brooded upon these topics. He would digest new thinkers and ideas, but he would always return to a position of modified skepticism. He would doubt all claims to social truth. Yet he would assert the baseness of racial privilege.

The Social Identity of African Americans

The year 1942 saw the publication of the longest essay that came out of Fontaine's years at Southern. "The Mind and Thought of the Negro" outlined the progress of intellectual affairs in African American novels, poetry, and scholarship, and the growing complexity of mental outlook. Surveying black literary expression from Reconstruction to 1940, the article reformulated the ideas of his course on black history at Lincoln and in some ways typified ideas that African American academics were purveying in literature and the arts. Black intellectuals looked to Locke's *New Negro* as the source of many of these attempts to understand the evolution of African American culture.[15] But Fontaine had a larger and different aspiration. He employed the African American literature of the years since the emancipation of the slaves to identify the growth of a communal consciousness. Such consciousness had grabbed attention in the philosophy of Hegel and his European interpreters, and of the more audacious American pragmatists. Fontaine thus outlined the social sources of an altering group mentality in a wide-ranging synthesis.

Like many philosophers and intellectual historians before the dominant era of social history in the late twentieth century—and like Du Bois—Fontaine believed in the integrated mind and character of a people. The scholar could understand this character by examining high culture, with an emphasis on the people's great thinkers. But "the Negro of the United States" had "not as yet attained this . . . level of intellectual expression." Fontaine proposed instead that the scholar look to the "imaginative literature [,] the poems, novels, and poetic prose of Negro writers." This literature would reflect the status of blacks as an "oppressed minority" and their "dominant wish" for equality. A "social situation" and an inherent yearning for group "self-realization" produced the developing self-consciousness of African Americans. Thus, Fontaine reconstructed the Hegelian notion of the becoming of spirit in the cosmos.[16]

Fontaine saw this development in black America going through a succession of stages from the time of the Civil War. In examining each of these stages, he looked at the contingent historical circumstances that had propelled certain changes. Variables included demographic shifts in the black population from rural to urban areas and from the South to the North, the role of religion, and the rise of even elementary education for blacks. He also found crucial the fraudulent element of American democracy—the contrast between the rhetoric of equality and the certainty of inequality. Fontaine depicted the operation of these variables at the level of thought and culture. But he also evaluated how white consciousness altered and how changes in the black self influenced whites.

In the first stage in the quarter-century after the Civil War, the era of "the disillusioned freedman," Fontaine argued that circumstances virtually replicated the experience of slavery in the South. As a consequence of the evaporation of the goal of equality, blacks postulated a "transcendental" self that was exempt from the trials of time and culture. This self had an inner positive worth that social frustration could not challenge. For Fontaine certain characteristic traits displayed this social self: a religion of fatalism and resignation, a humor of self-ridicule, and an art of dissimulation. In each of Fontaine's stages, he explicated the work of creative artists during the period in question to corroborate his ideas. In this stage he emphasized, as he had before, Paul Lawrence Dunbar, whose writing for Fontaine expressed little pride or race consciousness and even looked to the slave past with nostalgic yearning. Dunbar's dialect poetry in particular used laughter to hide inner misery.

The lack of racial consciousness contrasted to events in the next stage, from the turn of the century until World War I. Economic advances on the part of the Negro and conflict with the white power structure on that account went hand-in-hand with a dawning self-consciousness. African Americans began to see their own subjectivity as a function of what Fontaine called a dominant and hostile "other." A first generation of Negroes issued a "counter literature" to challenge the white status quo. Using Mannheim's words in a different context, Fontaine noted that (black) "utopian" ideas defied (white) "ideological" ones. The literature of 1900–1917 undermined white claims to authority and ran counter to the writing of the previous period that perpetuated the existing social order. In the early twentieth century, Negro culture began the long process of devaluing organized spirituality. Literary figures only sporadically rescued religion when it had radical social implications as a living force.

Fontaine noted the writing of Du Bois, James Weldon Johnson, and Waters Turpin, but he explicated that of Charles W. Chestnutt most thoroughly. In his novel *The Marrow of Tradition* (1901) Chestnutt repudiated the "Negro me" that was the convention of the white world. Instead Chestnutt illuminated the "I" out of which black individuals reacted to "the social [white] estimate." In Chestnutt the basic urge to equality disclosed to the African American that his social standing did not convey an immutable fact. A questionable authority constantly fabricated the Negro caste.

Fontaine's third stage from World War I to the Great Depression generated "The New Negro." The main material factor consisted of the kind of social change that he had witnessed in Chester in the 1920s. African Americans came back to the United States after fighting in France. Rural southern blacks adjusted to their move to the urban North. In the preceding stage, utopian thought had challenged the dominant culture. Now Fontaine intimated that the discovery of collective self-consciousness led to an overstatement of the autonomy of this novel black self-consciousness. Dunbar's worldview legitimated the lowly position of African Americans. For Chestnutt whites had imposed their values on blacks, and blacks could aspire to the highest culture. The New Negro made the aspiration actual. Fontaine said that while before 1917 the present was only *auspicious*, thereafter it was *historic*. The decade of the 1920s accompanied a "yea-saying to the power, glory, abilities and intrinsic worth of Negroes." The New Negro valued his African heritage and the beauty of his own women. The war transformed the cautious sense that whites made many black troubles. African Americans after World War I excessively exalted the black self. For Fontaine this exaltation defined the Harlem Renaissance. An African American public aesthetic came of age. Black creative work demanded attention in the white world. Fontaine called attention to Claude McKay, Jean Toomer, Countee Cullen, Jessie Fauset, Langston Hughes, Edward Sivera, and Waring Cuney—the last three Lincolnians of the 1920s.

Yet, wrote Fontaine, the consciousness of the Harlem Renaissance was flawed. He worked out a complicated chart on "Color Preferences in Novels, 1914–1930." Writers ostensibly celebrated blackness, but the consensus in the fiction told Fontaine of a brown American Negro ideal, in between white and black. The contradictory impulses, for Fontaine, showed that in reality white society had influenced the New Negro, whatever his rhetoric in salute to negritude. "In evaluating his own skin color the Negro does not think in a vacuum," wrote Fontaine. "Standards of the total culture and the desire for status affect his thinking." The yea-saying could only partially privilege the black man. This stage of self-consciousness had within it the seeds of greater complexity. The New Negro implicitly recognized the equality of the black "I" and a dialectically joined white "other."

The implicit, half-hidden, and semi-disguised tensions in the writing of the New Negro "mark[ed] . . . a great step forward" not just in understanding the mind of the other but in understanding oneself. The New Negro, however, still displayed a "dominant . . . racis[m]." In his recognition that white America had degraded him, he identically scorned white America.

In the final stage from 1930 until Fontaine's present, the philosopher postulated a "trans-racial trend." The economic collapse that commonly affected black and white caused this trend; so too did the liberal politics of the New Deal, which were especially influential in labor relations. Fontaine conceived a stage of thought in which "the self is known by assumption of the attitude of the 'other' toward the self, and [by] the understanding of the other and the self as products of a common ontological source." That is, while America exploited the Negro, the exploitation had a corrosive effect on the white social system as well. As the black struggle for equality progressed, a goal of "self-realization" involved each racial group in a "striving upward."

Fontaine spent some time here analyzing Langston Hughes's short story "Little Dog." Hughes wrote of a white woman's psychic struggle with her discovery of her passion for her African American janitor, who remained ignorant of her emotional trial. The complexities of self-conception in the story illustrated the "higher" stage of self-consciousness that Fontaine's last stage displayed. But in this stage he highlighted Richard Wright's *Native Son*, where it seems to me he had a more difficult time making his case. Moreover, in just two years, he would argue, scholarly thought, and not only poetry and fiction, could typify the latest evolutions in the Negro mind.[17] The exploration of black self-consciousness might now include thinkers in addition to writers of imaginative literature. Like the novelists and poets, the early generations of black scholars could also be investigated, for they would also have a consciousness that mutated in conjunction with a mutating white consciousness. But we can hardly argue that Fontaine had a finished sense of where he was going, since he was dealing with his own present.

"The Mind and Thought of the Negro" made an impressive argument in the style of Hegel, Marx, Mead, and Mannheim. Fontaine had his own distinctive sort of pragmatic-Marxist social analysis. In it he had found a way to think around the problems of African American nationalism versus assimilation; he understood the interdependence of black and white culture in the United States. The longest piece he wrote between 1936 and 1967, the essay comprised forty-five printed pages. Its thesis bypassed the standard terms of the old debate. But Fontaine published it in 1942 in an obscure magazine of Southern University, the *Southern University Bulletin*. The *Bulletin* served as the university's catalogue and mainly described the school's academic offerings and listed the courses taught. With the help of Fontaine, one issue a year from the early 1940s on focused on faculty research.[18]

Looking North

Fontaine thought about leaving Southern from the time he arrived in 1936. He got away in the summers as much as possible and then accepted a grant for a year off for research in 1942–43. In the early summer of 1943 he decided to take leave for a second year, though he had only another minor stipend for scholarly work to support himself and his family in 1943–44. In August 1943, finally, he wrote briefly and mysteriously to Felton Clark that he would not return to Louisiana.[19]

CHAPTER FIVE

Social Change and World War II

Wartime Opportunities

FONTAINE HAD LEFT Louisiana in the middle of a war. In 1940 and again in 1941 he applied to the Julius Rosenwald Fund for support of a project called "The Mind and Thought of the Negro," the title that he gave to his 1942 essay. An illustrious Jewish philanthropist, Rosenwald had made a fortune in retailing at Sears, Roebuck and Company. In the 1920s he had symbolized the rapprochement between American Jewry and African Americans in the struggle against prejudice. Rosenwald had spent considerable sums of money constructing schoolhouses for rural blacks in the South. Shortly before his death in 1932, and thereafter, the fund continued this practice and began regularly to award grants, usually to African Americans, for higher-level study. In 1942, on his third try, Fontaine succeeded. He received a stipend close to his Southern salary of $2,300 to study in 1942–43.[1] In 1943 he collected another small grant of money from the American Council of Learned Societies.[2]

The first stipend returned him to the University of Pennsylvania for the summer of 1942 and the first half of the academic year 1942–43. As part of "post-doctoral study" he sat in on graduate courses. He surely loved being a student. Fontaine took more advanced philosophy, but his program also incorporated American and Latin American history to master the cultural aspects of his planned effort. In the spring, as a further part of his project, he journeyed to Fisk University in Nashville, Tennessee, where he consulted with the sociologists Robert Park and Charles Johnson. Park had led the

"Chicago School" of sociologists of urban life and race relations. After he retired from Chicago, he went to Fisk, where his (black) student Charles Johnson was creating an independent African American center for the study of race. Fontaine was supplementing his philosophic views with insight both from the historical sources and from those knowledgeable in the sociology of race.[3] His stay at the University of Chicago in the summer of 1940 had probably increased his interest in an empirical effort, in addition to philosophy, that he felt necessary to comprehend race. Philosophy did the heavy lifting, although it now had more distinctive substantive material on which to work.

By this time a founding generation of African American sociologists had contributed to a respectable body of knowledge on race relations. Many white thinkers still believed that they could employ race as a critical biological concept. It allowed scientists to categorize human groups on hierarchical scales that might involve intelligence or quality of culture. Because groups inherited the genes determining race, scientists might rightly expect peoples lower down on such scales to change only slowly. If higher and lower groups mixed their gene pools, the argument went, the culture or intelligence of the higher group might diminish. Building on the work of turn-of-the century cultural anthropologists, the African American social scientists attacked the validity of race as a workable scientific concept that whites could use to defend a pecking order of peoples. Instead, men such as Du Bois, Johnson, Ralph Bunche, Allison Davis, and Carter Woodson used culture as the dominant variable to comprehend the differences between the races in the United States. Some white academics, most notably the sociologist Park, supported the black academics, but African Americans characteristically criticized the biological approach.

These men, however, did not just argue that social arrangements mutated and resulted from more than genetics. Power and entitlement grounded perceived racial dissimilarity. Even sympathetic white scholars usually understood racial prejudice as a function of individual or even group training, or as a natural, if regrettable response to observed distinctions. In contrast, the African Americans found such prejudice systematic. It had the function of maintaining the supremacy of one group over another; the prejudice was *racism.* Intellectual historians have come to believe that in this discussion blacks saw more clearly that the organized nature of discrimination took precedence over the white emphasis on individual failings.[4]

In the early 1940s, Fontaine mastered this literature. At both Fisk and

Penn he additionally took part in an initiative to fund new programs and centers for the study of Africa.[5] At both schools these schemes petered out after a few years for lack of white interest and money, but besides sociology Fontaine wanted cutting-edge knowledge of the black continent. One could not understand race in the United States without information about the African diaspora.

In the fall of 1943 Fontaine left Fisk and Nashville and came back again to the University of Pennsylvania, auditing yet more courses "courtesy" of his Ph.D. His return to Philadelphia had much to do with what was clearly surfacing as a provincial orientation and a desire to be near home. But the combination of Fisk and Penn showed that Fontaine knew the locus of the action in this area of African studies he was exploring. Continuing to sit at the feet of white professors also had a point. Fontaine was absorbing all that he could of the West's ageless wisdom, and he might have thought that learning would vault him into a realm of racial truth. Did he also want to continue in the good graces of the established professoriate? His small award from the American Council of Learned Societies for the academic year 1943–44—the grants averaged about $400 per recipient—funded postdoctoral research on his project under the supervision of his old teacher Edgar A. Singer.[6]

In his reports to the Rosenwald Foundation on what he regularly called his "book," considerable evidence suggests how Fontaine was expanding the ideas of the essay that the *Southern University Bulletin* had printed the year before. The analysis would now clearly bring together his pragmatic ideas with factual study of racial consciousness. Fontaine would explore the history of black America, both before and after slavery. And he would look at slavery in Latin America and in African culture itself. His time at Fisk enhanced his philosophical understanding with the scholarship on race relations that Park and Johnson had fostered. Thus, the title of the proposed book was "The Historical Development of the Mind of the American Negro."[7]

Two other dimensions of the book-in-the-works require discussion. First, his reports convey not just a greater scope but an enlarged ambition. From the time he entered Lincoln, Fontaine toyed with the idea of using imaginative literature to express his concerns. Du Bois's *The Souls of Black Folk* did not merely express sociological and philosophical ideas but put forward lyrical accounts of black life. Locke's *The New Negro* anthology made its point through a combination of literature and literary criticism. In a long report Fontaine wrote on his progress, he said that he would narrate one of the four

parts of "The Historical Development of the Mind of the American Negro"
as a series of ideas passing through the mind of a young Negro.

> The youth, weary of the black ghetto, emerges from it to stand upon
> a great arched bridge across the Mississippi River. There he beholds
> upon one bank . . . the towering world of stone where white men
> dwell, upon the other the shrinking cabins of the dark world behind
> the levees. This leads to thoughts of self, of other selves, and the
> dark flood of shadows barring mankind from the spiritual unity. . . .
> As the story proceeds, the reasons for the title [of this part of the
> book] *The Sorrows of Brown Dionysos* will become more obvious.[8]

A second new dimension also needs to be underscored. Conscious of his
overriding dilemma, Fontaine called it at one point the struggle of *Volkgeist*
and *Weltgeist*, the spirit of a group and the spirit of the whole. African American aspirations and a sense of injustice comprised the former; the latter was
the truth of the matter. But how did anyone escape his *Volkgeist*? Did anything exist beyond competing *Volkgeisten*?[9] Individuals had worldviews only
in a community, and a social locus shaped a community, so how did the
scholar draw an objective bead on what was going on? Did one have to
believe in a spiritual Hegelian absolute to find a place to stand? Even if such
a belief were necessary, was it possible to have it?

Fontaine showed a greater appreciation for Dewey's belief that "historical—cultural—anthropological" social knowledge might acquire experimental corroboration and might be made as safe as knowledge of the physical
world. He returned to Karl Mannheim, as he was often to do. Mannheim
had argued that "relational" knowledge depended on its cultural matrix and
therefore could not escape the partial or perspectival. But then Mannheim
turned standard arguments on their heads. Suppose we wanted a viewpoint
that synthesized conflicting outlooks in a broad and conciliatory fashion.
What group would have such a viewpoint? If knowledge were socially determined, what class could be constructed so that it would be caused to grasp
the world in a way that would look to a coherent synthesis of competing
interests? What circumstances best promoted this synthesis?

Mannheim answered by elaborating on the class of "the free floating
intelligentsia." It was composed of university-based thinkers who indeed had
a social locus. But distinctions such as birth, status, or wealth—or race, for
Fontaine—did not bind these thinkers together. This class had a less firm

social footing than others. Instead a common educational heritage, scholarship, and intelligence bound it together.[10] Fontaine was not so otherworldly as to think that members of Mannheim's intelligentsia avoided the bourgeois society in which they flourished. Nonetheless, they still might procure "warranted" moral and political judgments. Mannheim received a reading that fit him into Fontaine's (and Du Bois's) wish that learning might convey a "universal . . . beyond 'the Veil of Race.'" The free-floating intelligentsia might look toward a truth that might "be ever-hopefully approached like a Kantian *Grenzbegriff* [limiting concept]."[11] Part of Fontaine knew that only the imaginations of philosophers created neutral scholars. But part of him, interpreting Dewey and Mannheim, had faith that in an idealized philosophical community, he could evade American racial distortions.

Fontaine's Social Analyses

One extraordinary publication of 1944, "Social Determination in the Writings of American Negro Scholars," came out of Fontaine's work with, and his reading of, the African American social scientists. He learned from them in detail the way black scientists of society viewed race. Moreover, he also thought that at long last black scholarship in America, in addition to creative literature, might give the student insight into the African American mind. It had progressed to such an extent that the communal spirit might spring from higher academic thought, and not just literary culture. Yet the extraordinary quality of "Social Determination in the Writings of American Negro Scholars" derived from Fontaine's turn in a skeptical direction. He made a brutally effective assault on the logic of the black social scientists. The most acute essay Fontaine wrote, "Social Determination" had attention called to it as an exemplary study almost thirty years later by the premier sociologist of the era, Robert K. Merton.[12]

African American experts on race, Fontaine said, did not write in a void. Like all social scientists, their lived environment defined their position. Fontaine queried whether "psychoses" centering in "resentment, aggression, rage, and the desire for equality" formed the "mental set" of the scholar of color. "As undergraduate and graduate student, he learns that certain kinds of knowledge lend support to race discrimination" and therefore would tend to dismiss this knowledge. In such circumstances African American scholarship developed an "angle of vision" based on visceral reactions to the abuses.[13]

To prove his point, Fontaine (in his early thirties) tore into the studies of the black thinkers on race. Their ordinary claims, such as the premise of environmentalism and the dismissal of analyses of heredity, mirrored the cultural locus of black Americans as much as the demands of evidence and logic. "The practical interest in group status" diminished the scholarship. Fontaine also wrote that these scholars nonetheless committed themselves to American democracy, and their commitment might also result from the power of a society prejudiced in favor of whites. African Americans might have a false consciousness, a "defense psychology" wherein they might find counterfeit prospects for the future.[14]

The enraged reply of his chief target measured the accuracy of Fontaine's aim and the penetration of his critique. The famous black sociologist E. Franklin Frazier retorted *ad hominem* that *Fontaine's* beliefs might result from social rage and resentment. Maybe "logomachy," a confusing bit of false logic, produced them. Or the beliefs were, in Frazier's most contemptuous language, "wuzzleheaded."[15]

Fontaine had entered a debate in which he was in effect advocating a synthesis of American and African American cultures. But for some white theorists, race mixing created "brown crosses," that is, confused mental defectives or "wuzzleheads." When miscegenation blended the "disharmonious" and "conflicting instincts" of each race, the progeny were *worse* than your run-of-the-mill low-intelligence American blacks. Racial mixing led to overall degeneration. By extension African Americans categorized wuzzleheads as black men trying to act white, muddled about their racial identity. The wuzzleheads were dupes and more. Metaphorically speaking, we could say they remained black only on the outside. We might view them as white men in blackface, foolish characters out of a minstrel show. Fontaine had struck deep at Frazier and his ideas, but the prominent sociologist had struck back. Frazier had spiteful disputes with a lot of scholars, but in calling Fontaine wuzzleheaded, Frazier was telling African American intellectuals that, in a more derogatory way, the philosopher was an Uncle Tom or, in later parlance, "an Oreo."[16]

Fontaine had an ambiguous message. On the one hand, he denigrated these black scientists of society and observed that they could improve their understanding if they incorporated more fully the theories of (white) scholars who had different and perhaps antithetical notions. On the other hand, Fontaine hinted that vicious racial institutions in the United States and its sham ideology of democracy distorted the vision of learned African Americans. He clarified some matters. Philosophical pragmatism and Fontaine's color had sensitized him to the subjectivity of social knowledge and to the rootedness of the knower in a certain order. He had worked out a novel position on the ancient questions of the autonomy and value of African American culture. Black culture was inextricably linked to the dominance and quality of white culture. Each would change only in tandem, and the African American social scientists displayed the dialectical complexities of social consciousness as much as black literary figures did.

Two other matters remained unclear. Fontaine did not talk about the nature of the white perspective from which African Americans could benefit. Nor did he say what the synthesis of conflicting outlooks would mean to the projects of the black—or white—social scientists.

Did examining the mentality of men such as Frazier show us any evolution in the black American communal consciousness? The scholars seemed to be stuck in the realm of the New Negro, which could only validate negritude and had little sense of the enduring marriage of blacks and whites in America. Using Kantian language, Fontaine said that "absolute truth" was "at best" a regulative ideal that might only be approached as a possibility. Adopting a dialectical stance such as Mannheim's, the scholar could only advance by making the "empathic assumption" that social knowledge always required melding opposed perspectives.[17]

Change of Plans

In the fall of 1943, Fontaine enrolled at Penn to sit in on even more graduate courses and was living in Philadelphia. Nonetheless, he was working in Chester. In a striking transformation of undertakings, he joined up with his friend and former student, Kwame Nkrumah. Nkrumah had gotten his B.A. from Lincoln in 1939 and then, while a part-time assistant at his alma mater, had taken courses at Penn. With Fontaine at the university, in 1942–43, Nkrumah had set up there what he called the "African Studies Section."[18] But in 1943–44 Penn no longer had a place on Nkrumah's agenda, or on Fontaine's. The African and the American, together once more, went to labor in the Sun Shipbuilding Company in Chester to fight segregation.[19] As had happened in Louisiana in the late 1930s, politics briefly lured Fontaine from the classroom. World War II and Nkrumah, a man who always placed himself on the revolutionary left, had stirred Fontaine into social activism.

In the late 1930s the mass labor union, the Congress of Industrial Organizations, had begun a long struggle with the great Sun shipyard. In 1937 the CIO's Union of the Marine and Shipbuilding Workers initiated an attempt to unionize Sun's yards during the period of the New Deal's support for big labor. In 1942, at the start of World War II and with an enormous demand for shipping, Sun schemed to avoid unionization. The company hoped to sap African American collaboration with the CIO and created a "Negro Yard." A segregated facility within the larger plant, Yard Number 4 still provided thousands of positions for blacks. At Sun, Fontaine and Nkrumah joined a work force in which for the first time African Americans were involved in every phase of shipbuilding instead of getting stuck with only the worst jobs. But the business did not befriend blacks, nor did it receive their gratitude. In mid-June 1943, during a tense work stoppage, company guards at the yard fired on black employees and wounded four of them.[20]

Again, we lack much evidence about Fontaine's unexpected decision or its meaning, or exactly when he and Nkrumah first appeared at Sun. In late August 1943 Fontaine had sent in his cryptic resignation to Southern. He announced his "retirement" by saying "in the next few days, who knows where who shall be."[21] The resignation came around the same time as African Americans were demonstrating all over the United States about the segregated conditions of their wartime employment. A huge riot in Harlem had occurred in early August.

Sun had a complex strategy during the war. Many black groups criticized the explicit segregationist premise at work, and the company did not intend that blacks would get managerial positions. Moreover, the Negro Yard performed poorly, and later the CIO successfully forced Sun to recognize an all-shipyard union that included African Americans.[22] Fontaine recalled his connections to these developments with less complexity and took positive lessons from the experience. At first, he wrote, management relegated the black men to the single yard. But soon the labor force to which Fontaine and Nkrumah belonged was challenging segregated employment. Then Sun hired blacks for all jobs throughout the entire plant. Nkrumah only wrote that they labored outside on the midnight to 8 AM shift and that every night he came home chilled to the bone.[23]

The work reinforced Fontaine's belief that war powered social change. No practice was so "taboo," he wrote, as not to win approval if it could assure victory. "Time-honored mores begin to take on the quality of flexibility." To win the war Americans might swallow desegregation. They might trade it for something they wanted even more than racial superiority—victory over the Germans and Japanese.[24]

Nkrumah went to London in 1945, the first step in his journey back to the Gold Coast, but in another twist, Fontaine had left Sun long before that. Did the United States offer more than false hope for the black man? Did it proffer something to commit oneself to in preference to Nazi Germany? Fontaine's writing in the early 1940s had expressed doubts about the ethos of American democracy. Collective action in which he participated against segregated shipbuilding tested this ethos. Another test came in the American army. It drafted Fontaine at the end of 1943.

Engaged with Private Pete

By early 1944 Fontaine was encamped at the Holabird Signal Depot in Baltimore, Maryland, a military teaching installation just to the south of Lincoln, Chester, and Philadelphia. Holabird educated men in the use of radar, and so the facility also repaired radar, photographic apparatus, telephones, and mobile radio equipment. In the fall of 1943 it had absorbed a new group of teachers—one hundred men who would instruct illiterates.[25]

When the United States entered World War II, the nation immediately faced the predicament of how to train various substandard inductees. A primary problem arose from illiterates, who were formed from three groups. The first group consisted of non-English-speaking personnel. The second consisted of those who scored below 69, later 59, on the army-administered IQ test that had a norm of 100. The army categorized this group as consisting of "very slow learners" or "Grade V's," the bottom of the scale the army used to figure out job placements. The third consisted of "intelligent illiterates," men whom the military deemed normal except for the fact that they could not read or write. Until the middle of 1943, haphazard procedures governed the training of all these men. The service minimally educated some of them. It assigned others to low-level jobs or dismissed them from the army. But manpower needs so overwhelmed the nation, and the country generated so many draftees, that the military worked out a more systematic program that had conspicuously effective results.[26]

While the navy had its own program, the army sent illiterates who passed all the induction requirements except for the fourth-grade literacy test to Special Training Units around the nation. There they received pre-basic army training and schooling that might last from twelve to sixteen weeks. In this time the army expected them to acquire the requisite basic skills in reading, writing, language expression, and arithmetic. Eighty-eight percent did so and went on to basic training. The army sent the rest home. The military would not say publicly why it was entering the field of elementary education, but the national security requirement to draw on all available men obviously impelled the program. Because blacks suffered from educational discrimination, the STUs disproportionately represented African Americans.[27] From June 1943, when the army began to keep careful records, until it concluded the program in the fall of 1945, the service provided work in "the three r's" to over three hundred thousand soldiers. Almost half were black.

Fontaine taught at the Holabird STU from early 1944. In the segregated army of the time, he instructed only African Americans, although his STU had a white officer corps. He had a standard class size of sixteen students, with a median age of twenty. After testing the students-to-be, the army placed them at their appropriate level from kindergarten to fourth grade. The recruits then made their way through the school as their progress warranted, although the typical course lasted twelve weeks. The Holabird STU signed up two thousand men a month during the first part of 1944. Even in the last year of the war one thousand new men a month registered in Baltimore, and the school graduated six to eight hundred each month. The army job demanded much, as one report noted, for teachers had to have "a sympathetic understanding of frustrated people" and some notion of how to awaken in them "latent possibilities."[28] In addition to the class work, Holabird provided a social life for the illiterates, including weekly dances with young African American women, a sports program, and graduation ceremonies.[29] Receiving two rare E's for excellent in the periodic army evaluations, the Holabird STU did an outstanding job. Of the one hundred instructors, Fontaine and one other held doctorates.[30] Even as a corporal Fontaine was advanced to duties supervising the teaching staff, and he dealt with long-serving black sergeants and the white officers who commanded the blacks. At the beginning of January 1945, he was named "G.I. of the week" and featured in the camp newspaper.[31]

Fontaine taught from *The Army Reader* that mimicked the "Dick and Jane" books that educators in the United States used to teach children in elementary school. In the army, however, stories centered around Private Pete and his friend Daffy, who go into the army (first grade), write a letter home (second grade), and take care of their pay (third grade). The teachers employed a basic "look-say" method in initial teaching and advanced to some phonetic concepts. Illustrations profusely accompanied the material in *The Reader*, which dealt with everyday experiences. Drill exercises correlated reading with skills in speaking, writing, and arithmetic. The army trained these African Americans at Holabird in ways that would directly assist the service. The brass wanted the men to do rudimentary map reading, to understand written orders and signs, to tell time, and to count money. They wanted the draftees to send letters to their families and to assure them that they had put their sons in good hands in the army.[32]

Fontaine taught grades three and four, and the course of study culminated in the final grade. It conveyed a series of lessons in elementary civics, tutoring the draftees about "the characteristics of the good soldier, the United Nations, and global war," "what World War II is all about." Holabird produced a special primer for this grade, "Why We Fight," and students could contribute to a sort of literary magazine, "Our War." Supplementary reading material had special "Negro stories" talking about "Negro exploits" in the American military.

In the January 1944 issue of "Why We Fight," Private Pete wrote a letter saying "Dear Mom: . . . I know what I am working for in this war. . . . I want to be able to say what I think without being afraid. I want the right to do what I like." In *The Army Reader* a corporal tells Private Pete and his buddies about the Revolutionary War and George Washington's trial at Valley Forge. The corporal says, "We, too, must have courage. We must stick to our guns and win this war for freedom." In the last paragraph of *The Reader*, Private Pete says, "Now I begin to understand. We are still free men. We must always be free in the United States of America and in the whole world. That is why we are fighting. That is why we must win."[33]

Fontaine's classrooms held all black students. We do not know if the non-segregated treatment of Nazi prisoners of war in Louisiana had penetrated his consciousness. He may even have avoided such knowledge in Baltimore. For at Holabird the army interred Germans into whom Americans were instilling the principles of American democracy, but the army segregated the blacks, though not the whites, from the soldiers of the self-styled master race.[34] I cannot help but wonder what went on in Fontaine's fourth-grade civics class.[35]

The army program triumphed in astonishing ways. A woman had someone write to her son: "Mother was so proud to get your letter, to think you could write a letter yourself. God bless the man that taught you. It means so much to me to hear directly from you." At Fort Holabird one student attempted to give a teacher a sum of money. "You see," said the student, "I have just received a letter from home, and for the first time in my life, I was able to read it all by myself." Just as Horace Mann Bond took over the presidency of Lincoln in 1945, he wrote a deeply felt congratulatory letter to the army. Not only had the methods worked. Bond also found the educational improvement striking and thought that the United States should promote the training everywhere.[36]

A Wartime Meeting

The war in Europe ended in May 1945 and in Asia that September. The army closed the Holabird STU at the end of October 1945, and thereafter Fontaine perhaps spent some time giving occupational guidance to African American soldiers due to leave the service. He had reached the grade of sergeant, and the army mustered him out in Philadelphia in December 1945.[37] The evidence suggests that at some point during the last six months of his service, while waiting for the government to demobilize him, Fontaine struck up a companionship with a white sergeant a few years his senior, who was also waiting for orders home.[38]

Nelson Goodman had spent World War II in Virginia and Washington State. He gave psychological tests to inductees and soldiered himself as a member of an STU. A wealthy man, he had run his own art gallery in Boston for a decade preceding the war. But another curious civilian pursuit cemented a friendship that in miniature displayed how superior education together with World War II could turn traditional relationships topsy-turvy: Goodman had a Ph.D. in philosophy too. We have already met him offering Fontaine a ride to the Charlottesville APA meeting over Christmas in 1948. Goodman had studied in graduate school under C. I. Lewis at Harvard in the late 1920s and early 1930s. But Harvard's entrenched anti-Semitism had imperiled Goodman's academic progress. During the 1930s he had cultivated the fine arts at a profit and did not finish his dissertation until 1941, after a long period of gestation. In postwar America, Protestants lost their hold on the academy, and Goodman went on to a career, first at Pennsylvania and finally at Harvard, that would stamp him as Lewis's greatest professional student and as a stellar university philosopher.

An impressive figure in his time, Goodman still commands respect. He had absorbed the new logical specialties that Lewis pioneered and applied them to the theory of knowledge in unparalleled ways. But while Lewis was committed to the superiority of the one conceptual scheme of natural science, Goodman's work mirrored more his apprenticeship in the art world and its discriminating but subjective standards. We could not measure alternative schemes of thought against any outside standard, said Goodman, though all might prove useful for different purposes. We could favor no one of them. Goodman elaborated this point in his dissertation, "A Study of Qualities," that in revised form came out as a book in 1951. A dense treatise, *The Structure of Appearance* received more honor in scholarly footnotes than in conversation. The volume's first sentences read:

> The definitions of an uninterpreted symbolic system serve as mere conventions of notational interchangeability, permitting the replacement of longer or less convenient definientia wherever they occur by shorter or more convenient definienda. These conventions are theoretically unnecessary because the elimination of definitions and defined terms would affect the system only by making its sentences much longer and more cumbersome. Furthermore, notational conventions are of course arbitrary and cannot be disputed so long as certain formal requirements are satisfied, such as that no term be adopted as an abbreviation for two nonequivalent expressions of the system.[39]

Goodman's arguments did grip the philosophical community in a spin-off project that began with a 1947 essay, "The Problem of Counterfactual Conditionals," printed in a premier professional magazine, the *Journal of Philosophy*. He made his vision more intricate in the publication of another book, *Fact, Fiction, and Forecast*.[40]

A contrary-to-fact conditional is a statement like the following: "If Neville Chamberlain had repudiated Hitler at the Munich Conference of 1938, the West would have avoided World War II." Lewis had initiated the study of such statements. They legitimately showed, for him, that real alternatives abounded in the world. Chamberlain might have faced down Hitler and in doing so would have changed the history of the 1930s. On the contrary, for Goodman, counterfactuals offered only a language to redescribe the actual. The redescription might serve different needs than those that might come to the fore through some other description. The actual exhausted all there was.

Talk about what Chamberlain might have done had no point except to have us think, let us say, about what we might actually do in the present and future if confronted by a bully.

Goodman's thought opened up the possibility that philosophy might return to the ideas of cultural pluralism prominent during the era of William James. Counterfactual analysis might have led intellectuals to think in novel ways about the contemporary social world. But Goodman rather emphasized the semantic sleight of hand that might defend his position and did not liberate philosophy from technique. Professional colleagues associated his logical legerdemain with the rise of ingenious argumentation. Colleagues sometimes even accused Goodman of a fussy formalism. He had, in any event, a redoubtable intellect with unsurpassed abilities in specialized thought. With the logician Willard Quine of Harvard he created yet another professional position, "pragmatic analysis," that ranked as the most prepossessing branch of the post-war movement of analytic philosophy.

Once out of the service, Goodman married into a rich family of connoisseurs and art patrons. He spent a year at Tufts University before the University of Pennsylvania hired him to begin teaching in September 1946. From that time he kept up a graceful rural retreat in Schwenksville, Pennsylvania, some distance from Philadelphia, where he pursued his abstract study and where his wife, Katharine Sturgis, painted.[41]

At the same time, Morgan State College, an African American institution in Baltimore, Maryland, called Fontaine to chair its Department of Philosophy and Psychology. The Methodist Centenary Biblical Institute had founded the school to train ministers in 1867. Renamed after the first head of its board of trustees, it became Morgan College in 1890. It awarded its first B.A. in 1895 and moved to its Baltimore location in 1917. After a governmental report urged more opportunities in higher education for black students, Maryland made the school part of the system of state education. Fontaine got his appointment for 1945–46. However, because the army did not discharge him until after the fall semester had almost ended, he did not start his teaching until the spring.[42] Despite his position at Morgan State, Bill and Belle lived in Philadelphia, where she had relocated during the war. From Philadelphia he commuted to Baltimore, staying over a couple of nights a week. By the middle of the spring semester, he was yet again sitting in on graduate classes at Penn, a practice that he continued into the summer session of 1946.[43] Fontaine still identified himself with Mannheim's free-floating intelligentsia. He looked both to elevate himself intellectually beyond the racial divide and to find a way practically to overcome it.

He maintained his friendship with Goodman. The white man later criticized the affirmative action impulses of the 1960s in withering and daunting ways. Like many Jewish scholars, he stressed that only impartial measures of ability should govern academic appointments. But from the late 1940s on, he zealously championed Fontaine. Throughout the black man's career, many knew that he could always "count on Nelson."[44] Sixty years later Goodman was the only one of Fontaine's colleagues Belle Fontaine could easily remember. The Goodmans entertained them, she recalled, and Bill "worshipped" Nelson.[45]

In the spring of 1947 Quine of Harvard, Goodman, and Morton White, another successful professional philosopher whom I have already mentioned, had a famous three-way correspondence and discussion group. They debated the notions of meaning and possibility, which Goodman was ruminating about in his writing on counterfactuals and which attracted overriding importance in postwar philosophy.[46] During this period "Nelson and Kay" asked "Bill" to spend a day in Schwenksville with them, while White was also visiting. Fontaine enjoyed "the comradeship, the . . . wine & . . . food." He also admired the Goodmans' art collection, which included Kay's paintings as well as those of more notable artists.[47] It is easy to see that Fontaine might have believed he had reached a place "beyond the Veil."

A New Job

Soon after, the University of Pennsylvania invited Fontaine to teach as a visiting lecturer. Goodman had won a prestigious Guggenheim Fellowship and thus Penn needed a replacement for him for the 1947–48 year. Goodman arranged for Fontaine to take his place.[48] Fontaine went on leave from Morgan State, which seems hardly to have touched his life, although he apparently had enjoyed his usual success there as an instructor.[49] Penn repeated the arrangement in 1948–49. According to Morgan State, Fontaine "continue[d]" in Philadelphia as a "guest Professor of Philosophy."[50] In February 1949, Penn's Department of Philosophy proposed that, since Fontaine had succeeded at these temporary jobs, he receive a standing faculty appointment as an assistant professor to begin that autumn. This probationary post would run three years, followed by another "term" appointment of another three or four years. But after a total of six or seven years, such "tenure track" positions held out the promise of employment with tenure, a lifetime position. His initial salary amounted to $4,000, some $200 less than that of comparably qualified white assistant professors that the university had hired at the same time.[51]

We can only make educated guesses about the motivations involved at Penn. Racial changes, in part the product of African American militancy at many levels, ripened toward the end of the war and the immediate postwar period. Fontaine's work in the Chester shipyards illustrated this development, as did the earlier upheavals in Louisiana that he had witnessed.

On the national scene, the economic policies of the New Deal had a spillover effect that benefited African Americans, but President Roosevelt himself would not upset the racial order of the South, where much of the strength of the New Deal lay. Only his wife, Eleanor Roosevelt, and New Dealers on the fringe spoke out about the rights of citizenship—"civil rights"— that whites regularly denied to black Americans. When Harry Truman ascended to the presidency on Roosevelt's death in 1945, he acted as cautiously as Roosevelt had, but Truman had less control over his liberal troops and they were more able to extract at least symbolic reforms from him.

Truman would not immediately propose legislation to attack segregation in America, but at the end of 1946 he established the President's Committee on Civil Rights, which served as a forum for inquiry into racism. The committee prompted Truman to appoint a Fair Employment Practices Commission that, though it did not have much power, achieved a public relations coup for Truman with the liberals. More important, Truman started to desegregate the armed forces in the United States and moved against the worst anti-black employment practices of the federal government. Outside the executive branch, the Supreme Court reconsidered rulings that had supported segregation. The judiciary and African Americans in local communities energized a new movement in favor of civil rights.

Events of 1947, when Fontaine got his initial offer from Penn, probably grabbed most of the attention of the general public. During World War II the United States had an alliance of convenience with the Soviet Union; with Hitler defeated, ideology and economics now made adversaries of the two nations. In March 1947 in the Truman Doctrine speech, the president announced a global Cold War against this new enemy, between the United States and a totalitarian order that was enslaving people wherever its influence could reach. How could white Americans prevent blacks from voting in the

South and deny them basic amenities all over the United States when the government simultaneously proclaimed a foreign policy to make men everywhere free? Soon after the enunciation of the Truman Doctrine, Jackie Robinson, number forty-two, broke the color line in professional white baseball when he stepped onto the playing field for the old Brooklyn Dodgers. The black activism on display in Louisiana in the late 1930s and Chester in the early 1940s was having a nationwide impact.

The political highpoint took place at the Democratic nominating convention in Philadelphia in 1948, at Convention Hall, within a stone's throw of the campus of the University of Pennsylvania. Hubert Humphrey, the mayor of Minneapolis, called on his party to "get out of the shadow of states' rights and walk forthrightly into the bright sunshine of human rights." The speech split the party and caused extreme segregationists in the South to form their own States Rights Party; they were known as the "Dixiecrats."

The rhetoric of freedom defined foreign policy, and the rhetoric made an impact at home. In short, in the mid-1940s, the United States began a thirty-year period in which the domestic civic agenda centered on race. The outcome of the political battles would transform American life. The legal system of segregation in the South and the less formal one in the North would end. Although racial aspects of employment, education, and economics would still come between Americans, they would all accept greater tolerance as the norm. The racial politics of these years continually engrossed Fontaine, and first of all at the University of Pennsylvania.

There in the late 1940s, the Department of Philosophy had built a liberal enclave. Jews and Catholics had a voice, and at the same time that the university was hiring Fontaine, it was also employing a single woman philosopher (her salary was even less than his).[52] Fontaine had a Pennsylvania doctorate in an era when many schools had difficulties looking outside their own ambit. Did he try to create a role and a job for himself? The years of auditing graduate courses may have reflected strategic thinking on Fontaine's part as much as a love of learning. Of Fontaine's two dissertation directors, Singer had retired in 1944. But for the next two years he had an active appointment as a lecturer, and Penn still felt his influence through students determined to carry on his left-leaning experimentalist legacies.[53] Francis Clarke, now a senior faculty member, chaired the department. We need also to factor Goodman's stature and friendship into the appointment. Finally, in 1939, the university had called another philosopher, Glenn R. Morrow, to Philadelphia. An upright Quaker, Morrow was admired as an expositor of Adam

Smith and later had an international reputation as a scholar of Plato.[54] Penn respected Morrow's authority and leadership, and from 1944 to 1952 he served as dean of the College of Arts and Sciences. A high-minded man, Morrow felt he must always do the right thing but also came close to possessing moral excellence. He "enthusiastic[ally] support[ed]" the department's proposal to hire Fontaine[55] and was resolutely to back him.

Fontaine quickly decided to go to Pennsylvania for good, but complicated considerations went into the decision. The wish for acceptance "into the social order on the same terms as any other human being," said Fontaine, dominated the "inner consciousness" of black Americans. He wanted more than anything "to be an American and a Negro." Yet to "attempt to live in accordance with [these] double aims . . . dissipates . . . energies and impairs . . . quality of performance." Only people who knew "the enormity of American color prejudice can appreciate the difficulty." Did Pennsylvania really think him worthy? Everyone knew, he wrote, that "a Negro teacher, though educated in the best universities of the world, could not conceivably measure up to the pedagogical standards for white professors."[56] Lincoln University surely was predisposed to think that only whites could teach the higher wisdom. Did the philosophy faculty at Penn believe Fontaine worthy, or was it trimming its standards to show its tolerance? Was Fontaine being true to himself, or was he just trying, as he put it, to "act 'white' in the white world"? Would applying "white man's standards to the values of Negroes" result in "shame, diminution of the value of self"? Were his new colleagues only interested in having themselves feel better about their racial bias? Who were these white men anyway to make the judgment? The Negro did "not think in a vacuum" wrote Fontaine. "Standards of the total culture and the desire for status affect his thinking."[57] Whatever the forces at work, their outcome influenced both sides significantly. Even the lectureships had the specific approval of Pennsylvania's president.[58] In early 1949, Fontaine resigned from Morgan. He had taught there for a mere eighteen months, and he had not instructed at the institution for two years.

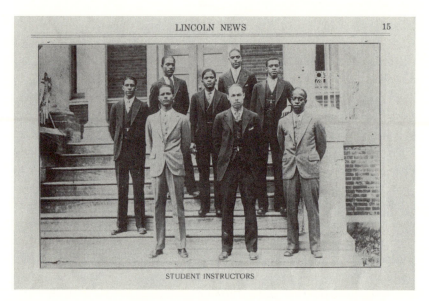

STUDENT INSTRUCTORS

Figure 1. Fontaine as a student instructor at Lincoln University, 1930. Fontaine is in the top row at the left (Lincoln University of Pennsylvania, Langston Hughes Memorial Library, Archives and Special Collections).

Figure 2. Belle Fontaine in the 1930s (courtesy of Pamela Harris).

Figure 3. Fontaine, a newly minted Ph.D., 1936 (Lincoln University of Pennsylvania, Langston Hughes Memorial Library, Archives and Special Collections).

Figure 4. *The Présence Africaine* Conference in Paris, 1956. From left to right are Richard Wright, Leopold Senghor, an unidentified man, William Fontaine, and Horace Mann Bond (Southern University Archives).

Figure 5. Fontaine about 1960, University of Pennsylvania faculty photograph (Collections of the University of Pennsylvania Archives).

Figure 6. Fontaine, with Saunders Redding and others at a conference at Howard University on southern Africa in transition, 1963 (Southern University Archives).

CHAPTER SIX

The Ambiguity of Success

Storming the Citadel

THE LOW-LEVEL APPOINTMENT at the University of Pennsylvania held momentous long-term prospects should Fontaine thrive. When African American scholars taught at the college level at all, they had careers at black institutions, all of which were economically constrained. The white scholar now rarely taught at them and left when he could. Howard University and its tradition of African American research epitomized the desires of most blacks. Academics at Howard (and Fisk and Atlanta) found it impossible to move into any other major research university—white segregated schools— where a few, by dint of perseverance, had gotten graduate degrees. Nonetheless, the atypical white institution of any sort that invited a black scholar to teach received an acceptance with alacrity.

A survey of 1940–41 related that no black professor held a permanent appointment in all of white academia. A 1943 study had six African American doctorates at white schools, one apparently with a lifetime appointment. By the end of 1947 the magazine *Ebony* reported some sixty African American teachers at nonblack schools, and even if we suspect this number, the postwar period was opening up white institutions. A much later and perhaps more reliable survey took appointment at "flagship" state universities as a criterion. This study showed that African Americans did not appear on many of these faculties, even in minimal numbers, until the 1960s. So change occurred very slowly. Most black teachers in white schools had modest instructorships at peripheral schools clustered in Chicago and New York City. But by the late

1940s, Cornell employed a black musicologist, and Columbia a microbiologist. Some older scholars were spending their last active years out of the segregated world. The sociologist Allison Davis received a full-time appointment at the University of Chicago in 1942. Chicago, which led in breaking down the color line, proudly proclaims him the first African American to have had such a position in a white institution. But administrators relegated Davis to the Department of Education, a program peripheral to the traditional arts and sciences, and only a grant of money from the Julius Rosenwald Fund made his job initially possible. Chicago tested other black men differently: the university did not permit the recently appointed Abram Harris to teach graduate students in his field of economics.[1]

Philosophers were most unusual. The single prominent one, Alain Locke, taught most of his life at Howard but by the late 1940s lectured at the New School for Social Research in New York City. From the time Locke received his doctorate in 1918 until the late 1940s, ten black men had gotten the advanced degree in philosophy. No blacks taught the subject in the Ivy League.[2]

Moreover, for the fifty years after World War I, the discipline of philosophy occupied a central role in the collegiate system. The philosophers adapted a conception of the thinker in higher education from nineteenth-century Germany. They perceived themselves as the bearers of the tradition of Western thought that began with the Greeks, progressed through the medieval period, and reached a pinnacle in modern philosophy: Descartes, Spinoza, and Leibniz; Locke, Berkeley, and Hume; Kant; Hegel, and those who followed. The men in this pantheon had reasoned about the human niche in the universe and presented the accumulated insights to an educated elite. Now philosophers in American higher education carried this elevated enterprise upward and forwarded the foundational values of the West. Essential to the growth of moral integrity, philosophy represented the best way for (usually male) undergraduates to understand human beings in the cosmos, but the field also offered conceptual assistance to the natural and social sciences. Finally, the philosopher had a prudent social function, tendering aids to reflection about the soul's anxieties but warning against untoward political expression.

Fontaine believed deeply in this conception. His peers in philosophy often delivered on it at the undergraduate level, where students would take a range of courses in the history of Western thought, and in selected areas of expertise such as logic, ethics, metaphysics, and the theory of knowledge.

But the constricted nature of graduate training displayed the self-serving and interested nature of philosophers' conceptions of their studies. Their cramped professionalism contrasted with the claims of wide-ranging genius and social insight. We can see these limitations by focusing on the cultural context in which professional philosophy existed in the United States in the period from the 1930s to the 1970s. The evolving appeal and prestige of logic, and the honor paid to rigor, determined what counted as philosophy. Thinkers at schools with the most authority maintained the boundaries of the subject. For example, the religion that had tinged philosophy all through the nineteenth century in the United States almost vanished. Philosophers also downgraded the societal concerns of thinkers such as Dewey. People whom the educated public would formerly have considered philosophers the profession defined as social commentators, popularizers, or cultural critics. Moreover, although philosophers did not grasp the point, social scientists moved into the civic sphere that men such as Dewey had wanted to inhabit. More to the point of the present book, professional thought placed outside its boundaries matters of consequence to people of color.[3] Fontaine knew that philosophy was *white*, as we can demonstrate from the nature of some of his work and some of the tactical decisions he fixed on and was about to fix on.

Fontaine's published essay of 1942, "The Mind and Thought of the Negro," made an ambitious statement, and he had worked on it since the end of 1938. The article exemplified his thinking in respect to the larger book project, "The Historical Development of the Mind of the American Negro." He took the publication as a brief version and a trial run for the project he would bring to fruition in his Rosenwald Fellowship of 1942 and his grant from the American Council of Learned Societies of 1943. I can guess that Fontaine allowed President Felton Clark to print the piece in the *Southern University Bulletin* because Fontaine thought the ideas would get wider exposure in a later book. In the eighteen-month period from mid-1942 till the end of 1943, he did substantial writing that elaborated his concerns, and he had the backing of the Rosenwald Fund and the ACLS. He told an interviewer for a black Baltimore newspaper in September 1944 that the war had broken off his progress on the effort, and he repeated the story to an army reporter in early 1945. Military service had interrupted his "almost finished" volume.[4] Yet he never went back to it after the war. Why?

In the study of the history of philosophy, scholars regularly cite Hegel's disquisition on the master-servant dialectic in the *Phenomenology of the Spirit* as evidence of his greatness as a thinker. More empirical and more focused on the despised subordinate group, Fontaine imitated Hegel in the 1942 essay. It had a powerful thesis elaborated at some length. Nonetheless, "The Mind and Thought of the Negro" was the only article Fontaine *never* mentioned in any of the various résumés he prepared for the University of Pennsylvania from the late 1940s to the late 1960s.[5]

The university and its Philosophy Department could not have cared less about this sort of scholarship that touched on race knowledge. Did Fontaine conspire with them to ignore his own scholarship? Would he have destroyed his chances had he *not* conspired with them? How did his decision cohere with his obvious hope that he was entering a higher realm where race did not count? These issues of social understanding complicated Fontaine's personal life and his publishing career just as he argued such issues confounded the racialized society as a whole.[6]

White Philosophy

White or not, the Department of Philosophy at Penn in the twenty years after World War II, with the institutional clout of Clarke and Morrow and the intellectual leadership of Goodman, became a star-studded place for graduate training in this hallowed area of inquiry. As philosophy shifted from historical and social concerns to those of technique and formalization, young men committed to professorial careers might go to Penn to study contemporary problems of logic, as well as the history of ideas. Surveys ranked the philosophers right behind those of Harvard, Yale, Columbia, and Chicago. The department located itself in the middle of campus, in College Hall, the main building that also housed administrators.

Penn in fact maintained segregation: the school had no black faculty, and at any given time only a minuscule number of black students, if any. Some fifty years before, Penn had released W. E. B. Du Bois after a brief appointment. This nasty episode, the institution's chief experience with African Americans, indicated that the university did *not* want an extended association with a black man. Now a standing faculty appointment gave Fontaine the first African American ticket to the inner sanctum of white learning. In part we can read Fontaine's opportunity as an illustration of liberalizing attitudes in the postwar period, but this would neglect its exceptional nature. This interpretation would also neglect the drama of the appointment. Fontaine had never taught whites before 1947. That year he offered them a course on Kant's *Critique of Pure Reason*. Two years before, after laboring in a ship-yard, he had instructed black illiterates in third and fourth grade.

In preparation for his entrance into the world of white philosophy—"the big brethren of lighter hue,"[7] as Fontaine said about that time—he forsook his racial writing priorities of the early 1940s. Martin Luther King, Jr., was studying at the Crozier Theological Seminary in Chester in the late 1940s, and he lived some ten blocks from Fontaine's Aunt Nettie, to whose home Fontaine still regularly returned. King also audited philosophy courses at Penn. One of Fontaine's colleagues, who did teach King, later surmised that he also might have sat in on Fontaine's lectures. Mutual friends may have introduced the two thinkers. William Gray, a well-known Philadelphia churchman, had a relationship with Fontaine that went back to their days in Scotlandville together, and Gray also had a connection to King's father. We do know that Martin Luther King, Jr. and Fontaine used to have coffee together in a Horn and Hardart's eatery, one hundred yards from College Hall.[8] Did they talk about race? Back in College Hall, Fontaine returned to the cast of mind he displayed at Harvard and Penn in the 1930s when he deliberated on the history of philosophy and on the foundations of knowledge. He published essays from which philosophers could draw no social implications. When the University of Pennsylvania's public relations people asked whom he favored as philosophers, Fontaine did not mention Alain Locke or W. E. B. Du Bois. He mentioned Edgar Singer, C. I. Lewis, and Nelson Goodman.[9] In practice he added a fourth who contributed to the asocial nature of American philosophy and Fontaine's own contributions to it. Indeed, C. L. Stevenson told him of the cognitively meaningless nature of cultural issues.

Meet C. L. Stevenson

A constellation of European ideas known as logical positivism boosted the late-1940s fashions of analytic philosophy. The positivists had begun to arrive in the United States in the 1930s with the Nazification of Europe. They did not make their mark in America, however, until after World War II, when many native thinkers assisted the positivists. As a group they stressed the exclusive claims of science to the title of knowledge and outlined the ways science was presumed to operate. While commentators have found it easy to caricature the positivists, one group of them did argue for a "criterion of empirical meaningfulness" associated with scientific statements: if we could verify a proposition as true or false, we could say it had meaning. Statements of science met this test, but other sorts of statements—for example, those of religion or of metaphysics—did not have cognitive meaning, if we spoke strictly. We could not specify the conditions under which we could credit or discredit a proposition such as "God is omnipotent" or "Racism is despicable" or "The segregated social system of the United States contravenes social justice." Philosophers could not denigrate theology, metaphysics, and social ideals as false; such inquiries rather made no sense at all.

I have already introduced A. J. Ayer of Oxford, who had sprung into prominence for his 1936 tract, *Language, Truth, and Logic*.[10] He most famously propounded positivism to speakers of English. At Harvard in the 1930s a young graduate student and friend of Goodman's, Charles Leslie Stevenson, was modifying the views of Dewey, to which he had adhered. He traveled to England, where he studied with Ayer. In 1944 Stevenson himself published *Ethics and Language*, which applied positivist ideas to ethics.[11]

To say "X is good" did not make an empirical claim but expressed an emotion of approval. The statement had an imperatival force designed to get the hearer to join in action with the speaker. "Evaluative language" did not describe the world factually but persuaded people to do something. Science elaborated on the realm of belief and the descriptive. Morality encompassed the realm of attitude. Ethical terms had "emotive meaning" and typified, as the positivists delighted in saying, one variety of the cognitively meaningless. Stevenson rapidly became known for the exposition of a "non-cognitive" theory of morals, "emotivism," or the "emotivist theory of ethics." Moreover, Stevenson helped to make famous the notion that philosophers did not themselves engage in moral discussion but rather clarified the language of morals. In emotivism Stevenson had formulated a "meta-ethical" position explaining how we "deployed" our moral concepts and how we could "unpack" them.

Stevenson himself in turn was attacked most notably by C. I. Lewis, who tried like Dewey to restore some practical content to morality. Nonetheless, the influence and popularity of Stevenson's position potently demonstrated how philosophers of this era had lost contact with the social order that made it possible for them to get jobs. From the late 1930s the United States had called upon its citizens to defeat the wickedness of Nazism and then had embarked in a death struggle with Communism. The future of the West was at stake. Yet philosophers clung so strictly to professional standards that, according to the reigning ethical theory, these global confrontations had no rational basis.[12] Between the public and the philosophical an enormous gap had formed. What an outlandish discipline for Fontaine, as a black man in America, to have dedicated himself to!

Unsurprisingly, even many philosophers read Stevenson's intoxicating and influential book as an especially troubling example of moral "relativism," although they interpreted him less than accurately. For Stevenson people did not have conflicting and equally legitimate moral beliefs. They did not have moral *beliefs* at all; they had opposed attitudes, feelings about the world. Stevenson himself certainly did not deal with actual moral questions; to use language of the twenty-first century he would not be considered an "ethicist." He wrote formally and even formulaically on substantive matters. He did, however, explore how people might overcome moral conflict by circumventing the opposed attitudes that ethical confrontations displayed. Stevenson reasoned that when we did achieve agreement we avoided the fruitless venting of emotion. In arguments over values one common strategy involved finding a desired factual situation that opponents nonetheless mutually wanted to bring into being. They might then ignore divergent feelings in a shared cause. Stevenson implied that we might resolve moral disputes with something like skills at social engineering, a shrewd appraisal of the real-world possibilities contesting sides embraced. But adversaries could not rationally negotiate value opposition itself.

A careful and sympathetic reader of *Ethics and Language*, Fontaine returned to the book again and again. It added another level of complexity to his puzzlement about the legitimacy of competing worldviews. Fontaine now tested the ground between the hope of Dewey (and Lewis) for moral objectivity and Mannheim's more skeptical impulses. Stevenson too took up Dewey's argument but was convinced that values inhabited just that area that escaped scientific corroboration. Stevenson led Fontaine to believe that appeals to reason might not resolve cultural conflict. For Fontaine and Mannheim social position generated differences in worldview. Stevenson gave Fontaine a further way of talking about the ultimate subjectivity of varied human outlooks and refined his sense of the foundation of contrasting political obligations. More important, in grappling with Stevenson, Fontaine actively participated in a professional philosophy that was insulated from American society.

In 1948 at an elite discussion group for collegiate philosophers in and around Philadelphia, he delivered a paper titled "The Immediately Valuable in C. I. Lewis." In June 1949, the *Journal of Philosophy*, the journal that had introduced philosophers to Goodman on counterfactuals two years before, published Fontaine's "The Paradox of Counterfactual Terminating Judgments," the first of two essays he wrote on the topic for the *Journal*. To savor the shift in Fontaine's perspective the reader need only look at the first paragraph of the second of these essays: "Avoidability and the Contrary-to-Fact Conditional in C. I. Lewis and C. L. Stevenson."[13]

> C. I. Lewis's critique of conventional methods of implication and his solution to the problems of the meaning and truth of contrary-to-fact conditional statements provide an interesting critical supplement to Stevenson's conclusions regarding the question of avoidability. For Stevenson, quoting W. V. Quine, states that the counterfactual is "not directly identifiable with any truth functional mode of composition but calls for a more elaborate analysis." But in lieu of such an analysis he merely admonishes that we must pay particular attention to the case at hand, that the "if" clause must not be contrary to the law of nature, that actual choices are to be distinguished from choices that might have been, and that the if-then relation is to be expressed by "should-would" of the subjunctive conditional. He neither undertakes a critique of existing theories of implication as these apply to his definition of avoidability nor does he give any final answer to the question of the meaning and truth of counterfactual statements in relation to a definite theory of implication. Stevenson, nevertheless, speaks of "the force of the contrary-to fact-conditional" as if to assume a definite theory of implication and as if the if-then relation has a definite meaning and the compelling force of truth.[14]

Both of Fontaine's essays incrementally contributed to the dispute over counterfactual conditionals that sharpened the differences between Lewis and his student Goodman. Fontaine trod a narrow and not very far-reaching path. In the first essay he argued that Lewis's adherence to the genuinely possible might constrict philosophers more than Goodman's attention to the creative use of language about the actual. In the second, Fontaine argued that Stevenson's concerns about moral choice depended upon his unexamined commitment to Lewis's view of the contrary-to-fact conditional. Philosophers ignored the essays, just as they did most of what appeared in the plethora of journals. And it is indeed hard to see where Fontaine was going with his publications, except to show that he was becoming just another writer for professional magazines, adept at what his new colleagues were doing.

"All Things Flow," the Bitter and the Sweet

Fontaine, however, could not just be another philosopher. After the racial incident at the 1948 meeting of the American Philosophical Association in Virginia, he was briefly a cause célèbre. The next year the APA Eastern Division met in Worcester, Massachusetts, under the auspices of Clark University. The Executive Committee of the organization called a special meeting. It discussed the impact of the mushrooming "red scare" that would soon be labeled McCarthyism, after Joseph McCarthy, the belligerent anti-Communist senator from Wisconsin. Defending the civil liberties of their members, the philosophers passed a number of resolutions that a mail ballot then over-whelmingly validated. The first resolution, however, did not concern the rights of white philosophers under attack from ultraconservative politicians. The incident the year before in Charlottesville had galvanized a number of heavyweight professors—the first generation of Jews in the American academy and many liberal Protestants—to evince their support for Fontaine.[15]

> I. WHEREAS the democratic operation of our Association entails equality of treatment for all members, which is not provided by meetings at places where there is racial segregation;
> BE IT RESOLVED THAT meetings of the Eastern Division of the American Philosophical Association not be held at colleges or universities where it is impossible to provide non-segregated accommodations.[16]

Just as we do not know where Fontaine's interest in Stevenson and counterfactuals was going, we do not know what Fontaine made of this expression of solidarity. Simultaneously with his promotion to the tenure-track job to begin in the fall of 1949 and before the APA meeting in Massachusetts, he petitioned for sick leave. Doctors told him in the summer of 1949 that he had tuberculosis, a terrifying disease of the poor, particularly widespread among black Americans, that was never spoken of in polite society because of the disgrace and embarrassment associated with it. The illness struck many in Fontaine's family. In the early 1920s, did he give himself the middle name

Valerio, with its overtones of physical health, to ward off the disease? In the early 1930s two of his youngest siblings had died after the family took them to the Pocono Mountains of Pennsylvania in a desperate last-minute attempt to stave off the illness through outdoor living.[17] In all likelihood, Fontaine had previously had what is now known as "primary" TB, which by 1949 had advanced to an "active" stage because of a weakened immune system. Fontaine wrote that "the shadow" had "stalked" him from birth. Diagnosed with active TB, he blamed "a lowered guard" on "the compelling ambition to win the contract at Penn."[18]

When doctors detected Fontaine's ailment, they were just devising genuine remedies for tuberculosis after a fifty-year period during which they quarantined patients in sanatoria and subjected them to a variety of dubious regimens. The diet, exercise, injections, and various surgical procedures had outcomes that might ameliorate the illness. But just as often, the "cures" might accompany a prolonged and wretched death in which the victim slowly and painfully wasted away. Often in all-black facilities, African Americans almost always had the worst care. The other names for TB, "consumption" or "the white plague," aptly summarized the cruel and frightening course of the malady.[19]

In the time-honored way, Fontaine immediately faced the prospect of yet another kind of prolonged segregation. He was installed at Sea View Hospital, in the middle of Staten Island, New York. Sea View, an enormous, rambling facility, had first opened in 1908 and promoted the virtues of salt air and the healthful out-of-doors.[20] Belle visited every weekend, using train, bus, and ferry to get to Sea View from Philadelphia.[21] Although he had to take the first semester off, Fontaine still expected to begin his teaching as an assistant professor in the term starting in February 1950. From the hospital, at the end of 1949, a few weeks before the APA voted in his behalf not to sanction segregation, Fontaine wrote Dean Morrow:

Dr. Cherkov gave me his final word today. It would come on the day of my birth [December 2]. Briefly it is this: I cannot return to work until negative one year, five months of which have passed. Should a positive sputum appear during this time he suggests removal of the right lung, which, incidentally, is the speediest way of eliminating this type of trouble. Patients are at home in two months, at work from four to six. I certainly do not wish surgery but I am just today in my fortieth year & I am willing to take the risk for my family, my work, and one more crack at life.

He continued:

Life is not easy here, and sometimes the thought settles upon my mind of how singular my fate is that my health should fail at a time when I need it so much. And then I think of Heraclitus "All things flow," the bitter and the sweet. I will walk out of here in six months ready for work.

Developments at the university cushioned this crushing blow to Fontaine's psyche and sense of purpose, although again I am forced to ask myself what Fontaine made of this heart-breaking diagnosis. Speaking for the college and the Philosophy Department, Morrow requested for Fontaine a full salary for a year of leave from the higher echelons of the university. In the course of the negotiations, he forwarded the above letter to the provost, saying, "I think you will be interested in reading it."[22]

The provost acceded to the petition, but Fontaine did not walk out of the TB ward in six months. Nor did he have his lung removed. Of the cures to which he subjected himself for the rest of his life we know only that at one point physicians collapsed the lung in which tuberculosis existed, supposedly to rest the organ. We also know that the diseased right lung eventually healed—although not before tuberculosis poisoned the left lung.[23] We finally know that of his first six years as assistant professor, he spent three and one-half in the hospital or convalescing, which was unexceptional for TB victims. The University of Pennsylvania carried Fontaine on full salary for the first three semesters of his illness and inquired to ensure that he could get appropriate treatment at Sea View. He returned to work—sometimes only one-half time—for the spring of 1951 and for the academic years of 1951–52 and 1952–53.[24] The next two-year stint of medical leave, from 1953 to 1955, occurred without pay, and sometimes doctors hospitalized him in Philadelphia.

In this period we also know that to eat well—a common recommendation—he traveled across the Delaware River to neighboring New Jersey, where the long-time black boxer and sometime heavyweight champion "Jersey Joe" Walcott trained. At the camp Fontaine got to know Walcott, who was a few years younger than Fontaine, and his entourage. Fontaine believed he got appropriate food there, preferring fresh eggs and milk. When he was able to teach, he would take the bus home from school at lunchtime to make sure he got just the right nutrition. Then he would return to the university after a nap. He also lectured and ate standing up. This routine "assist[ed] his digestion," and allowed him to deal more easily with the chronic aspects of the affliction, although family members often thought him in pain that went unacknowledged. Fontaine additionally altered other aspects of his life. He stopped smoking, gave up alcohol for the most part, and became less inclined and able to participate in the social evenings Belle arranged.[25]

Fontaine never fully recovered, but in the fall of 1955 he had sufficiently regained his health to begin a productive period of ten years. His specialist saw "no evidence of recently acquired or active disease,"[26] although Fontaine made constant trips to the doctor and had never-ending encounters with the medical gear of the era, x-rays, straight films, Bucky films, and planograms.[27]

Although the TB went into remission in the decade from 1955 to 1965, the University of Pennsylvania did not know how matters would turn out during the better part of the 1950s. Officials at the highest levels of the university gave him steady and worried scrutiny. Fontaine received a low salary, but in the eyes of the university this fact did not compensate for a state of affairs in which Penn paid him when he did not teach. Deans and provosts nervously fretted about their moral responsibilities but also about the economic dimension of their decisions. Would they have to subsidize Fontaine were he indefinitely ill? Should they tenure the man, this long-term prospect upset the institution's managers even more: might they have to carry him on the books permanently even if he could not work? It also understandably vexed policymakers that someone with a communicable disease was lecturing to their students. It reinforced all of these concerns that, as a new employee, Fontaine had no track record and that he was black.

The philosophers could patronize Fontaine, but they adamantly wanted to retain him when officials would have breathed a sigh of relief to rid themselves of the man. In going along with the department's repeated requests for leaves of absence, Penn's administrators could "see no way to avoid . . . [the] arrangement." They did resolve that they should not decide about Fontaine's continued employment on "a purely humanitarian basis." By the middle 1950s, to receive approval for a reappointment of three years, Fontaine had to forswear in writing any claims to tenure. Otherwise, his service at the university, which included both time at work *and* more time sick and on leave, would have automatically entitled him to a position without term. He then had his trial period as an untenured professor extended in the hope that his health would improve and that the extra years would give him the chance to make a greater mark—in accepted areas of philosophical scholarship. The university expected a measure of repute in its tenured faculty—in recognized portions of the intellectual universe. Fontaine acknowledged this arrangement in writing. His "deepest wish" was to have a period of "good health and scholarly attainment."[28]

While Fontaine feared for the rest of his life that a doctor might pronounce the tuberculosis "active,"[29] the university additionally required him to get a medical opinion attesting to dormant TB. In the first of a series of agreements that occupied the chief officer of Pennsylvania's School of Medicine, Fontaine's reappointments occasioned codifications of hiring and tenure proceedings at the university, which had previously only been subject to the deliberations of white gentlemen, and of its medical benefits.[30]

In my opinion the university set the bar higher for Fontaine than it did for comparable white faculty members, but I have a complex opinion, and the bar was not much higher. Despite the fact that many less then stellar scholars flourished at the institution, the university did honor academic writing. Fontaine had a slender publication record, and he feared sharing a significant amount of his writing with his evaluators. The philosophers had reason to dismiss his work on Lewis, Goodman, and Stevenson as of little account. At the same time, his written work on African American culture had more than outstanding merit. But, crucially, Penn attached no importance to concerns for race and social identity, where the jugular of Fontaine's publications lay. The philosophers barely considered this writing as connected to their discipline, and the university had a minimal interest in African American matters. Fontaine could make no impact in white circles with these publications. His fear about letting his colleagues examine some of this writing was not unjustified, although since he kept it from them we will never be sure. Finally, in part, I think Pennsylvania appraised matters on the basis of how the illness might hamper Fontaine's usefulness to the school.[31]

CHAPTER SEVEN

Social Philosophy and Civil Rights

Teacher of Philosophy

As a PENNSYLVANIA FACULTY MEMBER, Fontaine oversaw instruction in the beginning course in philosophy. His ability became more apparent when his health improved. "Fontaine and staff" stamped this first course, Philosophy 1, "Intro to Phil," with his own wide-ranging and learned vision of the history of ideas in the West from the time of the Greeks. He made this initial experience famous at Pennsylvania among undergraduates. Quiet and soft-spoken, Fontaine had yet a personal magnetism and a sense of his office at Penn. Elegantly dressed by Belle, he would arrive slightly late for the first class of a new semester, just when the (white) students were getting restless and complaining. He would enjoy their being taken aback as he walked in and introduced himself, in a perfect transatlantic accent, as their teacher, *Dr. Fontaine.* Alternatively, he would arrive *early* and seat himself to one side of the room and listen to the students complain and make snide remarks about the supposed tardiness of the professor. Then he would stand up and introduce himself as that professor.[1]

The students seldom left after the first meeting, for Fontaine taught effectively and instructed with dedication. He "receive[d] raves," said the Penn Guide to Courses.[2] "Phil 1" had a thematic organization. Although Fontaine lectured on metaphysics and the philosophy of religion, he emphasized epistemology and the various luminaries who exemplified certain theories of truth. Fontaine would make his points with maximum gesticulation, long bony fingers grasping for the correct formulations. He might sometimes cough slightly, bringing his hand quickly to his mouth; or throat clearing would interrupt his speech. In carefully enunciating his words he would smack his lips as if making a tiny effort at breathing.[3] Later, many of the undergraduates repeatedly remembered him as "kindly," "gentle." He might shame them into working. Those who were unprepared were never humiliated with words—he would merely shake his head and suck his teeth.[4] Perhaps Fontaine had his greatest influence on the more reflective of his pupils. He jolted these well brought up young people into a realization of the derogatory racial categories that defined their world. A man who represented for them a debased race first guided them to the highest ideas of (white) civilization.

At the same time students could not get their minds around the fact that he was an "American" Negro. In 1950 MGM released the film *King Solomon's Mines,* which was based on H. Rider Haggard's book of the same title. In this popular movie fantasy, a great white hunter, Allan Quartermaine, acted by Stewart Granger, led an intrepid band across the wilds of Africa. Umbopa, the king of the Watusi, a handsome black race said to have originated in Egypt, joined the group. The Watusi actor Siriaque, who was thin and almost seven feet tall, played the king. At Penn the undergraduates who had studied with Fontaine and knew him to be tall and thin told one another of his background as a Watusi. Or, because they did not know the difference, a Zulu or a Ubangi.[5]

In his more advanced teaching Fontaine cautiously concentrated on social issues in the mid- to late 1950s. One can easily attribute this shift to renewed health, growing confidence, and the prominence of a national political struggle for civil rights. Truman's Committee on Civil Rights, the Fair Employment Practices Commission, and the 1948 Democratic convention had made segregation and rights for African Americans hot topics in national politics even before the Supreme Court delivered its famous ruling in *Brown v. Board of Education* in 1954, which outlawed segregation in public schools. Fontaine returned at last to full-time work in 1955, after meditating about these issues on the sidelines for several years. His signature course, Philosophy 26, and its graduate equivalent also took many of his scholarly concerns into his lecturing. He titled the courses "Philosophy of the Social Sciences" and refused the name that others favored, "Problems in Social and Political Philosophy."[6] He still thought within the parameters of pragmatic analytic philosophy, but he now did so with his own accent. Philosophy majors took Philosophy 26, but the class also courted campus intellectuals. "Phil 26," many students recalled, introduced them to otherwise marginalized thought, "whole areas that were otherwise left out of our curriculum." As one student wrote, the class read authors and took up topics that "I doubt I would have otherwise encountered": Hegel, the early humanistic writing of the young Karl Marx, and that of the more heavy-handed Russian Marxist Georgi Plekhanov; the philosophers of history Oswald Spengler and Arnold Toynbee; the sociologists of knowledge Karl Mannheim and Karl Popper; the feminist social thinkers Ruth Benedict, Margaret Mead, and Simone de Beauvoir; and the contemporary students of the philosophy of the social sciences Isaiah Berlin, Charles Beard, Morris Cohen, Sidney Hook, and Ernest Nagel.[7]

Fontaine always worried that the social locus of the scholar influenced, perhaps tainted, the supposed knowledge in the human sciences. This worry provided the underlying theme of the course. "Is the genesis of a proposition," he would ask, "relevant to its validity?" "I didn't know exactly what this meant," recalled one former undergraduate student, "but I knew it was important."[8]

Fontaine sent graduate students to Pennsylvania's social scientists to get a sense of the actual texture of work in substantive disciplines and an idea of the practices of social knowledge.[9] In the seminar for doctoral candidates, much discussion and criticism arose from the floor, and the candidates consensually banned smoking, which was common at the time in philosophy teaching rooms. If Fontaine were ill, his teaching power was displayed when the graduate students trooped to his home for instruction.[10] Fontaine pressed his long fingers together at their tips while pursing his lips as he considered a response to questions put to him. As one former student put it, "His painstaking care in choosing his words came from a felt need to give his best to you."[11] In the 1960s when conventions permitted explicit talk about racial matters, he related to the graduate students the alternately sickening and comical stories that summed up much of his life at Southern in the 1930s. But he turned deadly serious in illustrating the injustices that his white students might find difficult to believe. He would conclude with a little laugh: "Do you see? Do you see?"[12]

By the late 1950s, Fontaine was thus coming back to interests dormant for more than a decade and, albeit in chastened form, responding to the lure that public responsibility and race had had for black leaders since Reconstruction.

Life and Politics

After Bill and Belle moved back to Philadelphia in the mid-1940s, Belle was always employed as a secretary and administrative assistant. She also regained custody of her two daughters, Jean and Vivian. The enlarged family underscored the need for a supplement to the household income, although Jean and Vivian, who were now grown up, left the house after a few years. In 1951 Vivian herself gave birth to a daughter, Pamela. Bill and Belle raised Pamela, who lived with them until she went off to college. Bill told his kin that the experience of being raised in poverty with many children underfoot had discouraged him from having children himself, but his fatherly inclinations were finally expressed in his connection to Pam. He took her to the movies, the circus, major league baseball games, and most regularly to the Penn Relays, an annual track and field event at the University. He bought Pam her first set of high heels and taught her to dance. With her he would still express his interest in music and especially jazz, but he would also lecture her on the importance of education, steering her in his own direction of educated gentility. "Try to remember what really counts—not money or titles," but how we treat others.[13]

When Fontaine started his professional life at Pennsylvania, he entered a parallel universe to that which existed at Lincoln, Southern, or Morgan. On his job he played a part in the white collegiate world and was subject to its customs and rituals. He both witnessed and participated in, even if unwillingly, its racial stereotyping and assumptions of superiority. His employment cut him off from his world in the intersecting black communities that had previously defined his lived experience. His profession now separated him from the world of the black academy and even from his life with his family and his roots in Chester. Belle added to Fontaine's disconnection by her desire to keep her less successful in-laws at a distance. Perhaps most important, and not without its own irony, even an assistant professorship at Pennsylvania, which Belle especially relished, immediately lifted Fontaine into the local black elite. Politicians, judges, religious leaders, teachers, and local literary figures populated this universe—men such as Robert N. C. Nix, a powerful congressman, and William Gray, the prominent leader of the Bright Hope Baptist Church and a long-time friend. But Fontaine's fraternizing with this group, again, moved him away from the social world of Penn that had originally given Bill and Belle their cachet. He wrote about whites and blacks: "They may meet daily . . . as fellow workers, but at the end of the work-day 'truce,' each withdraws behind the 'invisible wall' of his narrow world to the company of his own kind."[14]

Like the white elite, the black elite honored meritocracy only at the fringes. Often family connections and class position most firmly supported membership in this latter elite. It admired light complexion and found status in tracing ancestry back to white folk or to free blacks and to education in white institutions. But attachment to the elite rarely entitled its members to entrée into the white world. Rather, the black elite negotiated the ever changing boundaries between the segregated territories.

Fontaine joined the black elite primarily because of his education and not at all because of any tribal pedigree. Simultaneously, he did not adjudicate the borders of the color line so much as he scouted in the foreign land far over the line.[15]

The African American leadership measured itself in some way in relation to the separate society of Caucasians. But the blacks self-consciously prided themselves on a morality that was higher than that of the comparable white elite. The compromised racial standards that sullied the white leadership and even its racial liberals did not stain the African Americans. They were not racists. Fontaine suspected such claims to virtue. He had said in print long before that as a product of social position the ethics of a group or individual could not demand absolute standing. He also believed that a racist culture reciprocally gripped both African Americans and whites. It is hard not to think that he felt uncomfortable with the ethos of the "talented tenth." He strove to balance African American social insecurity with justified fury about its cause. Belle had fewer qualms; she loved her position.[16]

Fontaine's housing choices displayed these ambiguities. As a graduate student in philosophy, he had lived in a marginal black area at the city limits. After his appointment at Penn, he and Belle had moved to a better part of the large black ghetto of North Philadelphia; then they moved to the edge of West Philadelphia, which white members of the university community and prosperous African Americans inhabited. Later, the Fontaines moved again to Center City, a white enclave, and finally to a stylish condominium there.[17] Here Belle gave parties for their black friends, who rarely interacted with Fontaine's colleagues at the university. Here also, as Fontaine wrote, "black bearded males and blond- and russet-haired females" as well as "long-haired white boys and shapely brown-skinned girls walk[ed] hand in hand."[18] From Center City too Bill and Belle and Pamela went off on Sunday mornings to attend Belle's choice of an elevated and biracial Episcopal church, the Church of the Advocate in North Philadelphia. By the 1960s, under the leadership of Father Paul Washington, the church had involved itself in progressive civil rights activities that Fontaine favored.[19] The Christ to whom he prayed to at night "was but . . . a very wonderful man," "an idealized person that once existed in human form and now existed only in his continued influence upon human lives." In black churches Fontaine could find "the influence of Christ, the man, very much alive in fact, in act, and in song."[20]

Bill could not move up fast enough for Belle. Although she was informed and smart, she found the academic world a little pokey. She was, one of his colleagues claimed, "ambitious and high maintenance."[21] Bill's illness had additionally changed his priorities. His interest in their social existence diminished, while Belle's handsome energy craved a less staid lifestyle, more entertainment, not less.[22] Just as important, Belle never thought Bill's salary enough, and she felt she never got a respite from full-time work. Professors existed at the financial bottom of the professional class, and in addition Penn underpaid Fontaine. As Pamela put it, the couple would have "words."[23] Tuberculosis put a strain on the marriage, not least its sexual dimension. It was widely rumored within the elite black community that Belle had an ongoing affair with a black prizefighter,[24] and she surely made her own life, often leaving Bill alone with Pam. What had begun as a complementary relationship evolved into a connection between opposites. Bill and Belle now enjoyed a problematic union.

The available fragmented evidence makes it hard to reconstruct some of Fontaine's political party beliefs. As I have suggested, he resisted Chester Republicanism in the 1930s. Moreover, his writings from the late 1930s and such activities as attendance at the New Orleans Youth Conference and employment at the Sun Shipyard tell us that even if he was not radical in his politics, he made it to the left border of the New Deal. By the Truman era, 1945–53, things had changed. Eugene Holmes, a philosopher who taught for a time at Howard but who also recruited black intellectuals for the American Communist Party, reported that his overtures to join the party did not tempt Fontaine.[25] The Cold War between the United States and the Soviet Union had shifted American political expression to the right. During the early 1950s, Senator Joseph McCarthy of Wisconsin and those who followed him sought out politically untrustworthy Americans in a frenzy that most commentators have deprecated. A fear of the corrupting power of Communism swept the land and made ordinary citizens afraid to express any nonconventional beliefs. Political officials raised spiteful questions about the loyalty of many teachers. Temple University, in North Philadelphia, dismissed Barrows Dunham, a Marxist philosopher, for his views, and the Philadelphia public school district expelled a large number of high school instructors from their jobs.

In the late 1930s and early 1940s Harold Stassen had prominently and successfully governed Minnesota. In 1948 and again in 1952 he ran in Republican primaries for the presidency. In the second campaign Fontaine coordinated "Negro activities" for the Stassen for President Committee.[26] Although he came from the Midwest, Stassen adhered to a moderate internationalism, making him a member of a dominant group of politicians whom less interventionist and more conservative elements of his party called "the me-too Republicans." Their liberalism, said the Republican right, made them indistinguishable from Democrats. Stassen lost his bid in 1952 to Dwight David Eisenhower, the one moderate who had an undeniable chance to beat the Democrats—and did.

Fontaine's support for this style of Republicanism was a minority position in the black community, but it was not unheard of. From the era of Franklin Roosevelt, African Americans had left the party of Lincoln in droves and lodged as an accepted part of "the New Deal coalition" from the 1930s to the late 1960s. Later the Democratic Party counted even more on the black vote. But Stassen's racially liberal kind of white politics had a history in the Republican Party from Abraham Lincoln to Teddy Roosevelt to Earl Warren, who was appointed chief justice by Eisenhower in 1953. The line of thought attracted blacks who most wanted to be seen as socially respectable. It produced a number of significant African American public figures—the major league ball player Jackie Robinson, Senator Edward Brooke from Massachusetts, and Secretaries of State Colin Powell and Condoleezza Rice.

This explanation of the move in Fontaine's politics, however, does not attend to the fact that in between Stassen's runs for the presidency in 1948 and 1952 he took the job as president of the University of Pennsylvania from 1948 to 1953. He had at least formally supervised Fontaine's hiring. We might easily conclude that the philosopher, a family man and the father of two young adult girls, had a more rosy view of the United States than he had had fifteen years before. He may have trimmed his sails at Pennsylvania.

A Modest Political Stance

Still, the Republican right and southern Democrats often tried to associate the stirrings among blacks for voting rights with Communism. For these whites it was un-American to press for an end to segregation in the South and for full equality for blacks in the North. In the late 1940s Democratic liberals and African American activists predicated their initial push for freedom at home on a worldwide struggle against Communist tyranny. Conservatives countered this declaration with the argument that Communists almost always backed battles for domestic changes. Fontaine would have none of this talk he considered reactionary. He was now a settled anti-Communist. Long study of the writing of Marx and social theorists on the left had enriched his understanding of the connection between ideology and economic and social exploitation. Yet he rejected the policies of the Soviet regime that had come into existence espousing these Marxist ideas. Fontaine found Communist practices far more intolerable than the racial views of the Western democracies. He thus promoted anti-Communism at home and abroad, but he did so in the context of pointedly advocating global civil rights. His political evolution made him into a liberal internationalist Cold Warrior, a label more often used to describe some foreign policy Democrats such as Adlai Stevenson (the Democratic nominee for the presidency in 1952 and 1956) and Dean Rusk (the secretary of state under John Kennedy and Lyndon Johnson from 1961 to 1969).

Periodically in the 1950s and 1960s Fontaine spoke out on foreign policy in the pages of the student newspaper, *The Daily Pennsylvanian*. He supportively criticized the initiatives of Truman, Eisenhower, and Kennedy in foreign policy and adopted their anti-Communism.[27] At the same time he stood at home in an intellectual forefront of the burgeoning civil rights movement.

The Truman administration positioned itself as one friendly to black ventures, but steps toward equality did not end when the more hostile Eisenhower administration came to power in 1953. By this time the Supreme Court was smiling on the arguments of the NAACP's lawyers, and the decision rendered in the *Brown* case of 1954 concluded one phase of the Court's efforts. Yet desegregation of schools in the South proceeded at a glacial pace and the results were dubious. Nonetheless, grass-roots activities had shaped the Court's decision, and the decision stimulated more local movements, chief among them protests in Little Rock, Arkansas. These demonstrations led an irritated Eisenhower to use federalized troops in aid of African Americans in 1957. The same year brought the passage of an ineffectual Civil Rights Act, but the first in the United States since 1867. More important for Fontaine and his work, the politics of the era gave greater legitimacy to a concern for race and for the sort of reasoned discussion of racism at the heart of his labor.[28]

Social Philosophy in the 1950s

C. L. Stevenson corroborated Fontaine's fear that rationality could not adjudicate social policies. But although Stevenson argued abstractly, he also proposed various techniques by means of which people might manipulate facts and values to secure agreement on concerted action and avoid the clash of attitudes. Clever stage management became a priority.

Using Stevenson, Fontaine combined his white philosophical expertise with his views on race relations in the United States. The implicit examples with which he operated came out of his own experiences with America in wartime. Politicians put the African American male to work in northern defense industries in World War I. They did not desire decent employment for the black man but did want to avert defeat by the Germans. Blacks might not think that a German defeat was a great good, but they were certainly willing to engage in war work as a start at obtaining better jobs for themselves. In World War II, African Americans might doubt the commitment of the United States to domestic freedom, but they would support the war effort. In exchange, to get black support, American authorities would break down segregated employment in the defense industries. In a pragmatic focus on what blacks and whites could trade for what, they could steer clear of a dispute about racial superiority or inferiority, which they would not settle. Instead, shrewd negotiation could reach goals that both races sought.

An explicit example Fontaine used from another field also showed how he was thinking. The United States and the Soviet Union might care not at all for the survival of the society of the other. They had opposed attitudes essential to their moral evaluations, but each nation cared very much for its own survival. The enemy threatened this survival. If scientific calculation could persuade each nation that general disarmament would make each safer, then emphasizing the scientific facts of disarmament might eventuate in each side's being willing to disarm. It did so not to help the other, or because it embraced a joint ethic, but to save itself. Thus, we would resolve the moral issue of the nuclear arms race, even though non-shared attitudes steered the disagreement.[29]

Using language indebted to Stevenson, Fontaine called his position a "modified ethical relativism." Dewey argued that empirical beliefs might prove decisive in practical life but did not convince Fontaine. Nonetheless, observing the cognitive emptiness of social clashes did not flummox him. Leadership might orchestrate beliefs and attitudes to move to a social morality that might not otherwise attract opposing sides. A factual state of affairs that a group desired might alter the attitudes essential to its ethical stance. A morality Fontaine disparaged might give way when it no longer served high-level interests, or if incentives could be offered to amend it.

If one is not a philosopher, this more general formulation of Fontaine's position will seem well nigh empty. Fontaine looked on at a lofty height and examined social problems through complex lenses, as the philosophical writing he did in the mid- to late 1950s testifies. The flurry of work resulted in the first instance in a paper delivered in Paris in 1956 and then at the Inter-American Congress on Philosophy in 1957 in Washington, D.C. He elaborated abstractly how meta-ethics might subvert segregation. His presentation earned special mention in a report on the congress. Even the respectful *rapporteur*, however, worried about the method's applied "poverty": a Southern philosopher in the room had offered a rebuttal, rearranging the same ideas to shore up segregation.[30]

Fontaine thought that racial problems might dissolve themselves if only he could convince people to ponder appropriately his custom-made "modified ethical relativism." But he was also chary in print of showing how to apply his ideas concretely. He had drawn on some basic "types" of analysis in Stevenson's *Ethics and Language*, and a quotation from a 1958 publication, "The Means End Relation and Its Significance for Cross-Cultural Ethical Agreement," gives the full flavor of Fontaine's theoretical thinking:

Summing up the several factors now involved in the agreement of [two people in different cultures] C_1 and C_2, we have divergent ends S_1 and S_2, which have become in part convergent, and also E_1 or the intercultural program, which is approved both as means and as end. In so far as E_1 is approved by C_1 and C_2 as a means to divergent ends we have [of several varieties of complex ethical agreement an example of] basic type IV. In so far as E_1 is approved by C_1 and C_2 as a common end we have basic type II. Finally agreement of C_1 and C_2 on E_1 as an end exemplifies basic type I. C_1 and C_2 thus agree on E_1 simultaneously in a manner involving three different basic types.

The result is a complex ethical agreement involving basic types I, II, and IV.[31]

By the early 1960s, Fontaine was teaching his hypothetical approach in his classrooms.[32]

Tenure

When Penn extended Fontaine's appointment as an assistant professor in early 1956, the dean of the college told him that the institution expected more in the way of publication if he were to receive tenure. And indeed in the two years after the dean conveyed this expectation, Fontaine gave a series of talks that resulted in the publication of two essays and the submission of others for publication. This work applied the "modified ethical relativism" to social problems in its deracinated way. At the end of 1957 Chairman Francis Clarke delivered a "strong" departmental recommendation for an appointment "without term" as assistant professor. Fontaine would receive tenure in his rank. Universities had created three "professorial" grades, assistant, associate, and (full) professor. The promotion to an associate professorship usually went with tenure but not necessarily. Pennsylvania reserved *promotion* for faculty it thought of as strong scholars. The school gave tenure *in grade* to special cases. Nonetheless, Clarke wrote, aside from Fontaine's "technical competence," he was "particularly fitted" to deal with problems of "social studies." The department had a "considerable advantage" to have them "presented . . . in terms of critical analysis and not emotional rhetoric . . . by a Negro of such ability."[33]

The department's letter accompanied a dossier with references from a range of experts. Fontaine had sent a telegraph to one of these referees. Fontaine considered it "most important" that the authority respond favorably to the department's request for an appraisal.[34] And the Philosophy Department removed from the file sent to the dean and the provost a letter that declined to comment on Fontaine's writings.[35] But at a time before the inflation of praise in writing academic recommendations, the references spoke modestly but positively of Fontaine's scholarship. The most illuminating noted that philosophers put a premium on a "theoretical job" and that Fontaine was refreshing in "applying our theories to mundane and practical concerns."[36]

No one spoke the dreaded word "tuberculosis" in public, but in early

1958 the university administration acquiesced to the departmental recommendation only after medical examination again showed an "arrested" case of the disease. In addition, the president of the university, its chief medical officer, and the provost carefully wrote and rewrote the memorandum of agreement that stipulated the conditions under which the school would tenure Fontaine.[37] Pennsylvania's managers did not intend to provide medical care or to limit Fontaine's choice of such care. Yet his tenure depended on consent to twice yearly chest x-rays in order to ensure "a proper hygienic environment for the student body." Fontaine also agreed that the university would not pay his salary should he become "a hazard to the health of others."[38]

In the late 1950s Penn debated how the school's academic standards would square up with Fontaine's performance, but found it acceptable, and it surely was so, especially if we factor in the debilitating influence of his disease. Fontaine could probably not have put out of mind the conditions placed on his appointment, but he still had a tenured professorship in the Ivy League. As Fontaine wrote about this time, "Human existence is notoriously ambiguous. The individual who successfully maintains his life partakes of a grim, universal experience—the inexorable demand of death."[39]

CHAPTER EIGHT

Conservative Pan-Africanism

Back to Africa

IN THE TWENTY YEARS of the Cold War that Fontaine witnessed, the U.S. government displayed almost no independent interest in Africa, or its connection to American citizens of African descent. In the late 1950s and early 1960s, however, when the European powers gave independence to many of their African colonies, the United States adjusted its view of what was called the developing world, the third world, or the southern world. American diplomats rightly worried that the new nations might find anti-Western revolutionary politics attractive and that the Soviet Union might take advantage of such events. In Africa, U.S. policymakers engaged in behind-the-scenes diplomatic activity or covert operations to secure the support of pro-Western political groups. At home, events pushed the new presidential administration of John Kennedy into hesitant encouragement of the civil rights movement in part to show to the new countries the anti-racist and pro-black intentions of the United States. America sympathized with African goals. The same motivation led Kennedy, from 1961 to 1963, to place black citizens in the diplomatic corps and in ceremonial and public relations positions in the armed forces.[1]

For Fontaine these events corroborated his philosophy. He observed, in respect to Africa, that a threat to concrete and factual *interests* could guide politicians to actions that might change *attitudes*. White Americans might find desegregation worrisome—they had negative attitudes. Nonetheless, they might accept it to avoid the triumph of Communism in Africa—a certain factual situation. With his examination of Stevenson, Fontaine had defined these issues theoretically. If he had an appropriate theory, he might influence the moral shifts. But when Fontaine confronted the reality of Africa, he could hardly make the theory relevant. Nonetheless, the complexities of international politics, the Cold War, and domestic anti-Communism did all reinforce a new role for him as an engaged scholar of color.

African American intellectuals and intellectuals on the European left, both black and white, had begun to explore the possibilities for transforming Western race relations on the basis of what was taking place in African politics. American blacks had for a long time looked east to Africa with preoccupied concern. The artists of the Harlem Renaissance prominently attended to the African roots of their culture. And not just the whites in the old American Colonization Society wished for repatriation. As Fontaine knew, the "Back to Africa" movement of Marcus Garvey exerted a pull on poorer blacks in the early part of the century, and Fontaine spent more time studying it in the 1950s and early 1960s.

Black intellectuals who studied African affairs wondered how the fledgling ruling groups on the continent might construct the national identities that would emerge in the absence of a dominant white presence. Would Marxist suppositions, if not Communist politics, assist in banishing the remnants of colonial thought? This possibility kept American diplomats awake at night. Communism terrified black academics in the United States less. They saw that the evolution of African nationalism might aid African Americans striving to have their culture accepted on equal terms with white culture. How could African Americans integrate their own culture into a new multicultural American ideal? Here African American thinking connected to the issue of Communism. The Communist Party–USA had attracted blacks much earlier because, whatever its defects, it was confidently committed to racial equality. By the end of his life W. E. B. Du Bois, whose thought Fontaine always took seriously, believed both in Communism and in the African origins of African American culture. Finally, Fontaine realized that however bad the position of American blacks, they were in material and educational terms far better off than the great majority of the African populace.

In the context of American politics, Fontaine adhered to a Cold War liberalism, though he thought more unconventionally in the area of civil rights. In discussing Africa's place in global affairs, he located himself as what I call a "conservative pan-Africanist." Whether out of genuine anti-

Communism or from fear of how an association with Communism might contaminate all efforts for reform in America, he resolutely wrote off the Communists. He distrusted the authoritarian left, surely in the United States but also in other countries. He had difficulties dealing with all of those who put the Soviet Union of Joseph Stalin and his successors on a pedestal at the expense of the United States. Fontaine even dismissed the "Western Marxist" intelligentsia, who were far less enamored of Communism and Stalin. Fontaine would have reappraised his own position if anyone had shown any of the accusations of Communism to be true of civil rights advocates in America. He sought a middle way between two political stances. On the one hand, the extreme left linked its criticisms of American segregation to American imperialism. America's policies at home consisted of "internal colonialism." On the other hand, the American rhetoric of desegregation in the late 1950s had only a minimal real impact on everyday life outside the South. Fontaine wanted to see how America might assist the new African countries, and how these new countries might provide models for race relations in America, north and south. But he wanted to keep away from the Marxist left.

Traveling in Behalf of Africa

Although we lack the evidence for making the case, I find it plausible to argue that Fontaine's friendship with Nkrumah and Azikiwe galvanized his study of pan-African ideas. When colonial rule in British West Africa collapsed, both of them had risen to great power, Nkrumah in the old British Gold Coast—Ghana—and Azikiwe in Nigeria. In 1954 Fontaine had spoken to alumni at the one hundredth anniversary celebration of Lincoln's founding and called attention to the university's original commitment to Africa.[2] In addition, Fontaine had connected with the political scientist John A. Davis, who studied African politics. The brother of the more famous sociologist Allison Davis, John Davis had spent much of his career at Lincoln but by the 1950s had gone to City College in New York. In 1956, Fontaine and John Davis formed part of the American delegation that traveled to the First International Congress of Negro Writers and Artists held at the Sorbonne in Paris. The rest of the U.S. contingent included Horace Mann Bond, Lincoln's president; Mercer Cook, who taught at Howard; and James Ivy, the editor of *Crisis*. The American novelists Richard Wright and James Baldwin also made appearances.[3] The congress gathered an extraordinary worldwide group from African colonies, the Caribbean, India, Europe, and the United States. The center of gravity rested with Francophone intellectuals who had a romance with international Communism. The French-speaking poets and politicians Leopold Senghor from Senegal and Aimé Césaire from Martinique attended, and so did Frantz Fanon, the Martinique-born theorist of colonialism who had authored *Black Skin, White Masks* (1952) and was later to publish *The Wretched of the Earth* (1961).

These French-speakers had for years labored in the Négritude movement that looked on colonialism as practiced by France as the key issue for understanding black-white relations. In their celebration of a common African heritage, these men had something in common with the Harlem Renaissance, though politics absorbed the Franco-Africans far more than it did the African Americans.[4]

At the conference, Fontaine for the first time delivered his paper on the application of his "modified ethical relativism" to American segregation. According to Davis, the representatives widely discussed the paper and praised Fontaine at the congress.[5] The American delegates, including Fontaine, promoted independence for the African colonies but opposed Communism there. They thus embraced a studied and unadventurous position in the Cold War struggle over the third world and clashed with the French-speakers, who were more hostile to the United States and more cavalier about Communist infiltration in Africa. During the meeting Fanon excoriated what he took to be the conservatism of Fontaine and the other U.S. nationals, and Horace Mann Bond reported that the French Communist press attended the conference and attacked Fontaine.[6] The publicity prompted Fontaine, on the planeride back, to lecture the American delegation on Marxism, a topic he knew well and about which he could not keep quiet after the interchange with Fanon.[7]

The Francophone thinkers of the African diaspora had run the conference under the auspices of the magazine *Présence Africaine*, which was managed by the Parisian left. The journal generated revolutionary ideas and had a high profile in Europe. Out of the conference came the Society of African Culture, which closely associated itself with *Présence Africaine*, although the SAC had an international clientele. The society aimed to preserve and defend African values and traditions. It additionally voiced the need for African independence and harshly criticized American policies in Africa. From the perspective of the Americans, the Society of African Culture was naïve to believe that the Soviet (or Chinese) Communists could provide a helpful alternative to African engagement with the United States. But despite this political cleavage, in 1957, a year after the conference, the Americans founded in their home country a sister or suborganization of much less importance. The American Society of African Culture (AMSAC) blossomed with Fontaine as a charter member. He served first as the secretary of the organization and then for some years as a member of its executive committee, although he never had much organizational responsibility.[8]

For Fontaine, one did not do business with Communists. Moreover, the glorification of blackness was racist and did not account for the mutual dependence, everywhere, of black and white consciousness. Yet Fontaine wanted Africa freed from imperialism, and he acknowledged the crucial fraternity of Africans and African Americans. The latter might have something to learn from upheaval overseas.

John Davis created AMSAC and he ran the organization from New York City. He had formed it from a group originally called the American Information Committee on Race and Caste,[9] and the committee had paid for Fontaine's trip in 1956. The U.S. Central Intelligence Agency (the CIA) liberally funded this group and its successors as one of many vehicles to promote anti-Communism among intellectuals around the world. I cannot tell if Davis knew where his money was coming from, though I fear he did, despite his denials.[10] He certainly designed AMSAC to replace more radical black groups in the United States that were interested in pan-Africanism and that had Communist affiliations.[11] Fontaine almost certainly did not know of the society's tainted origins and cash flow and had nothing to do with AMSAC's finances. He primarily wanted to invite men of professional quality into the organization, and Davis employed him to that end.[12] When scandals exposed the group's funding in the late 1960s, the connection aroused more of an outcry than seems warranted today, and in any case by that time Fontaine's sickness had removed him from the group's affairs.[13]

Africans and non-African Francophone blacks, Fontaine thought, knew little about African Americans and their status in the United States. "Communist propaganda" had convinced the outsiders of colonialism in America. But, wrote Fontaine, African Americans did not occupy a colonial position. They rather had to obtain "complete political, economic, and social equality" in a different sort of social setting. Davis intended the U.S. branch of the Society African Culture to correct the perspective of the French fire-eaters. Indeed, Fontaine led in rejecting the elevation of Du Bois and Paul Robeson

(another famous American black Communist) to AMSAC's executive committee.[14] At the same time Fontaine gladly joined this global vehicle that
would promote an extraordinary civil rights agenda in the United States and
pride in African ties for American blacks. In foreign policy AMSAC took a
pro-American line despite the fact that the society was only supposed to
sponsor African American interest in Africa. In its activities in the United
States, however, AMSAC backed civil rights goals that were in the vanguard,
even though the leadership directed activities to an elite.

The society's written aim, which Fontaine helped to draft, unambigu-
ously recalled this old priority of Du Bois. The society opened membership
"to all accomplished . . . men . . . of Negro descent in America." It would
"unite by bonds of solidarity and friendship the men of culture of the Negro
world."[15] Fontaine also forsook one of his own priorities in involving himself
in AMSAC: although neither shrill nor strident, the organization limited
itself to blacks.

In 1959, Fontaine delivered a paper at the Second International Congress
of Negro Writers and Artists. For this one he flew to Rome courtesy of
AMSAC, and the twenty-five participants were a roll call of the world's politi-
cal intellectuals of color concerned with anti-colonialism in Africa. Senghor,
Césaire, and Fanon again graced the event. So too did Cheikh Anta Diop (the
Paris-based Senegalese historian of Africa), John Mbiti (a Kenyan Christian
thinker), Ezekiel Mphahlele (a South African writer), Jean Price-Mars (the
head of the University of Haiti), Sékou Touré (a political leader from
Guinea), and Eric Williams (a future leader of Trinidad).[16] In addition to
Fontaine, the other American participants were Robert L. Carter (Fontaine's
old student and a NAACP legal strategist) and St. Claire Drake (an important
black sociologist from Roosevelt University in Chicago).

Fontaine played a part in several of AMSAC's meetings in the United
States. Most prominently, in 1960 he assisted in arranging a large event titled
"African Unities and Pan Africanism" that was hosted at the University of
Pennsylvania.[17] The same year he traveled to Africa when Penn sent him to
Lagos for the installation of his old classmate Azikiwe as governor-general of
Nigeria.[18] On this trip Fontaine met Du Bois on board the ship to Africa,
although Du Bois's age and well-known standoffishness might have made the
meeting perfunctory.[19] Two years later Fontaine returned to Africa as a dele-
gate to the Conference on African Socialism in Dakar, Senegal.

Fontaine wrote some brief essays for AMSAC's short-lived journal, *African Forum*, as well as for the more significant *Présence Africaine*.[20] But his

politics remained guarded, and distance precluded much of a renewed attachment to Azikiwe and Nkrumah, who were militants. Nkrumah made several trips to the United States in the 1950s. But his leftist reputation during this heightened era of anti-Communism curtailed much of a renewal of the old friendship. And, according to Fontaine's family, on one occasion authorities prevented Nkrumah from visiting Fontaine in the large black enclave of Philadelphia where the philosopher was then living.[21] Fontaine did entertain Azikiwe in his home, when the African leader spoke in Philadelphia, and also hosted Diop, and he met Touré in New York.[22]

Fontaine radiated anti-Communism, but he did want to understand the rise of neo-Garveyite thought in the United States. Why did some African Americans stress a black nationhood in Africa? Why did a separatism that looked to Africa lure them? Fontaine worried about the inflexibility of the racial climate in the United States. If African Americans could never escape the evil effects of second-class citizenship, Garvey's thought made sense. Yet Fontaine would not relinquish belief in the potential for a non-segregated America, and a colorblind society that would display elements of both the old white and African American cultures. And he could not really see why Africa might magnetize blacks in the United States. At the same time, he did investigate how the new nations of Africa might illustrate the development of black culture released from worry about hegemonic white leadership. His writing in these areas only described and explored. But again it was striking how eagerly Fontaine expanded his horizon. He built upon his older reading in African history and in the links between African and black American ideas, but now came to grips with contemporary African affairs.

Penn and Africa

In 1963 the University of Pennsylvania promoted Fontaine to an associate professorship. In its deliberations about promotion, the school acknowledged that he published as a professional academic and dispensed with the humiliating provisos about his health. Although Glenn Morrow wrote the testimonial for the Philosophy Department with measured words, once again scholars who said they knew nothing of Fontaine's writing did not have their letters transmitted to the dean and the provost.[23] The philosophers, said Morrow, "esteem[ed]" Fontaine, and everyone knew of the "devotion" of students to his teaching. His "unostentatious kindness" and the "goodness" of his personality had a "steadying influence." His scholarship had not yet come to fruition, but it grew in promise. Altogether in Fontaine the university enjoyed an "honorable asset."[24]

The department did not desert Fontaine, although more than a hint of faint praise comes through in Morrow's letter. It appears a fair summary of the now more skeptical views of senior faculty members who did not see that their investment in Fontaine had yielded much of a return. The philosophers, and Morrow in particular, had an awareness of Fontaine's interest in matters African, but the institution had virtually no sense of the international arena in which Fontaine had made a mark.

More important, Penn was just beginning to work with the American diplomatic establishment in creating a favorable impression of the United States among Africans. The university now advertised itself as a place for Africans to study, although the institution still did not want blacks from the United States in its midst. The school's commitment to the American Department of State may have occasioned its outlay for Fontaine's trip to Nigeria in November 1960.[25] Moreover, the next year Fontaine chaired a university-sponsored lecture series—the "AMSAC Seminar"—on the political philosophies of African leaders.[26] But while Fontaine's engagement with the intellectual dimension of the African diaspora had pierced Morrow's consciousness, the university only dimly realized Fontaine's connection to black intellectuals in Europe or Africa. To the extent that the connection registered at Penn, the institution hardly deemed these concerns worth comment, and no one thought they had anything to do with philosophy. When Fontaine proposed to the provost that Penn invite the speakers on African political theory to campus, the academic chief wanted assurance that the program would not conflict with the *philosophical* symposia Fontaine's department offered.[27]

Fontaine did not lead in the "new" Négritude movement that the end of African colonialism had revitalized. Yet he did maintain a presence in a worldwide network. He had traveled widely and lectured in Europe. His global scholarly acquaintances gave him important recognition. Yet his reputation in Europe and elsewhere among those interested in Africa did not impress his own university. Africa was terra incognita for Penn, and even more for his discipline. Indeed, his area of inquiry really did not recognize his brand of social thought as philosophy at all. As a form of cultural knowledge, professional philosophy in America had intellectual standards that reflected factors other than an impartial ideal of excellence. The norms of the discipline relegated to the periphery the thinking that engrossed Fontaine. Philosophy banished from its purview notions about the creation of social personality. Equally important, Pennsylvania barely counted intellectual activity that encompassed Africa as an enterprise of much value. The epistemology of the counterfactual conditional, *yes*; social thought, *maybe*; the construction of identity in Africa and America, *no!*

A studious professor, Fontaine unsurprisingly did not achieve the public eminence of someone such as Du Bois. But from 1956 to 1963 he contributed to a global dialogue. The failure of Pennsylvania and philosophy to comprehend this fact remarkably comments on the racial dimension of scholarship in the United States during that era. Fontaine could have ignored the blind spot of his discipline and of his university only with difficulty.

But even as Fontaine's social philosophy oriented itself to the new global environment that connected Africans and African Americans in the 1960s, the man himself lagged behind what was going on in the streets of the United States.

CHAPTER NINE

White Racism and Black Power

The 1960s Begin

FROM THE LATE 1950S politics had a claim on Fontaine's life. Ferment at home and overseas drew his attention. He felt most comfortable in the early 1960s when exhortation and political pressure combined to move the Kennedy administration in the correct direction, both in foreign and domestic affairs. Kennedy's intellect sided with progressives in racial matters. Black activism, including the work of Fontaine's former acquaintance Martin Luther King, was edging the United States toward desegregation. The administration would propose a more potent civil rights bill than that of 1957. Anti-Communism was complementing the quest for African independence overseas. After Kennedy's death in 1963, Lyndon Johnson proved a far more effective advocate for civil rights, and the 1964 and 1965 Civil Rights Acts eventually ended the segregated southern way of life and ushered in a new era of racial tolerance in the North.

At Penn in the early 1960s, the issue of "discrimination" discomfited white liberals. They favored desegregation in the South as a matter of law. Yet talk about de facto segregation in their own neighborhoods prompted them to sweat and exposed the racism endemic in the North to much of white America. Even if administrators at the university tried to maintain the status quo, issues of fairness troubled them, and they struggled with their prejudices. Again and again, combative black Americans and pushy students on the left exposed the limits of northern egalitarianism as it pertained to daily life on campus. A biracial coalition at Penn pointed to bias in admissions policies, student housing, and the employment of low-level workers.[1] Suddenly, for the university, race had a high profile, and deans and provosts wanted eagerly to point with pride to whatever black presence they had. Suddenly, Fontaine had a considerable importance to the school, although he embodied the racial "tokenism" of an era that did not know how to cash out its promises of equality.

Initially, I conjecture that because African matters occupied Fontaine, Penn only slowly pushed him front and center. Then for a short time in the mid-1960s he had a role as the visible black faculty member, in the brief period before his tuberculosis finally did him in. Even when healthy, however, Fontaine was a thinker about civil rights, not a doer; he was always a bit standoffish, not an activist. He hardly capitalized on the new place of race at the school.

Between 1964 and 1966 Fontaine did not see much beyond the increased violence about racial matters all over the United States and the rise of political passion. The hopeful dialogue about race in the interchange between John Kennedy and Martin Luther King had barely begun before it had given way to a more strident era. The unpredictable enlargement of the struggle for equality, for all Fontaine knew, could eventuate in social regression. He noted several times the troubles of "the long hot summer" of 1966, when riots occurred in many black ghettos in American cities.[2] He worried not just about the progress of desegregation but also about the rise of black racism. He finally despaired because the war in far-off Vietnam undermined the anti-Communism that, he thought, allowed for the promise of democracy in Africa. He believed war would rework social mores at home, but he could not say how. The domestic fallout of the war in Vietnam burst forth less predictably than had such fallout in the past. And then, always cautious, Fontaine was once more ill.

A tiny number of black students at Pennsylvania in the 1960s could declare their U.S. citizenship, and in a period of social upheaval they had an uncharted position at a prestigious white institution. In 1959 John Wideman, later a notable novelist and writer, entered Penn's freshmen class, some twelve hundred strong, as one of a half-dozen African Americans.[3] A poor black young man, Wideman did not have an easy time. In his sophomore year he learned that Penn had a black professor, and Wideman thought that maybe such a person could help with his insecurities about his place at a white university. Wideman walked over to College Hall and spotted Fontaine near the offices of the Philosophy Department but walked past the man, afraid to introduce himself. As Wideman told the story, on his way he had come to fear that "if Bill Fontaine was teaching at the University of Pennsylvania, he must be a special case. He probably wasn't as good as the white professors. And so, if I wanted to do my best, I wouldn't ally myself with Bill Fontaine."

> That's the sort of self-delusion I had been laboring under. I had been told enough times that black was inferior that I had lost my capacity to image what black could be. And so Bill Fontaine, al-though I needed him, was somebody I couldn't talk to, because I was afraid—I was afraid that what other people had told me about who I was, was in fact true; and if it were true about me, then it would be true about this man, this teacher.[4]

In recalling this event, Wideman also remembered, however, that Fon-taine did not reach out to him—the philosopher kept himself aloof.[5] Five years later matters had improved slightly. In 1966 undergraduates formed the Society of African and Afro-American Students, the first such organization at Penn. As faculty sponsor, Fontaine spoke briefly to the assembled students at their opening meeting in October. While they concentrated on their exclusiv-ity as a group, Fontaine "hoped we would make an effort not to become isolated from the rest of the university."[6]

In the twenty-first century pundits still debate whether historically white colleges and universities do provide or can provide the nurture to students of color that they provide to white students, or that historically black institu-tions still offer to their charges.[7] The issue baffled Fontaine in 1966. He supported the few black students who made their way to him, but he also distanced himself from student activism. He implied that philosophic specu-lation would allow Americans to circumvent the racial issues that he saw at a crisis point. But his perspective, *The African American Registry* later said, had "a conservative aroma."[8] The *Registry* picked out Fontaine's opinion that the "Black Power" of the 1960s had the same defects as white racism. He equated African American militants with southern whites. But this opinion only skims the surface of Fontaine's anxieties. Despite his gloom about the mean reality of racism, he had made great strides, he thought, by philosophically "dissecting" white control of blacks. The students thought this trivial. Of course, American society had the defects he had shown. Who could doubt it? And who could doubt that conjuring up intellectual blueprints would *not* make it go away?

A Book in the Making

From the late 1950s Fontaine had pledged a book expounding his position, the promise of which Morrow had spoken. Fontaine had recorded as early as 1956 that he had completed three of the five chapters.[9] In early 1961, he announced it as "near completion."[10] By the spring of 1963, he had a finished manuscript that colleagues had read, and a year later he had an improved version of it.[11] *Reflections on Segregation, Desegregation, Power and Morals* appeared in 1967, a year before he died. It would, he believed, secure his reputation as a social theorist and his promotion to a full professorship. *Reflections* was "his pride."[12] At one point in its long gestation, Fontaine's old friend Zik, now governor-general Nnamdi Azikiwe of Nigeria, wrote to Pennsylvania's Philosophy Department about the book on its author's behalf.[13] On its publication in late 1967, a "Committee of Friends," composed of a white and black social and intellectual elite of Philadelphia, celebrated the volume's release and fêted Fontaine.[14] In addition to people such as the Reverend Bill Gray and Congressman Bob Nix, the company included John Saunders, the editor of Philadelphia's black newspaper, *The Tribune*; the African American judge Juanita Kidd Stout; Fontaine's old student Robert Carter, now general counsel for the NAACP; Walter Phillips, a patrician Philadelphian who had unsuccessfully run for mayor as a "reform" Democrat in 1963; and Marvin Wachman, the white president of Lincoln University. Kay and Nelson Goodman, who had left Penn for Harvard, came from Massachusetts.

An agonizing process had given birth to this volume, and only the efforts of another white philosopher, Marvin Farber, pushed Fontaine to finish it at all. A well-known professional, Farber had come to Pennsylvania in the early 1960s to chair the Philosophy Department. He styled himself a man of the left, and spoke out vigorously on racial issues.[15] He urged Fontaine on. A magazine Farber edited, *Philosophy and Phenomenological Research*, printed an essay that had begun as part of a chapter of *Reflections*. Farber finally published the book in a monograph series in American philosophy that he oversaw.[16]

Reflections

The changing times and, I think, the contemplation that he did not have much time left himself, impelled Fontaine to return to the themes of the unfinished project of World War II, "The Historical Development of the Mind of the American Negro." But the new book differed, displaying a long simmering anger. Fontaine's work in the late 1930s and early 1940s had often turned his fury inward. These youthful writings had elaborated on the upward sweep of black intellectual development in conjunction with a revamped white consciousness. Yet they had also highlighted the deficiencies of black intellectuals because of the disadvantaged position from which they wrote. *Reflections* had another tone. It lashed out against racism. Although Fontaine praised some white Americans for their leanings toward social justice, he censured others. He railed at the "Anglo-Teutonic culture of America" and condemned white liberals for their half-hearted support of integration. *Reflections* scorned both white and black churchmen for promoting segregated Christianity because they clung to their own priestly power.[17]

Some things remained the same. The book asserted that overcoming racial polarization hung on "the philosophic task" of "clari[fying] . . . issues and . . . positions." And so, for example, Fontaine supplied "the five forms of separation" that "comprehended . . . all the problems of segregation by race." As one friendly interviewer put it, "he is reducing a current social predicament—the racial question and its solution—to a philosophical question."[18] Most important, leaders needed "a method" to understand issues systematically.[19] How did Fontaine describe it?

He had discussed these issues for a long time, and the book implicitly laid out his mature reflections on the relativity of political ethics. The opposing contestants in racial battles, said Fontaine, all took for granted the "objectivity" of their moral positions, even though they contradicted themselves. Expounding pragmatism and the sociology of knowledge had long ago convinced him that cultural identity as much as reality grounded these divisions among worldviews. Rationality could not adjudicate basic differences, which survived beyond fact and science. He found an "emotive disagreement" fundamental to the conflict between his views and those of racists. At the same time Fontaine held that social choreography might get America to the point he wanted it to reach. The philosopher sought to order common factual beliefs so that individuals would unite behind programs encompassing divergent and incompatible evaluations. Fontaine had monitored how such political contriving had occurred again and again. The duress of World War I, World War II, the onset of the Cold War, and the early 1960s had forced egalitarian change. These examples showed how attitudes might shift to protect interests perceived as ordinary and accepted facts.

Fontaine reasoned that, although white Americans liked segregation, they had a greater commitment to making money. The philosopher envisioned circumstances in which, although whites might not promote desegregation, they would swallow it because they could get something they desired more. "The social philosopher," he wrote, "calls the attention of mankind generally to the loci of value and to new modes of living."[20] Fontaine did not assume that whites and blacks would arrive at identical moral judgments. Rather, for whites to get their highest goal, pecuniary reward, the theorist or planner must generate novel chances that would bring racial assimilation into being along the way. Blacks would contribute financially to this effort to obtain their *summum bonum*, full acceptance.[21]

Residential desegregation illustrated the theory. Fontaine supported the existence in every city of a body that, with deprecating humor, he called OOPS, the Organization for an Open Progressive Society. With contributions from many sources, including urban black professionals, OOPS would subsidize whites and blacks sharing neighborhoods. For example, material incentives might persuade upwardly mobile blacks not to move from their homes, and similar incentives might get whites, and not blacks, to move next door. The organization would grant mortgage relief, free home improvements, cheaper groceries, and cash payments. It would also better the schools in such neighborhoods and would afford urban amenities, parks, upscale shopping, and restaurants.[22]

Throughout *Reflections* Fontaine inveighed against the black power movement, as he had to the African and African American students, but now he made his reasons plain. For Fontaine black power asked for preferential treatment for blacks, asserted a special culture untouched by white America, and claimed that whites could not participate in black existence and organizations. This credo, for Fontaine, paralleled the unfortunate views of white Americans in the worst days of a segregated social order. Black power advocates and white racists had the same defective mentality. They paraded as the chief obstacles to an integrated public life.

Like Martin Luther King, Fontaine wished for a time when black men and white men, Jews and Gentiles, Protestants and Catholics would come together because of the equality of their souls. Fontaine envisioned an era in which the gap between the reality of American life and its egalitarian ideal would close, in which we would overcome, and America would at last come home. King manifested for Fontaine, as he did for many thoughtful Americans, responsible and effective leadership on racial matters. For Fontaine in particular, King's religious stewardship of the Southern Christian Leadership Conference had changed the philosopher's estimate of black religion. But Fontaine still suspected King's sort of commitment—Bill Gray, the Baptist leader and friend of both King and Fontaine, had reported to the family that King, who was known for his womanizing, had asked to be fixed up with Belle in one of his appearances in Philadelphia.[23]

Problems with *Reflections*

Early on Fontaine had titled his volume *The Ethics of Segregation and Desegregation*.[24] In 1964 Morrow recommended it to Random House, an important publisher in New York City, and Fontaine submitted it there.[25] He had "written & re-written sections many, many times" and he felt "satisfied with almost every word."[26] Random House rejected the effort, and Fontaine set to work on yet another revision for the much less significant series edited by Farber. But the more Fontaine tinkered with the manuscript, the more it lost its coherence, and during the 1960s he often lamented that he could not get the "transitions" correct. He could not repair the clumsy and unconvincing shifts from chapter to chapter. He fretted about minor topics, and the final title, *Reflections on Segregation, Desegregation, Power and Morals*, hinted at the further loss of focus. The book devolved into a series of barely connected essays, some of which dated from far earlier periods, such as the work in the *Southern University Bulletin* from 1942.[27] The man could not articulate a lucid framework for what he wanted to say. He did not know where he stood, or at least could not say where he stood.

In some ways Fontaine's book simply tried to do too much. On one level he had written a primer for white Americans on African American history and on race relations in the United States. Fontaine had spent twenty years in the white professional world. He was convinced of its ignorance of Negro life and culture. "The intellectual repertoire" of whites did not include knowledge of African Americans. "The black man and his subculture have been treated as an inconsequential thing apart."[28] Parts of *Reflections* instructed white people of good will in a friendly way. On another level he had published a memoir. If one knows anything at all about Fontaine, one can see the autobiographical aspect of much of the work. A biographer will find it a main source about Fontaine's experiences, and what he made of them. At yet another level Fontaine was attempting his hand at the literary expression that he had valued from the time he had read Du Bois and Locke. A form of creative writing captivated him. He consciously mixed historical narrative, the letters of third parties, philosophical asides, passages of fictional dialogue, and analysis. And then there was the analysis, which was compelling in many ways: a novel approach to the conflict of racial values joined an innovative implementation of the approach. But I have excavated Fontaine's views from 160 pages that he never managed to integrate. A skeletal form of the ideas I have reconstructed did exist in *Reflections*, but Fontaine muddied his arguments.

Robert Nix, the powerful black congressman from Philadelphia, had a tribute to the book put into the *Congressional Record*. Nix asked his fellow lawmakers to peruse what he thought was a brilliant and incisive piece of writing. Nix or someone in his office had carefully and intelligently read *Reflections*. But the tribute also urged that the quality of the work would stand "on its ability to compete in the market place of ideas and survive in the arena of intellectual challenge."[29]

A search in JSTOR, an online compendium of past issues of many magazines, uncovers *no* reviews of the book and *no* discussions of it for forty years after its publication.[30] The 450-page *Companion to African-American Philosophy*[31] of 2003 does not mention Fontaine once, either in its essays or in its bibliographies, despite the fact that early on he contributed to almost every issue the *Companion* examines.

During the period of the book's gestation in the 1960s, Fontaine also worried and protested that his colleagues ignored him and showed him little respect. He perceived matters querulously but accurately. By the 1960s, it was apparent that the department had hired him in the late 1940s as a tribute to the racial liberalism of that former period. The philosophers did not repeat the experiment, and in the institution's eyes Fontaine had turned out to be a far cry from Clarke, Morrow, or Goodman. Just so! The philosophical essays that he wrote for his colleagues to see were in a very minor key. He did not show them his best work on the social construction of race, and in any event they were interested neither in this issue nor in the African diaspora.

Fontaine was a black souvenir. Now he had piddled away his time on a problematic book. One of his colleagues remembered looking at it and thinking "it was much more social history than philosophy." His reputation was "nice but inconsequential."[32] From the extant but incomplete evidence, the conclusion may be easily drawn that the book's flaws corroborated what may have been the underlying views of his fellow philosophers about black brainpower. At least Fontaine sensed their lack of favor. He wrote in *Reflections,* "Specialists in a segment of a discipline are the stars; all others, including those having expertise in history and generalities, are boresome expendables. . . . Specialization and the cult of stars are . . . sources of insecurity, vindictiveness, dogma and envy."[33] Penn paid him some $6,000 a year during this period, less than 60 percent of Goodman's annual salary, and the disparity increased.[34] In the last year of Fontaine's life after *Reflections* appeared, the philosophers at Pennsylvania and its administration did not promote him to a full professorship.

Fontaine did have the intellectual ability. His World War II articles on the sociology of knowledge and on the development of social consciousness, as I have tried to demonstrate, cut at the bone. His peers at Penn may not have known "The Mind and Thought of the Negro," from 1942, and "Social Determination in the Writings of American Negro Scholars," from 1944, but he had produced first-class essays. They had without doubt more merit than his later book. *Before Fontaine had irrevocably hooked himself up at a white institution, he had shown great facility in discerning the strengths and limits of social knowledge.*

One might argue that in interpreting the book and finding it wanting, I have—like Fontaine's white colleagues?—applied irrelevant criteria; perhaps other criteria are appropriate to judging it. But how might we grasp such alternative criteria, since virtually no one, black or white, has found the text worth cogitating over? To comprehend these issues has posed a well-nigh insoluble problem for me. Like Fontaine, I believe that standards colored by race permeate the society—period. But like Fontaine, too, I believe that the social locus of the knower does not compromise some matters. The book exhibited a breakdown of control. If we can point out why such a breakdown might have occurred, we might better grapple with its reality.

Partially Explaining *Reflections*

Several reasons explain the misfortunes of the book. Tuberculosis comes first. From the early to mid-1960s Fontaine's health declined, and his writing evidenced a heated activity different from his previous scholarly endeavors. His correspondence about the book regularly commented on his fight against his disease. Again and again he set deadlines for the completion of the manuscript, and again and again he failed to deliver. He often parenthetically noted to his editor some new turn in the course of his illness:

> July 1963: I have made pretty good progress on the book. Now & then I become concerned about the body (health) but my weight is fine [,] lbs up.

> October 1964: I have been working on weekends. I think you will like the revision & and new sequence. . . . My health is good. Xray is clearing fast.

> April 1965: The good news is that my health is good. I am working away at the completion of the book.

> November 1965: I am re-working the final chapter . . . My health has been somewhat uncertain during the last month. However, it was my good fortune just yesterday to learn an exercise which pulls up my receding ribs. For two days it has worked, so I keep my fingers crossed.

> April 1966: I am trying very hard to get my manuscript into your hands by the first of June. . . . My health is good.

> Telegram, April 1967: Bill Undergoing minor exploratory surgery will communicate later. W. Belle Fontaine

> May 1967: I think it is very important for this footnote to be added. . . . My health is just a wee bit better.

> Telegram, May 1967: Completed galleys mailing today. Bill

> September 1967: Enclosed is the dedication page. . . . Bill dictated the attached to me over the telephone. I am not sure about correct form and punctuation. W. Belle Fontaine.[35]

Fontaine only feverishly finished *Reflections* after going on indefinite medical leave in January 1967 for the tuberculosis that was now slowly killing him. Belle later said that, because of "his disability," he "did not write his book in the normal fashion." She had to type his manuscript "from small pieces of paper, backs of envelopes, etc."[36] The dying man did not have the energy to straighten out the muddled scholarly apparatus, and friends ineffectually assisted him.[37]

A second reason for the shortfall of the book stems from Fontaine's philosophically trained incapacity to think concretely about social problems. His career distanced him somewhat from the untidy racial world of mid-twentieth-century America, and he intellectualized what he could not ignore. Philosophy, Fontaine wrote, comprised not a "strictly academic" field but rather a "foundation for human society."[38] On the contrary, professional thought in America from the 1930s to the 1970s only half-heartedly—maybe less—sponsored perception into his predicament, or the human predicament. Despite its historic claims to wisdom, the discipline to which Fontaine had devoted his life had ironically made it difficult for him to understand his life. In his thirty-one years as a scholar, from 1936 to 1967, writing on social identity easily played out as his strong suit. But the white professionalized discipline of twentieth-century American philosophy did not judge Fontaine, by choice and chance, on this writing. His discipline ignored his significant work.

We can instructively contrast Fontaine here with other more prominent African American academics who contributed more effectively to a conversation about race in the United States. Black college administrators lobbied as a critical group for these concerns. Consider Charles Johnson at Fisk, with whom Fontaine had consulted in 1943. Johnson took over as Fisk's president in 1947 after running its social science programs. Look at Fontaine's acquaintance Horace Mann Bond, who directed institutions in the South and served as the first black president of Lincoln in 1945. Bond gave up his career writing social-historical analyses of African American life for life as an educational leader. His biographer has written that for Bond to have remained a faculty member at a black college would have meant "a life with high teaching loads, poor pay, [and] little research support."[39] Along with men such as Johnson, Bond influenced white philanthropists. While he did not have a perfect record, Bond (along with Johnson) did help to shape the contours of higher education just at the time African Americans were breaking the color line. Like Bond and Johnson, Fontaine escaped the trying professional life of most black practicing scholars at needy schools. Yet the managing official at a black university more easily made an impact than did a philosopher at a white university.

The black social scientists who made names for themselves in the black collegiate system overshadowed even black administrators. They attracted the notice of professors in white institutions through the study of race relations. In addition to conferring with Johnson in 1943, Fontaine had crossed swords in print with E. Franklin Frazier a year later. These sociologists and others like them rarely got outside African American schools; and white sociological theory conventionally refuted their views, which turned out to be more right than wrong. Yet the black sociologists defined part of a circle of academics, and race relations commanded consideration as a mainstream area of social science. African American sociologists had a voice and debated their white colleagues in the academy.[40]

Surely other debates about prejudice in the United States had theoretical overtones, and other communities of inquirers, black and white, addressed racial thought in the intellectual life of the era. But Fontaine's white discipline allowed for no community of inquirers into a philosophical problem of race; there was no one to talk to, and no one to listen. By the mid-twentieth century, if you wanted to understand the world, you did not want to get into the field of philosophy.[41]

We can make a final revealing comparison between Fontaine and John Hope Franklin, a scholar six years younger than Fontaine. Franklin studied in history, an area in which Fontaine had subsidiary interests. Franklin had worked in black colleges in the South, but by 1956 he had gained employment at Brooklyn College in New York City and later at the University of Chicago. Like Fontaine, Franklin uniquely taught in his field as a black man in white institutions. But Franklin found in American history, as had African Americans in sociology, a discipline more hospitable than philosophy. Historians of the United States, with its long history of slavery, could not avoid a dialogue about race. More than Fontaine, however, Franklin showed bulldog-like fortitude in publishing material that demanded the attention of his white peers. He justly rose to great prominence in the white academy.

Franklin and Fontaine make for a key comparison. Both men can be called deep cultural conservatives: they revered scholarship and in some way identified with the Greco-Roman and European world that they thought promoted learning. "Western civilization" offered sophistication and refinement that they treasured. It somehow occupied a realm beyond the color line. Colleagues knew Franklin for his rarified hobby of growing orchids. At the same time, as his autobiography makes clear, Franklin could barely contain his rage at the inequities of the racial system of the United States. Over and over again, as he recalled, white people subjected him to slights, snubs, and subtle reminders that they thought African Americans, and him specifically, as worthy of something less than respect. The contrast between what the nation supposedly stood for and the actual behavior of its dominant group of citizens constantly crowded in on Franklin's mind. Yet it did not turn him into a radical; quite the contrary. Moreover, the contrast did not noticeably damage him psychically; indeed, it may have spurred his accomplishments.[42]

The same cannot be said for Fontaine. To get a final insight into the troubles of *Reflections*, we must keep in mind not just the breakdown of his health and the unresponsive nature of the philosophical disciplines. We also need to look at the way being a cultured American and a disdained Negro affected Fontaine. While Franklin found a functional way to direct his wrath, Fontaine did not. His place in the world rather contorted his awareness and certainly the investigations of his book.

Double Consciousness

Fontaine's academic discipline did not help him. It had no time for what he did well and dismissed his mainstream philosophical work. Fontaine was cruelly destined to walk through the valley of the shadow of death, and this fate certainly subverted his ability to write. A complex set of social circumstances makes up a final reason for the deficit performance in the book. Singular pressures burdened Fontaine as the only black person in a white professional environment. They operated so as to exemplify the "double consciousness" that Du Bois had articulated long before and that Fontaine had returned to throughout his life.[43]

Commentators have made a great deal of the meaning and significance of Du Bois's concept.[44] They have debated its importance for Du Bois and for his readers, yet one version of the notion absorbed Fontaine, who had mulled over it on several occasions. Whatever one makes of the idea of a damaged black psyche, Fontaine thought that Du Bois attributed a troubled mental coherence to the black man, and Fontaine saw the idea as applying to himself. Such incoherence infuses *Reflections*.

Double consciousness for Du Bois meant that the African American male did not merely come to understand himself in a community of others, but did so knowing that, whatever he thought of himself, white culture regarded him as "a problem." The black man saw himself "through the revelation of the other world." The African American was alert to the contingency of conceptual schemes and worldviews. Human beings made them and need not take them as given. People could attack or defend frameworks of understanding. The dominant group, whose way of life appeared simply as social fact, had this depth of insight less available to it. Yet this black discernment also accompanied the "measuring [of] one's soul . . . by contempt and pity."[45]

In this aspect of double consciousness, marginal self-esteem wrestled with the acuity of black intellect. But Du Bois additionally outlined a related doubleness, between being black and being an American. He found "two thoughts, two unreconciled strivings; two warring ideals in one dark body, whose dogged strength alone keeps it from being torn asunder."[46] On the one hand, the man of color simply wanted to be an American, entrusted with a heritage of democracy, and to participate in the community of all men created equal. On the other hand, a harsh segregated culture molded his self. This aspect of double consciousness spoke to the torment of blacks because the master values of the United States embarrassed the American creed.

Both aspects of double consciousness applied in some measure to Fontaine. In his own account of Du Bois, Fontaine lamented that the Negro lived with double aims; the dual focus resulted in "feelings of shame, diminution of the value of the self." Elsewhere, Fontaine wrote that "when wishes deeply involving the self are denied, human beings resort to substitute forms of fulfillment."[47] He did not shroud himself from the realities of his Jim Crow society and instinctively understood alternative perspectives in a way that his peers in epistemology did not. Nonetheless, he lifted his predicament to the plane of reason through this same academic discipline. His uncommon position in the learned world dramatized the issues. He could personally attest to the guarantees of American democracy; this grandson of a slave and son of a common laborer had transformed himself into an Ivy League philosopher. But Fontaine's immersion in white institutions came with a penalty. His professional world had nothing to do with the world of most African Americans, including the world of Chester into which he had been born. He *had* joined the black elite, and by the time the civil rights movement blossomed in the late 1950s and 1960s, he had good contacts with the local black leadership. Yet for Fontaine courtesy and not right associated him with the world in which he taught and spent his working days. "The great illusion of most white liberals," he wrote, "is their secret assumption that, although segregation is immoral, white skin qualifies them for membership in a privileged caste." Members of the university community, Fontaine commented, would tell him "shamefaced" that they had never "been inside the home of a Negro."[48] As one faculty member recollected, "none of [Fontaine's] connection to the black community was part of his presence at Penn."[49]

A Terrible Price

How could Fontaine put his two worlds together?

On the one side, Fontaine lived as a black man in America. As he put it early in his career, within the black community scholars unquestionably had substantial status, but "before the bar of American public opinion a Negro is a Negro. Regardless of complexion, education, wealth, achievement, refinement, whether he is northern or southern, urban or rural, his social position is restricted."[50]

Sometime in the mid-late 1950s, the university renovated a broom closet, which was five feet by thirteen feet, to serve as Fontaine's office. Fifty years later workmen converted it to a small women's toilet. College Hall housed this office, in the same hallway where lay the suites of the president and provost.[51] When they determined at the end of the 1961 school year that the tiny area would have other uses, they gave Fontaine a week's notice to vacate the room. He knew of the lack of regard—or was it more?—that these men had for him.[52] In his own small way he mocked their lukewarm concern for a more egalitarian university.[53] Nonetheless, a long-dead Negro man, Albert Monroe Wilson, occupied a larger space in Fontaine's daily life than these administrators. Known as "Pomp," Wilson had cleaned College Hall for fifty years after the Civil War. As a janitor, he had waited on generations "of Pennsylvania men." The students had prominently placed an oversized picture and a condescending, if affectionately inscribed tablet to Wilson in College Hall as a "tribute to his zealous fidelity."[54] Fontaine saw the picture every day he went to his office.

On the other side, the university treated Fontaine with exquisite civility and respect. For departmental and university functions his colleagues opened their homes to "Bill and Belle."[55] Jewish and liberal professors had founded the Ivy Club as a non-discriminatory eating society at Penn.[56] In 1958 the club gave Fontaine its Lecturer of the Year Award, at that time the university's only teaching prize.

In 1964 the Philosophy Department imploded. A few years earlier, with the retirements of Clarke and Morrow imminent, the university had asked Goodman, easily the most prestigious figure, to take on duties as chair. He agreed but only for one year and demanded that the school find a philosophical administrator to allow him to continue his epistemological research unimpeded by busywork. With Goodman's high and warm recommendation, Penn had hired Marvin Farber, who succeeded Goodman as chair. But Farber proved a disaster, and his silly but autocratic rule led to clashes with the politically conservative and temperamentally finicky Goodman. Philosophic ideology also divided them—Goodman's pragmatic analysis conflicted with Farber's more wide-ranging ideas about philosophy.[57] Farber left Pennsylvania and so did Goodman. Fontaine had valuable ties to both men. Nelson, with affectionate regard, had always sustained him, and they had a friendship of long standing. Fontaine had much more briefly associated with Marvin Farber, but he was unshakingly committed to Fontaine's scholarship and determined to get Fontaine to produce his book. Fontaine's inability to adjudicate the struggle between the two men left him bitterly upset.[58]

In 1964 and 1965, the department hit bottom. The professional crisis and the university's new sensitivity to race elevated Fontaine. Before Farber left, Fontaine was deputed "assistant to the chairman" for a semester, and in July 1964 he became the acting chair of a diminished group of philosophers.[59] Fontaine oversaw a botched effort to restore the shine of the department by rehiring Goodman. In this effort administrators minimalized Fontaine's own power, and his impotence contributed to his personal feeling of distress. Then his failing health compromised his brief rise to authority. Shortly after he took over as chair, he was "sweating out an 'X.' "[60] By the end of 1964—he was 54—the tuberculosis had begun an inexorable course. The TB that had started in his right lung had healed; now the doctors found "progressive involvement with destruction of the left lung."[61] In the fall of 1965, he took on the less demanding job as graduate chair until he went on medical leave at the beginning of 1967.

How did Fontaine incorporate the back-of-the hand disrespect with the cultivated politesse? How did he deal with the genteel averting of the eyes about his race, which was the crux of the institution's dealing with the man?

Du Bois's double consciousness was theoretically manufactured, and it only partly encompasses the complexities of existence. John Hope Franklin had written explicitly about how the issues distressed him,[62] but just as Du Bois displayed a mental toughness, so did Franklin; and this toughness overcame many of the troubles of double consciousness. Evidently, African American psyches were more varied than double consciousness allowed. Fontaine's self-knowledge often relied overtly on Du Bois's formulations, but he too actually had a set of experiences too messy for double consciousness to accommodate. Like other high-aiming black men, he knew that he had been dealt a certain hand in life, and he did his utmost to make the best of it, irrespective of the racial divide. If he factored in his illness, which we must believe he did, he might well have thought that Pennsylvania's medical leave policies benefited persons of any race greatly. Lincoln or Southern or Morgan could hardly have continued to have him on their faculties with his medical condition. Moreover, the racial climate evolved in his favor over his years in Philadelphia, even if the enormous strides of the late 1960s came too late to profit him.

Nonetheless, as an African American, Fontaine lectured more or less alone in the first-rank institutions of learning in the United States. His elevation compromised his ability to comment on race relations in a way that many black intellectuals were doing. Where would he find the ground cogently to censure the racial attitudes of his colleagues or of the University of Pennsylvania or of the United States? Fontaine did not choose simply to come to terms with his supposed good fortune in the white university world, or to make a heartbreaking decision not to bite the hand that fed him. Would that it were that simple! As John Hope Franklin put it, the divisions between insight and self-esteem, black and American, cost Negro scholars dearly.[63] In his exceptional position for a score of years, Fontaine paid a price with the difficulty he had in articulating his vision of an alternative to segregated America. We may analogize the hurt in his mind, the psychic mystification, to the confusion shifts, and unevenness of his book.

Imagine that, instead of being dismissed, Du Bois had received a tenured professorship at the University of Pennsylvania. Suppose that his departmental peers treated him with regard, and that the university kept him on at his position with much leave time despite a discreditable and debilitating illness. Would we have lost the sharpness of Du Bois's social criticism? Had Fontaine stayed at Lincoln, Southern, or Morgan State, would his critique of American life have lacked clarity?

To grasp what we can of the disjointed nature of *Reflections* we must finally consider this last element, the impact of racism on the ability of both blacks (and whites) to understand the social world that had been created. The segregation of American society hurt everyone, as the restricted nature of white philosophy demonstrates. But segregation surely hurt African Americans and tortured people like Fontaine most. Almost every black scholar, even the most radical, set his sights on the white academy. For Fontaine travel to this promised land helped to spoil his understanding—*the failure went with the territory*. Therein lies for me the compelling and tragic dimension of this story. The social world charged a massive psychic fee to token black intellectuals who crossed the color line between 1940 and 1970. *Reflections on Segregation, Desegregation, Power and Morals*, said Fontaine, was not merely something he had written. "The book is my life."[64]

Fontaine's wager on the system and on his own abilities in it had not panned out as he had wanted. He spoke with "wry resignation."[65]

Journey's End

Reflections appeared in November 1967, and the Committee of Friends gave its reception for Fontaine at his home in downtown Philadelphia in December of that year, shortly after Fontaine's fifty-eighth birthday. Bringing together black and white, the party may have brightened Fontaine's hope for a racially homogeneous United States, although even at this event he made only a short appearance.[66] The event did demonstrate how far the country had come since he had first made the trip to Philadelphia in 1930.

In the new year of 1968 he briefly rallied, and while confined to his apartment he gave an interview about his book to a reporter at the University of Pennsylvania. From the book he prepared an article that Farber had agreed to publish, although Belle had to do much of the work. The family told people that he was convalescing, but clearly, in the summer and fall of 1968, the tuberculosis bit by bit was taking his breath away. He did not leave his home, and his closest companion became an oxygen tank. Friends and relatives visited for the last time. A young colleague from the university found Fontaine "personally philosophical" and more at ease with his impending death than anyone the white man had ever dealt with. Fontaine said he had been living on one lung for a long time, and he knew that the second would give out in a short time.[67] He lived through his birthday on December 2 but died less than a month later, on December 29, 1968. Belle said his fight "was long and hard."

The funeral took place in black North Philadelphia on January 3, 1969. The program quoted the extraordinary poem "We Wear the Mask," by Paul Lawrence Dunbar. Had Fontaine, who had studied Dunbar carefully, selected it before he died?

We smile, but O Great Christ our cries
To Thee from tortured souls arise
We sing, but O the clay is vile
Beneath our feet, and long the mile
But let the world dream otherwise
We wear the mask.[68]

West Goshen Township lies north of the city of Chester, in the direction of Lincoln University. In 1938 African American businessmen bought land in the sparsely populated area for an upscale cemetery for Negroes who could not use white graveyards. The white community of West Goshen at once protested about the possibility that living black people would inter dead ones in the neighborhood. A crisis ensued—secret midnight entombments—before African American cortèges could openly make their way to what became Rolling Green Memorial Park.

After the funeral service, family and colleagues buried Fontaine at Rolling Green. Soon thereafter Belle married again, this time to a well-to-do African American physician whom Bill had known at Lincoln. Sam Bullock practiced in Washington, D.C., and in early 1970 Belle and her new husband moved to Silver Spring, Maryland.[69] She had marked Fontaine's grave with a small and unadorned granite plaque. He rests near a large upright slab on which the Twenty-third Psalm is inscribed—"The Lord is my shepherd. I shall not want."[70]

Conclusion

ALMOST EVERY SCHOLAR in the last quarter century who has written about race in America has adopted a similar narrative stance, and I am no exception. Especially in biographies, the story recounts the toil of African Americans—sometimes successful, sometimes not, but always never ending—for a measure of equality. By now convention utterly drives the story. But even though simplified, overly heroic, and less ambiguous than truth, the story forces itself upon the mind and has a sure accuracy in framing the life of William Fontaine.

He came to maturity at the critical transitional time in American race relations. While in many ways a victim of segregated America—as were so many citizens of both races—Fontaine took advantage of the symbolic developments of the first half of the twentieth century. Too old to reap all the rewards of the civil rights revolution, he involved himself in its progress from the late 1940s onward. His career bridged the segregated university system of the early twentieth century and the desegregated system of the early twenty-first, with its greater diversity in talent and achievement, with its greater variety of personalities, and with its self-conscious quest for multiculturalism.

If only Fontaine had come along even five to ten years later, he would not have sacrificed so much of his life for some greater good. In constructing this biography, I have found myself again and again examining the evidence and saying "If only. . . ." A litany of "if only's" composes African American history in this period. Yet in some ways Fontaine contributed to the well-being of many. His classes at Pennsylvania whom his teaching and his humanity touched received a wonderful gift. In addition to the rarified learning into which he launched his students, he displayed to them the faults of their racial categories. As one of them wrote, "Professor Fontaine was a strong advocate for me, and I regarded him as a mentor . . . and advisor for many years. . . . He was a gentleman, a scholar, and an admirable person."[1] His careful language, wrote another, evinced "a form of respect . . . [at] the core of the man's impressive dignity and civility."[2] He taught, said yet another, "with such gentleness and generosity of spirit—and such a hint of sadness— that it is not surprising that so many of us remember him with fondness."[3] He personified the elegiac.

By the late 1960s Pennsylvania's Graduate School of Arts and Sciences was giving special fellowships for disadvantaged students. In 1969 the institution had designated them the William T. Fontaine Fellowships in memory of the philosopher. By 1974 the university had stopped describing nominees for Fontaine Fellowships as "culturally and educationally deprived."[4] Still later, when recruitment of minority graduate students had dramatically increased and had a higher priority, Penn brought all such fellowship programs under the rubric of the Fontaine Fellowships, and a prestigious Fontaine Society enrolled the students who held the fellowships.

Fontaine changed the lives of his own students by example. He assisted an egalitarian cause in ways that went beyond his own personal dilemmas. As he wrote toward the end of his life, he strove for a great social revolution, "helping to turn squalor into responsibility, arrogance into conciliation, antipathy into community, and color caste into a bygone episode in the history of social justice."[5] He added laurels to the crown of his ancestors.

NOTES

INTRODUCTION

1. *Addresses and Proceedings of the APA, 1948–49*, vol. 22 (September 1949): 461, 472.
The APA later would automatically enroll anyone who could pay its dues.
2. Morton White, email, September 21, 2004.
3. A. J. Ayer, *More of My Life* (London: Collins, 1984), 45.
4. White, email; *Addresses and Proceedings of the APA, 1949–50*, vol. 23 (September
1950): 88.
5. Although there are many varieties of African American thinkers, and although I
have put my own twist on the topic, the study of constellations of black intellectuals as
representative of a social type is common in the literature. For personal accounts see, for
example, J. Saunders Redding, *On Being Negro in America* (Indianapolis: Bobbs Merrill,
1951), and John Hope Franklin, "The Dilemma of the American Negro Scholar," in
Herbert Hill, ed., *Soon One Morning: New Writing by American Negroes, 1940–1962* (New
York: Knopf, 1963), 60–76. For generalizations, see, for example, Harold Cruse, *The Crisis
of the Negro Intellectual* (New York: William Morrow, 1967), esp. 451–75; William M.
Banks, *Black Intellectuals: Race and Responsibility in American Life* (New York: W. W.
Norton, 1996), esp. 242–46; and Hazel Carby, *Race Men* (Cambridge: Harvard University
Press, 1998), esp. 5–41. For specific thinkers, see, for example, Jonathan Scott Holloway,
Confronting the Veil: Abram Harris, Jr., E. Franklin Frazier, and Ralph Bunche, 1919–1941
(Chapel Hill: University of North Carolina Press, 2002), 33, 210–18; Jerry Gafio Watts,
*Heroism and the Black Intellectual: Ralph Ellison, Politics, and Afro-American Intellectual
Life* (Chapel Hill: University of North Carolina Press, 1994); and the unpublished work
of Barbara Savage on Carter Woodson and Benjamin Mays.

CHAPTER 1

1. See Charles Palmer, *A History of Delaware County Pennsylvania* (Harrisburg: National Historical Association, 1932). Population data in this and the following paragraph
are from John Morrison McLarnon III, *Ruling Suburbia: John J. McClure and the Republi-*

can Machine in Delaware County, Pennsylvania (Newark: University of Delaware Press, 2003), 255.

2. For biographical details, in addition to the sources cited, I am indebted throughout to the material in the Fontaine Papers and his Alumni File in the Archives of the University of Pennsylvania (hereafter UPA) and to interviews conducted with Evelyn Fontaine Prattis (Fontaine's sister) and Kathleen Prattis (his niece) on October 23 and 24, 2003, October 19, 2004, and July 24, 2007; and with Pamela Harris (his granddaughter) and Belle Fontaine (his wife) on August 7, 8, and 14, 2007. There is an obituary in the *Proceedings of the American Philosophical Association* 43 (1969–70): 200–203 by James Ross.

3. Fontaine, *Reflections on Segregation, Desegregation, Power and Morals* (Springfield, Ill.: Charles C. Thomas Publishing Co., 1967), 97; *Colored Directory of Delaware County 1906* (Delaware County), under Ballard and Hunt.

4. Fontaine, *Reflections*, 97; student transcripts, Fontaine, Lincoln University Archives (hereafter LUA).

5. Student transcripts, Fontaine, LUA.

6. Ibid.

7. Ibid.

8. McLarnon, *Ruling Suburbia*, 63–65.

9. "Black History" clippings, *Chester County Times, Chester County Democrat, Oxford News, Oxford Press*, 1922–24, West Chester Historical Society, West Chester, Pa.; Fontaine, *Reflections*, 35, 95.

10. Fontaine, "The Mind and Thought of the Negro of the United States as Revealed in Imaginative Literature, 1876–1940," *Southern University Bulletin* 28 (March 1942): 20–21. For the impact of these events on black intellectuals, see Michael C. Dawson, *Black Visions: The Roots of Contemporary African-American Political Ideologies* (Chicago: University of Chicago Press, 2001), 176–81.

11. McLarnon, *Ruling Suburbia*, 213–15, 246–49.

12. Harris and Fontaine interviews.

13. I have taken this depiction of his life in Chester from Fontaine's thinly disguised description in *Reflections*, v, 95–97. The same autobiographical echoes appear in "Segregation and Desegregation in the United States: A Philosophical Analysis," *Présence Africaine* 8–10 (1956): 166, 168. In addition to Fontaine's recollections, see Richard E. Harris, *Delinquency in Our Democracy* (Los Angeles: Wetzel Publishing Co., 1954), the section on Chester, esp. 22–29.

14. Fontaine, *Reflections*, 16.

15. Prattis interviews; Fontaine, *Reflections*, iv.

16. Student transcripts, Fontaine, LUA.

17. The best source on Lincoln is Horace Mann Bond, *Education for Freedom: A History of Lincoln University, Pennsylvania* (Lincoln University, 1976) (published in Princeton, N.J.: Princeton University Press, 1976), 232–510.

18. See the discussion in Arnold Rampersad, *The Life of Langston Hughes*, vol. 1: *1902–1942, I Too Sing America* (New York: Oxford University Press, 1986), 169–71.

19. A. L. Greenwood, "The Railroads of Chester County," *Tredyffrin Easttown History Club Quarterly* (February 1953): 86–94.

20. In his autobiography, *The Big Sea* (1940; New York: Hill and Wang, 1963), 279.

21. The only negative appraisal I have found is from J. Saunders Redding, who attended Lincoln for one year, 1923–24. See his *No Day of Triumph* (New York: Harper and Brothers, 1942), 34–35. There is an excellent survey of Lincoln in the 1920s in Raymond Wolters, *The New Negro on Campus: Black College Rebellions of the 1920s* (Princeton, N.J.: Princeton University Press, 1975), 278–93.

22. Student transcripts, Fontaine, LUA; for the dean's list see, for example, *Lincoln News*, October 1, 1930, 16; and on debating, see *Lincoln News*, January 1, 1929, 8, also in LUA.

23. *Lincoln News*, October 1, 1928, 6, LUA.

24. *Lincolnian*, January 19, 1934, 3, LUA.

25. *Lincoln News*, October 1, 1928, 1; January 1, 1929, 2, LUA.

26. See Martha Jane Nadell, *Enter the New Negroes: Images of Race in American Culture* (Cambridge, Mass.: Harvard University Press, 2004), esp. 34–67.

27. On the issue of literary expression, see Valery Sweeney Prince, *Burnin' Down the House: Home in African American Literature* (New York: Columbia University Press, 2005).

28. Nnandi Azikiwe, *My Odyssey: An Autobiography* (New York: Praeger, 1970), 147.

29. Robert L. Carter, *A Matter of Law* (New York: The New Press, 2005), 19.

30. *Pi Gamma Psi News*, 1930, LUA. The fraternity went out of business but was later resurrected in the late twentieth century at other schools.

31. Patrick B. Miller, "To 'Bring the Race along Rapidly': Sport, Student Culture, and Educational Mission at Historically Black Colleges during the Interwar Years," *History of Education Quarterly* 35 (1995): 119, 122.

32. According to Hughes, *The Big Sea*, 280–84.

33. Azikiwe, *My Odyssey*, 146–48.

CHAPTER 2

1. Robert Carter, *A Matter of Law* (New York: The New Press, 2005), 18.

2. Catalogues, 1928–36, Lincoln University Archives (hereafter LUA).

3. Catalogues, 1935–36, 1950–51, LUA; August Meier and Elliott Rudwick, *Black History and the Historical Profession, 1915–1980* (Urbana: University of Illinois Press, 1986); Wayne J. Urban, *Black Scholar: Horace Mann Bond 1904–1972* (Athens: University of Georgia Press, 1992).

4. Horace Mann Bond, *Education for Freedom: A History of Lincoln University, Pennsylvania* (Lincoln University, 1976) (published in Princeton, N.J.: Princeton University Press), 368. George Johnson, Alumni Files, Archives of the University of Pennsylvania (hereafter UPA).

5. See Husik, Alumni Files, UPA; and especially his *History of Medieval Jewish Philosophy* (New York: Macmillan, 1916, 1930).

6. The best way to get a sense of this vision is to examine Seymour G. Martin et al., *A History of Philosophy* (New York: Appleton-Century-Crofts, 1941), which has a "Patristic and Medieval" section by Clarke.

7. On Singer, see his Alumni File, UPA.

8. Singer's manuscript history of modern philosophy was required reading for generations of students. Copies can be found in the Singer Papers, UPA. Another version is Edgar Singer, *Modern Philosophy and Present Problems; an Approach to Modern Philosophy Through its History* (New York: Henry Holt, 1923). See also his "Foreword" to Martin et al., *History of Philosophy*.

9. See the discussion in Bruce Kuklick, *A History of Philosophy in America* (Oxford: Oxford University Press, 2001); "quest for certainty" is taken from Dewey's book of that name, which was published in New York in 1929 by Minton, Balch & Co.

10. Fontaine, student transcript, Box 9, UPB 7.62, UPA.

11. Henry James, ed., *Letters of William James*, 2 vols. in one (Boston: Little Brown, 1926), 2: 228–29.

12. I have taken up some of these issues in a review, "Modern Anglophone Philosophy: Between the Seminar Room and the Cold War," *Modern Intellectual History* 3 (2006): 547–57.

13. For Lewis, who is critical for understanding many aspects of the philosophical disciplines, see Murray Murphey, *C. I. Lewis: The Last Pragmatist* (Albany: State University of New York Press, 2005).

14. Summer School Catalogue, 1933, HU 75.25, Harvard University Archives.

15. Fontaine's later comments on Lewis appear in Chapters 5 and 6 of this book. For the background, see Bruce Kuklick, *The Rise of American Philosophy: Cambridge, Massachusetts, 1869–1930* (New Haven, Conn.: Yale University Press, 1977).

16. I have constructed the following analysis from the brief course description in the Lincoln University Catalogue of 1935–36, LUA; Fontaine, "The Mind and Thought of the Negro of the United States as Revealed in Imaginative Literature, 1876–1940," *Southern University Bulletin* 28 (March 1942): 5–50; Fontaine, "Toward a Philosophy of the American Negro Literature," *Présence Africaine* 24–25 (1959): 164–76; and Fontaine, *Reflections on Segregation, Desegregation, Power and Morals* (Springfield, Ill.: Charles C. Thomas Publishing Co., 1967), 3–40.

17. In *Creative Conflict in African American Thought: Frederick Douglass, Alexander Crummel, Booker T. Washington, W. E. B. Du Bois, and Marcus Garvey* (New York: Cambridge University Press, 2004), Wilson Jeremiah Moses locates Du Bois differently from the way I do or Fontaine did.

18. On Du Bois and assimilation I have found helpful Manning Marable, *W.E. B. Du Bois: Black Radical Democrat* (Boston: Twayne, 1986); for hyphenation, see Jerry Gershenhorn, *Melville J. Herskovits and the Racial Politics of Knowledge* (Lincoln: University of Nebraska Press, 2004).

19. Du Bois, *The Souls of Black Folk* (New York: Simon and Schuster, 1903, 2005), 6–9, 81–84, 108.

20. David Levering Lewis, *W. E. B. Du Bois—Biography of a Race, 1868–1919* (New York: Henry Holt, 1993), 94–95; Fontaine, *Reflections*, 11–12.

21. Alaine Locke, *The New Negro* (New York: Albert and Charles Boni, 1925).

22. For the impact Locke's writing may have had on Fontaine, see Caroline Goeser, *Picturing the New Negro: Harlem Renaissance Print Culture and Modern Black Identity* (Lawrence: University Press of Kansas, 2007), especially its illustrations.

23. *Lincolnian*, November 19, 1935; March 5, 1936, LUA.

24. The relationship can be followed in their correspondence in the Locke Papers, 164–29, Folder 37, Howard University Archives (hereafter HUA).

25. John Hope Franklin, "On the Evolution of Scholarship in Afro-American Studies," in Darlene Clark Hine, ed., *The State of Afro-American History* (Baton Rouge: Louisiana State University Press, 1986), 13–22 offers an elegant survey of this literature.

26. *The Lincolnian*, April 3, 1935, LUA.

27. Fontaine, student transcript, UPA.

28. *Fortune, Matter, and Providence, a Study of Ancius Severinus Boethius and Giordano Bruno* (Scotlandville, La., 1939).

29. Ibid., 41–42, 44, 46; Fontaine to Locke, n.d. [circa May 1936] 164–29, Folder 37, Locke Papers, HUA; Fontaine, student transcript, UPA.

30. *Fortune, Matter and Providence*, 1, 3.

31. For an overview, see James D. Anderson, *The Education of Blacks in the South, 1860–1935* (Chapel Hill: University of North Carolina Press, 1988), esp. 238–78, although this book does not mention Southern University in Louisiana, where Fontaine ended up.

32. An unusually helpful website by means of which these schools can be compared is www.petersons.com/blackcolleges/bacu. Jonathan Scott Holloway, "The Black Scholar, the Humanities, and the Politics of Racial Knowledge since 1945," in David Hollinger, ed., *The Humanities and the Dynamics of Inclusion Since World War Two* (Baltimore: Johns Hopkins University Press, 2006), 219–21 has a good survey of this constellation of schools. Information can also be gleaned from Marybeth Gasman, *Envisioning Black Colleges: A History of the United Negro College Fund* (Baltimore: Johns Hopkins University Press, 2007).

33. Fontaine to Locke, n.d. [circa May 1936], 164–29, Folder 37, Locke Papers, HUA; Fontaine to Wright, May 27, May 30, 1936, Wright Papers, LUA.

34. See the exchange of letters for 1936 in the Fontaine File, Southern University Archives.

CHAPTER 3

1. Adam Fairclough, *Race & Democracy: The Civil Rights Struggle in Louisiana, 1915–1972* (Athens: University of Georgia Press, 1995), 1–105.

2. Fairclough, *Race & Democracy*, 21–22.

3. Quote at ibid. Michael Likurtz and Morgan D. Peoples, *Earl K. Long: The Saga*

of Uncle Earl and Louisiana Politics (Baton Rouge: Louisiana State University Press, 1990), 196.

4. Fairclough, *Race & Democracy*, 25–28.

5. Horace Mann Bond, *The Star Creek Papers*, ed. Adam Fairclough (Athens: University of Georgia Press, 1997), in particular Fairclough's "Introduction," xxvii; Fairclough, *Race & Democracy*, 63.

6. Donald E. Devore, "Race Relations and Community Development: The Education of Blacks in New Orleans, 1862–1960" (Ph.D. diss., Louisiana State University, 1989), 63–73.

7. For helpful information on the land grants, see Roger L. Williams, *Origins of Federal Support for Higher Education: George W. Atherton and the Land-grant College Movement* (College Park: Pennsylvania State University Press, 1991).

8. Charles Vincent, *A Centennial History of Southern University and A&M College, 1880–1980* (Scotlandville: Southern University and A&M College, 1981), xii, 184.

9. Ibid., 64, 109.

10. Ibid., 101, 111, 114.

11. Felton G. Clark, "Introduction," *Southern University Bulletin* 29 (May 1943): 5.

12. Butler A. Jones, "The Tradition of Sociology Teaching in Black Colleges: The Unheralded Professionals," in James E. Blackwell and Morris Janowitz, eds., *Black Sociologists: Historical and Contemporary Perspectives* (Chicago: University of Chicago Press, 1974), 126–29.

13. Vincent, *A Centennial History*, 101, 111, 119, 140.

14. See the Redding Papers, 98.1, Brown University, Box 1, Folder 138; and especially the note on Fontaine's death in Box 13, Folder 42.

15. Wayne J. Urban, *Black Scholar: Horace Mann Bond 1904–1972* (Athens: University of Georgia Press, 1992), 62.

16. For a profile of the student body at the time, see J. J. Hedgemon, "A Study of Freshman Students Entering Southern University for the First Time in September, 1939," *Southern University Bulletin* 30 (May 1944): 4–14.

17. See Fontaine, "Foreword," *Southern University Bulletin* 27 (March 1941): v.

18. Vincent, *A Centennial History,* 143–44, 153, 155; Josiah Clark to Fontaine, June 25, 1936, July 14, 1937, August 6, 1938; on teaching, see Felton Clark to Barrett, December 16, 1938, all in Fontaine File, Southern University Archives (hereafter SUA).

19. Instructor's Schedule Sheet, April 7, 1938, Fontaine File, SUA.

20. My appraisal is not based entirely on my interviews with Evelyn Fontaine Prattis (Fontaine's sister) and Kathleen Prattis (his niece) on October 23 and 24, 2003, October 19, 2004, and July 24, 2007, which is hearsay evidence about distant events, but also the independent interview with David Goldblatt on October 15, 2004, and my reading of the various documents cited below.

21. For the basic facts in this and the following three paragraphs, I relied on interviews with Pamela Harris (Fontaine's granddaughter) and Belle Fontaine on August 7, 8, and 14, 2007; for the interpretative stance, although the conclusions are my own, I am

indebted to a conversation with Leonard Harris on November 8, 2006. Harris interviewed Belle in 1978–79. On Belle being mistaken for white, I relied on George Pappas's email, September 22, 2004.

22. Interview with Winifred Timberlake on August 14, 2007. Timberlake was Belle's half-sister.

23. Fontaine, *Reflections on Segregation, Desegregation, Power and Morals* (Springfield, Ill.: Charles C. Thomas Publishing Co., 1967), 48. Charles F. Robinson II, *Dangerous Liaisons: Sex and Love in the Segregated South* (Little Rock: University of Arkansas Press, 2003), discusses these issues, but he mainly covers an earlier period in southern race relations.

24. The best I have been able to do with this issue of trailing academic wives is Stephanie Y. Evans, *Black Women in the Ivory Tower, 1850–1954* (Gainesville: University of Florida Press, 2007), 194–97.

25. Fontaine, *Reflections*, 4. On this issue, see Anthony B. Pinn, *Terror and Triumph: The Nature of Black Religion* (Minneapolis: Fortress Press, 2003): 88–90.

26. Fontaine, "The Mind and Thought of the Negro of the United States as Revealed in Imaginative Literature, 1876–1940," *Southern University Bulletin* 28 (March 1942), 22, 26–38; and his statements of purpose in Rosenwald Fund Papers, Box 412, f.7 and f.8, Fisk University Archives.

27. Prattis interview, October 19, 2004; Harris and Fontaine interviews. Fontaine to Josiah Clark, n.d. [circa July 1937], Clark to Fontaine, July 14, 1937, Fontaine File, SUA.

28. Harris and Fontaine interviews. Daniel C. Thompson, *The Negro Leadership Class* (Englewood Cliffs, N.J.: Prentice-Hall, 1963), 49–50, has information about New Orleans college teachers just after 1940.

29. Fontaine, *Reflections*, 78.

30. Goldblatt interview. And see Pinn, *Terror and Triumph*, 72–75.

31. Fontaine, "Social Determination in the Writings of American Negro Scholars," *American Journal of Sociology* 49 (1944): 302, 303.

32. Fontaine to Clark, n.d [circa July 1937]; Clark to Fontaine, July 14, 1937, Fontaine File, SUA; Prattis interviews.

33. Harris and Fontaine interviews.

34. Jerry Purvis Sanson, *Louisiana During World War II: Politics and Society 1939–1945* (Baton Rouge: Louisiana State University Press, 1999), 181, 265.

35. See Matthew J. Schott and Rosalind Foley, *Bayou Stalags: German Prisoners of War in Louisiana* (Lafayette: Center for Louisiana Studies, 1981). Arnold Krammer, *Nazi Prisoners of War in America* (New York: Stein and Day, 1979) has the best overview.

36. Some of these issues are raised in Robin Kelley, *Hammer and Hoe: Alabama Communists During the Great Depression* (Chapel Hill: University of North Carolina Press, 1990). Keith P. Griffler, "The Black Radical Intellectual and the Black Worker: The Emergence of a Program for Black Labor, 1918–1938" (Ph.D. diss., Ohio State University, 1993), is an excellent treatment that gives the flavor of African American radical politics in the 1930s.

37. Some of these issues are covered in John Egerton, *Speak Now Against the Day: The Generation before the Civil Rights Movement in the South* (New York: Knopf, 1994).

38. Fairclough, *Race & Democracy*, 54.

39. Fontaine to Locke, May 9, 1940, 164–29, Folder 37, Locke Papers, Howard University Archives.

40. Fontaine to Wright, May 7, 1941, Fontaine File, Walter Wright Papers, Lincoln University Archives.

CHAPTER 4

1. "Philosophical Implications of the Biology of Dr. Ernest Just," *Journal of Negro History* 24 (1939): 281–90; "An Interpretation of Contemporary Negro Thought from the Standpoint of the Sociology of Knowledge," *Journal of Negro History* 25 (1940): 6–13; "The Mind and Thought of the Negro of the United States as Revealed in Imaginative Literature, 1876–1940," *Southern University Bulletin* 28 (March 1942): 5–50; "Social Determination in the Writings of American Negro Scholars," *American Journal of Sociology* 49 (1944): 302–13.

2. Fontaine to Locke, February 3, 1935, 164–29, Folder 37, Locke Papers, Howard University Archives (hereafter HUA).

3. For an overview, see Leonard Harris, ed., *The Critical Pragmatism of Alain Locke: A Reader on Value Theory, Aesthetics, Community, Culture, Race, and Education* (Lanham, Md.: Rowman and Littlefield, 1999).

4. Fontaine to Locke, n.d. [ca. June 1936]; June 1, 1936, February 18, 1939; January 25 and May 9, 1940, 164–29, Folder 37, Locke Papers, HUA.

5. See the material in 164–29, Folder 37, Locke Papers, HUA. Fontaine also had at least one other project, now unidentifiable: see Fontaine to Goodman, n.d [ca. June 1947], Quine-Goodman, 1947, Box 1, Series II, Nelson Goodman Papers, Harvard University Archives.

6. For example, Fontaine, *Reflections on Segregation, Desegregation, Power and Morals* (Springfield, Ill.: Charles C. Thomas Publishing Co., 1967), 15, 95–96.

7. Arnold Rampersad, *The Life of Langston Hughes*, vol. 1: *1902–1942, I Too Sing America* (New York: Oxford University Press, 1986), 66–70.

8. Locke to Fontaine, October 24, 1939 (misaddressed and not re-sent); and n.d. [ca. January 1940]; Fontaine to Locke, January 25 and May 9, 1940, 164–29, Folder 37, Locke Papers, HUA.

9. John Dewey, *The Quest for Certainty* (New York: Minton, Balch & Co., 1929), 4–5, 67, 254–56.

10. Fontaine, "The Mind and Thought of the Negro," 49.

11. See Karl Mannheim, *Ideology and Utopia: An Introduction to the Sociology of Knowledge*, trans. and ed. Louis Wirth and Edward Shils (New York: Harcourt-Brace, 1936), esp. 126–27, 147–57, 162–64, 189–91.

12. Fontaine, "The Mind and Thought of the Negro," 50. This dimension of Fon-

taine's thought, I believe, is beholden to Lewis in *Mind and the World-Order*, but the debt would not become clear until later.

13. Fontaine, "The Mind and Thought of the Negro," 6, 9, 49–50.

14. Fontaine, "Foreword," *Southern University Bulletin* 27 (March 1941), v.

15. In addition, compare Fontaine's essay to Rebecca Barton, *Race Consciousness and the American Negro* (Copenhagen: Arnold Brusck, 1934); Benjamin Brawley, *The Negro Genius, a New Appraisal of the Achievement of the American Negro in Literature and the Fine Arts* (New York: Biblo and Tannen, 1937); and Sterling Brown, *The Negro in American Fiction* (Washington, D.C.: The Associates in Negro Folk Education, 1937). For later essays, see Robert Bone, *The Negro Novel in America* (New Haven, Conn.: Yale University Press, 1965); Ross Posnock, *Color and Culture: Black Writers and the Making of the Modern Intellectual* (Cambridge, Mass.: Harvard University Press, 1998); and Martha Jane Nadell, *Enter the New Negroes: Images of Race in American Culture* (Cambridge, Mass.: Harvard University Press, 2004), esp. 113–14.

16. In this and the following paragraphs, I have followed the argument from "The Mind and Thought of the Negro," 5–48.

17. "Social Determination," 302.

18. According to both Southern University and the Library of Congress, copies of most issues of the *Bulletin* no longer exist.

19. Fontaine to Clark, August 27, 1943, Fontaine File, Southern University Archives.

CHAPTER 5

1. Rosenwald Fund Papers, Box 412, f.7 and f.8, Fisk University Archives (hereafter FUA). On the ambiguous nature of this philanthropy, see John H. Stanfield, *Philanthropy and Jim Crow in American Social Science* (Westport, Conn.: Greenwood Press, 1985); and Peter M. Ascoli, *Julius Rosenwald* (Bloomington: Indiana University Press, 2006).

2. *ACLS Bulletin* 36 (December 1944). He may also have been unsuccessful in obtaining money from the Social Science Research Council in 1939. See Felton Clark to Ballard, December 16, 1938, Fontaine File, Southern University Archives.

3. Rosenwald Fund Papers, Box 412, f.7 and f.8, FUA. For Fisk at the time, see Katrina Marie Sanders, "Building Racial Tolerance through Education: The Fisk University Race Relations Institute, 1944–1969" (Ph.D. diss., University of Illinois, Urbana-Champaign, 1997), esp. 88–96.

4. See the excellent study of James B. McKee, *Sociology and the Race Problem: The Failure of a Perspective* (Urbana: University of Illinois Press, 1993). See also John P. Jackson, Jr., *Social Scientists for Social Justice: Making the Case against Segregation* (New York: New York University Press, 2001), 17–59; Jonathan Scott Holloway and Ben Keppel, eds., *Black Scholars on the Line: Race, Social Science, and American Thought in the Twentieth Century* (South Bend, Ind.: Notre Dame University Press, 2007); and Vernon J. Williams, Jr., *The Social Sciences and Theories of Race* (Urbana: University of Illinois Press, 2006).

5. Jerry Gershenhorn, *Melville J. Herskovits and the Racial Politics of Knowledge* (Lin-

coln: University of Nebraska Press, 2004), 178–82. For Johnson see the less interesting Patrick J. Gilpin and Marybeth Gasman, *Charles S. Johnson; Leadership Beyond the Veil in the Age of Jim Crow* (Albany: State University of New York Press, 2003).

6. Fontaine, student transcript, Box 9, UPB 7.62, Archives of the University of Pennsylvania (hereafter UPA); *ACLS Bulletin* 36 (December 1944).

7. Rosenwald Fund Papers, Box 412, f.7, Project Description, p. 12, FUA.

8. Rosenwald Fund Papers, Box 412, f.7, Progress under Grant, pp. 3, 8; f. 8, Excerpt, *The Worlds of Silk and Velvet*, FUA.

9. Rosenwald Fund Papers, Box 412, f.7, Progress under Grant, p. 7, FUA.

10. Karl Mannheim, *Ideology and Utopia: An Introduction to the Sociology of Knowledge*, trans. and ed. Louis Wirth and Edward Shils (New York: Harcourt-Brace, 1936), esp. 126–27, 147–57, 162–64, 189–91.

11. Rosenwald Fund Papers, Box 412, f.7, Project Description, pp. 9–10; Progress under Grant, p. 6, FUA.

12. See Merton, "Insiders and Outsiders: A Chapter in the Sociology of Knowledge," *American Journal of Sociology* 78 (1972): 16. Fontaine's essay is reprinted in an instructive anthology edited by Leonard Harris, *Philosophy Born of Struggle: Anthology of Afro-American Philosophy from 1917* (Dubuque, Iowa: Kendall/Hunt Publishing Company, 1983).

13. Fontaine, "Social Determination in the Writings of American Negro Scholars," *American Journal of Sociology* 49 (1944): 302, 303.

14. Ibid., 310; "An Interpretation of Contemporary Negro Thought from the Standpoint of the Sociology of Knowledge," *Journal of Negro History* 25 (1940): 7.

15. Frazier, "Rejoinder," *American Journal of Sociology* 49 (1944): 313–15.

16. Fontaine, "Social Determination," 306; Frazier, "Rejoinder," 313–15. I have taken my understanding of "wuzzleheaded" from one of Fontaine's sources: W. Montague Cobb, "The Physical Constitution of the American Negro," *Journal of Negro Education* 3 (1934): 352–53; and from Leonard Harris conversation, November 8, 2006. "Wuzzlehead" and its variants do not appear in any of the slang dictionaries I examined. For a discussion of Frazier and Fontaine, see Vernon J. Williams, Jr., *From a. Caste to a Minority: Changing Attitudes of American Sociologists to Afro-Americans, 1896–1945* (Westport Conn.: Greenwood Press, 1989), 158–60.

17. Fontaine, "Social Determination," 302, 312–13.

18. Nkrumah, *Ghana: The Autobiography of Kwame Nkrumah* (New York: International Publishers, 1957), 43.

19. Ibid., 33; interviews with Evelyn Fontaine Prattis (Fontaine's sister) and Kathleen Prattis (his niece), October 23 and 24, 2003, October 19, 2004, and July 24, 2007.

20. Nkrumah, *Ghana*, 33; Fontaine, *Reflections on Segregation, Desegregation, Power and Morals* (Springfield, Ill.: Charles C. Thomas Publishing Co., 1967), 103. For white America's sense of these activities at just this time, a good source is *The FBI's RACON: Racial Conditions in the United States During World War II*, comp. and ed. Robert A. Hill (Boston: Northeastern University Press, 1995), esp. 18, 719.

21. Fontaine to Clark, August 27, 1943, Fontaine File, Southern University Archives.

22. For the issue, see Jerome Heartwell Holland, "Study of Negroes Employed by the Sun Shipbuilding and Dry Dock Company During World War II and Their Problems in the Post War Period" (Ph.D. diss., University of Pennsylvania, 1950); Bernard Mergen, "History of the Industrial Union of the Marine and Shipbuilding Workers of America, 1933–1951" (Ph.D. diss., University of Pennsylvania, 1968), 110–11; and Lester Rubin, *The Negro in the Shipbuilding Industry* (Philadelphia: University of Pennsylvania Press, 1970), 46. For the wider picture, see John Morrison McLarnon III, *Ruling Suburbia: John J. McClure and the Republican Machine in Delaware County, Pennsylvania* (Newark: University of Delaware Press, 2003), 155, 216–18; and David Palmer, *Organizing the Shipyards: Union Strategy in Three Northeastern Ports, 1933–1945* (Ithaca, N.Y.: Cornell University Press, 1998), 41, 218–19.

23. Nkrumah, *Ghana*, 33.

24. Fontaine, *Reflections*, 101, 103, 107, 108.

25. I have drawn my portrait of Holabird from its records, Fort Holabird Signal Depot, Baltimore, 1941–48, Record Group 111, National Archives Records Administration, Mid Atlantic, Ninth and Chestnut Streets, Philadelphia (hereafter NARA).

26. For a survey of programs, see Christopher P. Loss, "'The Most Wonderful Thing Has Happened to Me in the Army': Psychology, Citizenship, and American Higher Education in World War II," *Journal of American History* 92 (2005): 864–89.

27. Statistics and some of my information come from Samuel Goldberg, *Army Training of Illiterates in World War II* (New York: Teachers College Press, Columbia University, 1951). For an historical overview, see Paula S. Fass, *Outside In: Minorities and the Transformation of American Education* (New York: Oxford University Press, 1989), 139–55.

28. Quoted in Goldberg, *Army Training*, 29.

29. *Holabird Exhaust*, October 7, 1943 (Box 2); *Holabird Herald*, January 6, 1945, March 10, 1945 (Box 3), NARA.

30. Goldberg, *Army Training*, 174, 232.

31. *Holabird Herald*, January 6, 1945, March 10, 1945 (Box 3), NARA.

32. Goldberg, *Army Training*, 100–110; *Holabird Exhaust*, October 7, 1943 (Box 2); *Holabird Herald*, March 10, 1945 (Box 3), NARA.

33. Goldberg, *Army Training*, 110, 220–21; *Holabird Exhaust*, October 7, 1943 (Box 2), NARA.

34. Arnold Krammer, *Nazi Prisoners of War in America* (New York: Stein and Day, 1979), 61; Ron Robin, *The Barbed-Wire College: Reeducating German POWs in the United States During World War II* (Princeton, N.J.: Princeton University Press, 1995).

35. Estimates are complex about the impact of the war on black GIs. See John Modell, Marc Goulden, and Sigurdur Magnusson, "World War II in the Lives of Black Americans: Some Findings and an Interpretation," *Journal of American History* 76 (1989): 838–48; Neil A. Wynn, *The Afro-American and the Second World War*, rev. ed. (New York: Holmes & Meier, 1993).

36. *Holabird Herald*, March 10, 1945 (Box 3), NARA; Goldberg, *Army Training*, 270.

37. Fontaine's service records, obtained under a Freedom of Information Act (FOIA) request.

38. The evidence is again less than firm. I have relied on the Prattis interviews; Fontaine's entry in the Lincoln Alumni Directory for 1946 and an article in the Baltimore *Tribune*, September 16, 1944, in Alumni Files, Fontaine, Lincoln University Archives; a crucial letter from Goodman to Churchman, April 20, 1946, in Philosophy Department records, Goodman, UPA; and an August 15, 2005 email from the executrix of the Nelson Goodman literary estate, Catherine Elgin.

39. Nelson Goodman, *The Structure of Appearance* (Cambridge, Mass.: Harvard University Press, 1951), 3. A second edition was issued in 1966, a third in 1977. The dissertation itself, "A Study of Qualities," was published in 1990 by Garland Press of New York.

40. Nelson Goodman, *Fact, Fiction, and Forecast* (Cambridge, Mass.: Harvard University Press, 1955). The book prints the 1947 essay.

41. Good introductions to Goodman are Daniel Cohnitz & Marcus Rosenberg, *Nelson Goodman* (Montreal and Kingston: McGill-Queen's University Press, 2006); and Jakob Steinbrenner et al., eds., *Studien zur Philosophie Nelson Goodmans* (Heidelberg: Synchron Wissenschaftsverlag der Autoren, 2005), especially Oliver Scholz's essay, "In Memoriam Nelson Goodman (1906–1998)," 9–32.

42. Morgan State College *Bulletin* 11 (July 1945); 12 (April 1946), Morgan State University.

43. Fontaine, student transcript, Box 9, UPB 7.62, UPA.

44. Interview with Robert Schwartz on September 15, 2004. This evidence is hearsay but was heard by many.

45. Interviews with Pamela Harris (Fontaine's granddaughter) and Belle Fontaine on August 7, 8, and 14, 2007.

46. See Morton White, *A Philosopher's Story* (College Park: Pennsylvania State University Press, 1999), 64–67, 337–57.

47. Fontaine to Goodman, n.d. [ca. June 1947] Quine-Goodman, 1947, Box 1, Series II, Goodman Papers, Harvard University Archives.

48. Harris and Fontaine interviews.

49. Interview with George Rhoden on August 14, 2007. During this period Rhoden was a student at Morgan, where he met and married Fontaine's stepdaughter Jean.

50. Morgan State College *Bulletin* 13 (May 1947), 14 (October 1948), Morgan State University.

51. Clarke to Morrow, February 8, 1949, Appointment, Harris Collection, Fontaine Alumni File; Musser to Morrow, March 2, 1949, File 17: Fontaine, Box 74, Provosts Files, UPA.

52. Elizabeth Flower's career in some ways paralleled Fontaine's: Salaries, Philosophy, 1952–53, Box 50, Presidents Papers, UPA.

53. See Alumni Files on C. West Churchman and Russell Ackoff, two other students of Singer's who taught at Pennsylvania for a time, and Singer's own Alumni File, UPA.

54. Morrow wrote the brief but highly regarded *Ethical and Economic Theories of Adam Smith* (New York: Longmans, 1923), but he was best known at Pennsylvania for several studies of Plato, which included most famously *Plato's Cretan City: A Historical Interpretation of "The Laws"* (Princeton, N.J.: Princeton University Press, 1960), which made Morrow one of the great modern expounders of Plato.

55. Morrow to Musser, February 23, 1949, File 17, Fontaine, Box 74, Provosts Files, UPA.

56. Fontaine, *Reflections*, 10–11.

57. Fontaine, "The Mind and Thought of the Negro of the United States as Revealed in Imaginative Literature, 1876–1940," *Southern University Bulletin* 28 (March): 25–26.

58. Fontaine File, The College, 1946–47, Letters, #2, Box 3, McClelland Papers, UPA.

CHAPTER 6

1. Anthony M. Platt, *E. Franklin Frazier Reconsidered* (New Brunswick, N.J.: Rutgers University Press, 1991) has an illuminating discussion of this issue as it pertains to Frazier, 103–05.

2. See William M. Banks, *Black Intellectuals: Race and Responsibility in American Life* (New York: W. W. Norton, 1996), 96–100, 134, 234; "Negro Profs in White Colleges," *Ebony* 2 (October 1947): 15–19; Harry Washington Greene, *Holders of Doctorates Among American Negroes . . . 1876–1943* (Boston: Meador Publishing Company, 1946), 202–12, 216–19; and "The First Black Faculty Members at the Nation's 50 Flagship State Universities," *Journal of Blacks in Higher Education* 39 (spring 2003): 120–26. A survey of the nation may be found in Jonathan Scott Holloway, "The Black Scholar, the Humanities, and the Politics of Racial Knowledge since 1945," in David Hollinger, ed., *The Humanities and the Dynamics of Inclusion Since World War Two* (Baltimore: Johns Hopkins University Press, 2006), 220–26. Two other essays on the issue need to be noted: Ira De A. Reid, "New Designs in Teaching," *Phylon* 7 (1946): 383–85; and R. B. Atwood, H. G. Smith, and Catherine O. Vaughn, "Current Trends and Events of National Importance in Negro Education," *Journal of Negro Education* 18 (1949): 559–67.

3. I have taken up the relevance of milieu to thought in my essay "Philosophy and Inclusion in the United States, 1929–2001," in Hollinger, ed., *The Humanities and the Dynamics of Inclusion*, 159–85.

4. Clark to Ballard, December 16, 1938, Fontaine File, Southern University Archives; *ACLS Bulletin* 36 (December 1944); *Baltimore Tribune*, September 16, 1944, clipping in Fontaine alumni folder, Lincoln University Archives; *Holabird Herald*, January 6, 1945 (Box 3), Holabird Records, RG 111, National Archives and Records Administration, Mid-Atlantic.

5. In comprehending the social setting of the academic discipline of philosophy I have been helped by Jerry Gershenhorn, *Melville J. Herskovits and the Racial Politics of*

Knowledge (Lincoln: University of Nebraska Press, 2004); and Andrew Valls, ed., *Race and Racism in Modern Philosophy* (Ithaca, N.Y.: Cornell University Press, 2005).

6. Some African American philosophers of the twenty-first century have taken up the issues of identity that intrigued Fontaine and have explicitly considered the "whiteness" of professional philosophy in the United States. But with few exceptions these thinkers have lost sight of Fontaine himself. For the issues, see George Yancy, ed., *African American Philosophers: 17 Conversations* (New York: Routledge, 1998); and for the most recent discussion, Tommie Shelby, *We Who are Dark: The Philosophical Foundations of Black Solidarity* (Cambridge, Mass.: Harvard University Press, 2005), 11–21 and the notes thereto. The exceptions include Leonard Harris, ed., *Philosophy Born of Struggle: Anthology of Afro-American Philosophy from 1917* (Dubuque, Iowa: Kendall/Hunt Publishing Company, 1983); Joyce Mitchell Cook in Yancy, ed., *African American Philosophers*, 283; and the writings of James Spady for the *Philadelphia New Observer*.

7. Fontaine to Bond, n.d. [ca. spring 1950], Fontaine File, Bond Papers, Lincoln University Archives. The remark is made about white patrons of blacks.

8. Typescript memoir, Elizabeth Flower, Philosophy Department records, Archives of the University of Pennsylvania (hereafter UPA). On King in Chester, see David Levering Lewis, *King: A Biography* (Urbana: University of Illinois Press, 1978), 27–28.

9. Fontaine, Alumni File, UPA.

10. A. J. Ayer, *Language, Truth, and Logic* (London: Gollancz, 1936).

11. C. L. Stevenson, *Ethics and Language* (New Haven, Conn.: Yale University Press, 1944).

12. I have taken up these issues in relation to Stevenson in "Philosophy at Yale in the Century after Darwin," *History of Philosophy Quarterly* 21 (2004): 324–25.

13. Fontaine, "The Paradox of Counterfactual Terminating Judgments," *Journal of Philosophy* 76 (1949): 416–20; "Avoidability and Contrary-to-Fact Conditional in C. I. Lewis and C. L. Stevenson," *Journal of Philosophy* 48 (1951): 783–88. There is another unpublished essay from 1952, "Functionalism in the Social Sciences."

14. Fontaine, "Avoidability," 783.

15. Morton White email, September 21, 2004; *Addresses and Proceedings of the APA, 1949–50*, 23 (September 1950): 88.

16. *Addresses and Proceedings of the APA, 1949–50*, 88–89.

17. Interviews with Evelyn Fontaine Prattis (Fontaine's sister) and Kathleen Prattis (his niece) on October 23 and 24, 2003, and October 19, 2004.

18. Fontaine to Bond, n.d. [ca. spring 1950], Fontaine File, Bond Papers, Lincoln University Archives.

19. For a sense of how the disease changed lives, see Barbara Bates, *Bargaining for Life: A Social History of Tuberculosis, 1876–1954* (Philadelphia: University of Pennsylvania Press, 1992), which focuses on Philadelphia in a slightly earlier period; and Marion M. Torchia, "Tuberculosis Among American Negroes: Medical Research on a Racial Disease, 1830–1950," *Journal of the History of Medicine and Allied Sciences* 32 (1977): 252–79, which reaches the period in which Fontaine was sick. My thanks go to Janet Tighe, formerly of

the Health Science Program of the University of Pennsylvania, for discussion of the information on the 1940s and 1950s I obtained regarding Fontaine's TB. I have not been able to identify the doctor (Cherkov).

20. My information on Sea View comes from www:preservenys.org/seven/farmcolony.htm and similar websites about it as a historic but now forgotten set of New York buildings.

21. Interviews with Pamela Harris (Fontaine's granddaughter) and Belle Fontaine on August 7, 8, and 14, 2007.

22. Fontaine to Morrow, December 2, 1949, File 17, Fontaine, Box 74, Provosts Files, UPA.

23. Theodos to To Whom it May Concern, October 31, 1967, Harris documents, Fontaine Alumni File, UPA.

24. Sabbatical Application for 1961–62, ca. January 1961, Appointment, Harris documents, Fontaine Alumni File, UPA.

25. Interview with David Platt on September 15, 2003. Platt was a student of Fontaine's in the late 1940s and early 1950s and visited him in the hospital; Harris and Fontaine interviews.

26. Hetherington to Theodos, January 25, 1956, File 17, Fontaine, Box 74, Provosts Files, UPA.

27. Fontaine, *Reflections on Segregation, Desegregation, Power and Morals* (Springfield, Ill.: Charles C. Thomas Publisher, 1967), 50.

28. Fontaine to Daly, March 21, 1956, in File 17, Fontaine, Box 74, Provosts Files, UPA.

29. See the many letters in File 17, Fontaine, Box 74, Provosts Files, UPA.

30. File: Personnel Panel, Box 44, College Dean's Records, UPA.

31. The bibliography at the end of this book is the best indicator of his scholarly productivity. I take up the issue of his reputation in Chapters 8 and 9.

CHAPTER 7

1. This is according to Evelyn Fontaine Prattis, Fontaine's younger sister who attended his courses. Interviews with Evelyn Fontaine Prattis and Kathleen Prattis (Fontaine's niece) on October 23 and 24, 2003, October 19, 2004, and July 24, 2007.

2. See Guide to Courses, 1962–63, Folder: Daily Pennsylvanian, Box 58, College Dean's Records, Archives of the University of Pennsylvania (hereafter UPA).

3. Interview with Robert Schwartz on September 15, 2004. Schwartz was a student of Fontaine's in the late 1950s. Many former students joined Schwartz in recalling Fontaine's personal style.

4. Interviews with Pamela Harris (Fontaine's granddaughter) and Belle Fontaine on August 7, 8, and 14, 2007.

5. Student notebooks, 1960 and 1962, in author's possession.

6. College of Arts and Sciences, *Catalogues*, 1950–67, UPA.

7. Student notebooks , 1960 and 1962, in author's possession; Schwartz interview, Russell Goodman email, September 21, 2004.

8. Interview with Russell Goodman on September 23, 2004; other students remembered the same kind of question.

9. Alan Hart email, September 30, 2004; David Goldblatt email, October 15, 2004.

10. Harris and Fontaine interviews.

11. Jay Hullett email, September 28, 2004.

12. Goldblatt email.

13. Harris and Fontaine interviews.

14. Fontaine, *Reflections on Segregation, Desegregation, Power and Morals* (Springfield, Ill.: Charles C. Thomas Publishing Co., 1967), 44.

15. Wayne J. Urban, *Black Scholar: Horace Mann Bond 1904–1972* (Athens: University of Georgia Press, 1992) has inspired this interpretative remark. See especially 1–13, 206–9.

16. E. Franklin Frazier exaggerated and mocked these aspects of elite African American life in this period in his *Black Bourgeoisie* (Glencoe, Ill.: The Free Press, 1957).

17. I have compiled this record from various documents in the UPA: 6013 Race St. and nearby 6029 Spring St. in the 1930s; 2412 N. 15th St. in 1943; and nearby 2437 N. 17th St. as a newly hired faculty member; 5832 Spruce St. in the 1950s; and to Hopkinson House in Washington Square and later 1919 Chestnut St., both in Center City.

18. Fontaine, *Reflections*, 124–25.

19. Prattis interviews. For a sketch of Washington, whose politics seem to be more complex than Fontaine allowed, see Matthew Countryman, *Up South: Civil Rights and Black Power in Philadelphia* (Philadelphia: University of Pennsylvania Press, 2006), 195–98. For Washington's recollections of his ministry during the time Fontaine attended the church, see Washington, with David McI. Gracie, *"Other Sheep I Have": The Autobiography of Paul M. Washington* (Philadelphia: Temple University Press, 1994), 25–69.

20. Fontaine, *Reflections*, 127.

21. James Ross email, April 15, 2004.

22. Interview with Julia Williams on February 18, 2007. The interpretation is mine.

23. Harris and Fontaine interviews.

24. Interviews with Leonard Harris on November 8, 2006; John Wideman on November 30, 2006; and Robert Williams on February 18, 2007—each unconnected with the others.

25. Leonard Harris interview.

26. See the *Bulletin* of the University of Pennsylvania, March 9, 1952, UPA.

27. See, for example, *The Daily Pennsylvanian* for May 11, 1961, where Fontaine comments on the "botched" Bay of Pigs invasion.

28. See Manfred Berg, "Black Civil Rights and Liberal Anticommunism: The NAACP in the Early Cold War," *Journal of American History* 94 (2007). This article has an especially good summary of the black politics of the period of the late 1930s and early 1940s on pp. 77–84.

29. This is a simplified exposition of the reasoning found in Fontaine, "The Means End Relation and Its Significance for Cross-Cultural Ethical Agreement," *Philosophy of Science* 25 (1958): 160–61.

30. Samuel Gluck, "Report on the 5th InterAmerican Congress of Philosophy," *Journal of Philosophy* 54 (1957): 630. Fontaine's paper was published as "Segregation and Desegregation in the United States: A Philosophical Analysis," *Présence Africaine* 8–10 (1956): 154–73.

31. Fontaine, "The Means End Relation," 161, 162. See also Fontaine's review of Don Shoemaker, ed., *With All Deliberate Speed,* in *Harvard Educational Review* 28 (1958): 253–55, especially the last paragraph.

32. Student notebooks, 1960 and 1962, in author's possession.

33. I have rearranged Clarke's syntax in Clarke to Daley, December 3, 1957, File 17, Fontaine, Box 74, Provosts Files, UPA.

34. Fontaine to Davis, October 4, 1957, Folder 15, Box 1, AMSAC [American Society of African Culture] Papers, Moorland-Spingarn Research Institute, Howard University.

35. White to Clarke, November 14, 1957, Fontaine Alumni File, Harris Collection, UPA. I have compared material in this collection to that in File 17, Fontaine, Box 74, Provosts Files, UPA.

36. Alexander to Flower, November 5, 1957, File 17, Fontaine, Box 74, Provosts Files, UPA.

37. See the letters of February 19–21 from Vice Provost Bradley to others; and Bradley to Schrode, March 3, 1958, File 17, Fontaine, Box 74, Provosts Files, UPA.

38. Minute, February 20, 1958, File 17, Fontaine, Box 74, Provosts Files, UPA.

39. "Toward a Philosophy of the American Negro Literature," *Présence Africaine* 24–25 (1959): 165.

CHAPTER 8

1. See the insightful work of Thomas Borstelmann, *The Cold War and the Color Line: American Race Relations in the Global Arena* (Cambridge, Mass.: Harvard University Press, 2001); and Brenda Gayle Plummer, *Rising Wind: Black Americans and U.S. Foreign Affairs* (Chapel Hill: University of North Carolina Press, 1996). On the Soviet-American face-off in the third world, see Odd Arne Westad, *The Global Cold War* (New York: Cambridge University Press, 2005).

2. *Lincolnian*, April 7, 1953, Lincoln University Archives.

3. For a discussion of the complex politics of the conference and the people in attendance, see Richard H. King, *Race, Culture, and the Intellectuals, 1940–1970* (Washington, D.C.: Woodrow Wilson Center Press, 2004), 208–15, 246–50; and Plummer, *Rising Wind*, 253–54.

4. For background, see Gary Wilder, *The French Imperial Nation State: Negritude and Colonial Humanism Between the Two World Wars* (Chicago: University of Chicago Press, 2005).

5. Davis to Clarke, October 22, 1957, File 17, Fontaine, Box 74, Provosts Files, Archives of the University of Pennsylvania (hereafter UPA).

6. See Fontaine to Bond, September 20, 1956; and Bond's account of the congress, Folder 111, Box 35, Horace Mann Bond Papers, University of Massachusetts, Amherst (Reel 15 of the microfilm edition).

7. Conversation with Leonard Harris, November 8, 2006.

8. For background, see James H. Meriwether, *Proudly We Can Be Africans: Black Americans and Africa, 1953–1961* (Chapel Hill: University of North Carolina Press, 2002); and Penny M. Von Eschen, *Race Against Empire: Black Americans and Anticolonialism, 1937–1957* (Ithaca, N.Y.: Cornell University Press, 1997), 174–76. I have also relied on Folders 45–47, Box 87, of the Raymond Pace Alexander Papers, UPT 50 A374, UPA, for some of my knowledge of AMSAC. Alexander was an official representative of the group in Philadelphia. This collection is more substantial for my purposes than the AMSAC papers at the Schomberg Center for Research in Black Culture at the New York Public Library. The richest collection is that at the Moorland-Spingarn Research Center at Howard University, which I have cited as AMSAC-H. I have also used material from the Horace Mann Bond Papers at the University of Massachusetts, Amherst (hereafter AMSAC-Bond), which have a substantial amount of correspondence pertaining to the organization because of Bond's prominence in it. For the microfilm edition that I have accessed, the shelf list has been published: John H. Bracey, Jr., ed., *The Horace Mann Bond Papers, Parts 1–4* (Bethesda, Md.: University Publications of America, 1989), see esp. 33–38.

9. For the history, see File 1 (History of CORAC), Box 20, AMSAC-H; and Reels 10 and 11 (Folders 78 and 79, Box 30), AMSAC-Bond.

10. Davis to Harriman, April 1, 1968, Reel 13 (Folder 91, Box 33), AMSAC-Bond.

11. See the insightful pamphlet by Hollis R. Lynch, *Black American Radicals and the Liberation of Africa: The Council on African Affairs 1937–1955* (Ithaca, N.Y.: Cornell University, Africana Studies and Research Center, 1978).

12. See, for example, the material in AMSAC-Bond, Reel 11 (1957 Meeting, Folder 79, Box 30).

13. For the CIA connection, see Reels 12 and 13 (Folder 90, Box 32; Folder 9, Box 33) AMSAC-Bond; Wayne J. Urban, *Black Scholar: Horace Mann Bond, 1904–1972* (Athens: University of Georgia Press, 1992), 159–63; and Frances Stonor Saunders, *Who Paid the Piper? The CIA and the Cultural Cold War* (London: Granta, 1999). On the ideological struggles of AMSAC, in which Fontaine became too ill to participate, see Harold Cruse, *The Crisis of the Negro Intellectual* (New York: William Morrow, 1967), 499–512.

14. Fontaine to Diop, n.d. [ca. February, 1957], File 15, Box 1, AMSAC-H; and Diop to Davis, April 19, 1957, Reel 15 (Folder 111, Box 35), AMSAC-Bond.

15. "The Origin and Nature of the American Society of African Culture," n.d. [ca. September, 1957], in Fontaine to Redding, September 13, 1957 [mistakenly dated 1947], Folder 13, Box 1, Saunders Redding Papers, 98.1, Brown University.

16. See *Présence Africaine* 24–25 (1959).

17. See Files 2–4, Box 36, AMSAC-H. He was a chief panelist thereafter at a Howard University conference in 1963 and at another in Atlanta in 1965.

18. Azikiwe to Farber, October 11, 1963, Correspondence, Fontaine, Marvin Farber Papers, University of Buffalo.

19. Interviews with Evelyn Fontaine Prattis (Fontaine's sister) and Kathleen Prattis (his niece) on October 23 and 24, 2003, October 19, 2004, and July 24, 2007. And see David Levering Lewis, *W. E. B. Du Bois: The Fight for Equality and the American Century 1919–1963* (New York: Henry Holt and Company, 2000), 566.

20. See *Pan-Africanism Reconsidered*, ed. American Society of African Culture (Berkeley: University of California Press, 1962), v–vii; and Fontaine's essay therein, "Philosophical Aspects of Contemporary African Social Thought," 244–54. There are two other essays from this period. "The Negro Continuum from Dominant Wish to Collective Act," *African Forum* 3, no. 4; 4, no. 1 (spring/summer 1968): 63–75, appeared after Fontaine's death but also as the first chapter of Fontaine's book, *Reflections on Segregation, Desegregation, Power and Morals* (Springfield, Ill.: Charles C. Thomas Publishing Co., 1967), which had been published almost a year before. Portions of "Toward a Philosophy of the American Negro Literature," *Présence Africaine* 24–25 (1959): 164–76, appeared in *Reflections* too, but there was also a French version, "Vers Une Philosophie de la Littérature Noire Américaine," in the French edition of *Présence Africaine* 24–25 (1959): 153–65. The latter pieces borrow from Fontaine's early essay, "The Mind and Thought of the Negro of the United States as Revealed in Imaginative Literature, 1876–1940," *Southern University Bulletin* 28 (March 1942): 5–50.

21. Prattis interviews. See also Kevin K. Gaines, *American Africans in Ghana: Expatriates and the Civil Rights Era* (Chapel Hill: University of North Carolina Press, 2006).

22. Fontaine to Davis, October 23, 1957; Fontaine to Davis, October 14, 1959; Fontaine to Davis, March 3, 1961, File 15, Box 1, AMSAC-H.

23. See Beardsley to Farber, April 28, 1963, Fontaine Alumni File, Harris documents, UPA. I have compared the material in this collection to that in File 17, Fontaine, Box 74, Provosts Files, UPA.

24. See Morrow to Springer, April 26, 1963, Correspondence, Morrow Papers; and File 17, Fontaine, Box 74, Provosts Files, UPA.

25. See the folders Africa I, 1960–1965, and Africa, 1960–1965 in Box 50, Presidents Papers, UPA; *Daily Pennsylvanian,* November 21, 1960.

26. *Daily Pennsylvanian,* February 22, February 28, 1961; Fontaine to Davis, January 16, 1961, File 15, Box 1, AMSAC-H.

27. Fontaine to Eiseley, September 1, 1960, Africa 1960–1965, Box 50, Presidents Papers, UPA.

CHAPTER 9

1. Discrimination Folders, Box 127, Presidents Papers, Archives of the University of Pennsylvania (hereafter UPA). For the city of Philadelphia in this period, see Matthew

Countryman, *Up South: Civil Rights and Black Power in Philadelphia* (Philadelphia: University of Pennsylvania Press, 2006).

2. For example, Fontaine to Farber, July 25, 1966, Fontaine File, Farber Papers, University of Buffalo (hereafter UB).

3. University of Pennsylvania Freshman Directory Class of 1963 (1959), UPA.

4. John Edgar Wideman, "Imagining," *Pennsylvania Gazette* 84 (June 1986): 20–21. Wideman came to tell this story because he later learned that Fontaine had been associated with the *Présence Africaine* group, and thus, for Wideman, was an intellectual of world-class status (21).

5. Interview with John Wideman on November 30, 2006.

6. Folder: Minutes of Meeting, Fontaine Papers, UPA.

7. On this pertinent issue I am indebted to the ideas of Marybeth Gasman, "What Can Penn Learn from our Nation's Historically Black Colleges and Universities?" *Almanac* (University of Pennsylvania), November 8, 2005, 8. Wayne Glasker, *Black Students in the Ivory Tower: African American Student Activism at the University of Pennsylvania, 1967–1990* (Amherst: University of Massachusetts Press, 2002) takes up the issue in the period just after Fontaine was active.

8. See www.aaregistry.com/african_american_history/1533/William_Fontaine.

9. Morrow to Springer, April 26, 1963, Recommendations, Morrow Papers; Fontaine curriculum vitae, File 17, Fontaine, Box 74, Provosts Files, UPA; Curriculum vitae, 1956, in Fontaine, Philosophy Department Records, UPA.

10. Sabbatical Application, ca. January 1961, Appointment, Harris documents, Fontaine Alumni File, UPA.

11. Morrow to Dushkin, February 3, 1964, Correspondence, Morrow Papers, UPA.

12. From an essay by JAF in the *Pennsylvania Gazette* 66 (March 1968), in Fontaine, Alumni File, UPA.

13. Azikiwe to Farber, October 11, 1963, Fontaine File, Marvin Farber Papers, UB.

14. Announcement, December 17, 1967, Fontaine File, Marvin Farber Papers, UB.

15. Interview with Peter Hare on February 14, 2006.

16. Fontaine pays tribute to Farber in *Reflections on Segregation, Desegregation, Power and Morals* (Springfield, Ill.: Charles C. Thomas Publishing Co., 1967), v. Fontaine, "Josiah Royce and the American Race Problem," *Philosophy and Phenomenological Research* 29 (1968): 282–88.

17. Fontaine, *Reflections*, 50, 56–57, 114–15. "Anglo-Teutonic" is quoted from JAF, *Pennsylvania Gazette* 66 (March 1968), in Fontaine, Alumni File, UPA.

18. JAF, *Pennsylvania Gazette* 66 (March 1968), in Fontaine, Alumni File, UPA.

19. Fontaine, *Reflections*, vii–viii.

20. Ibid., 119.

21. Ibid., 11–13, 116–17.

22. Ibid., 117ff.

23. *Reflections* expressed these sorts of sentiments about King on pp. 39, 63, 110, 126; interviews with Evelyn Fontaine Prattis (Fontaine's sister) and Kathleen Prattis (his niece)

on October 23 and 24, 2003, October 19, 2004, and July 24, 2007; and with Pamela Harris (his granddaughter) and Belle Fontaine (his wife) on August 7, 8, and 14, 2007. The Gray and the King families were friendly, and Martin Luther King was often in Philadelphia. In addition, he had spoken at Gray's Bright Hope Baptist Church.

24. In various curriculum vitae, UPA.

25. Morrow to Dushkin, February 3, 1964, Correspondence, Morrow Papers, UPA.

26. Fontaine to Redding, n.d. [ca. 1964], Folder 138, Box 1, Saunders Redding Papers, 98.1, Brown University.

27. Fontaine Correspondence, Farber Papers, UB.

28. Fontaine, *Reflections*, 50.

29. "'Reflections on Segregation, Desegregation, Power and Morals,' a Statement by Rep. Robert N. C. Nix," *Congressional Record*, vol. 114, part 6, 90th Congress, 2nd Session (Washington, D.C: Government Printing Office, 1968), 8008–9.

30. I have located two: one by John Gillespie in *The Philadelphia Bulletin*, the city's evening newspaper, for February 4, 1968; and the typescript of another by W. Edward Farrison of North Carolina College at Durham, in File: Review, Fontaine Papers, UPA. I have also found one *mention* of the book, which does not turn up in JSTOR: Leonard Harris, "Philosophy in Black and White," *Proceedings and Addresses of the American Philosophical Association* 51 (1978): 415–24.

31. Tommy L. Lott and John R. Pittman, eds., *A Companion to African-American Philosophy* (Malden, Mass.: Blackwell Publishing, 2003).

32. James Ross email, April 15, 2004. Ross was a young philosophical colleague of Fontaine's in the 1960s.

33. Fontaine, *Reflections*, 14.

34. Philosophy, 1958–59, Box 49; Philosophy, 1960–66, Box 55, College Dean's Records, UPA.

35. All of this material is in Correspondence, Fontaine, Farber Papers, UB.

36. Willa Belle Bullock (Fontaine's wife had remarried) to Dallet, July 18 [n.d. ca. 1980], Fontaine, Alumni File, UPA. The scraps themselves are in the Fontaine Papers, also in UPA.

37. Fontaine, *Reflections*, 5.

38. See www.aaregistry.com/african_american_history/1533/William_Fontaine.

39. On Johnson, see Patrick J. Gilpin and Marybeth Gasman, *Charles S. Johnson: Leadership Beyond the Veil in the Age of Jim Crow* (Albany: State University of New York Press, 2003). On Bond, see Wayne J. Urban, *Black Scholar: Horace Mann Bond, 1904–1972* (Athens: University of Georgia Press, 1992), esp. 72–73, where the quote is from.

40. See my discussion in Chapter 5 and the work by James B. McKee, *Sociology and the Race Problem: The Failure of a Perspective* (Urbana: University of Illinois Press, 1993); and Jerry Gershenhorn, *Melville J. Herskovits and the Racial Politics of Knowledge* (Lincoln: University of Nebraska Press, 2004). Also consult Francille Rusan Wilson, *The Segregated Scholars: Black Social Scientists and the Creation of Black Labor Studies, 1890–1950* (Charlottesville: University of Virginia Press, 2006).

41. In the early twenty-first century philosophy still has a self-definition that barely includes the sort of questions of interest to Fontaine, but this fact does not explain why contemporary philosophers with such interests are unaware of him. See Young and Pittman, eds., *A Companion to African-American Philosophy*, and Joseph Young and Jana Evans Braziel, eds., *Race and the Foundations of Knowledge* (Urbana: University of Illinois Press, 2006).

42. Franklin's *Mirror to America: The Autobiography of John Hope Franklin* (New York: Farrar, Straus, and Giroux 2005) is itself a mesmerizing document and a useful primary source for studying the Negro intellectual.

43. The following examination takes issue with some themes in V. P. Franklin, *Black Self-Determination: A Cultural History of African-American Resistance*, 2nd ed. (Brooklyn: Lawrence Hill Books, 1992); Kevin Gaines, *Uplifting the Race: Black Leadership, Politics, and Culture in the Twentieth Century* (Chapel Hill: University of North Carolina Press, 1996); and Daryl Michael Scott, *Contempt and Pity: Social Policy and the Image of the Damaged Black Psyche, 1880–1996* (Chapel Hill: University of North Carolina Press, 1997).

44. Adolph L. Reed, Jr., *W. E. B. Dubois and American Political Thought: Fabianism and the Color Line* (New York: Oxford University Press, 1997) contains an excellent survey of the interpretation of double consciousness and its importance to Du Bois on 91–125. Most sensible on the basic issues is Mia Bay, *The White Image in the Black Mind: African-American Ideas about White People, 1830–1925* (New York: Oxford University Press, 2000), 187–229.

45. Du Bois, *The Souls of Black Folk* (New York: Simon and Schuster, 1903, 2005), 6–9.

46. Ibid., 7.

47. Fontaine, *Reflections*, 9–12, 4.

48. Ibid., 50.

49. Ross email, April 15, 2004; this recollection was independently confirmed in an interview with another colleague, Bernard Grunstra, on November 28, 2006.

50. Fontaine, "Social Determination in the Writings of American Negro Scholars," *American Journal of Sociology* 49 (1944): 304.

51. College Hall, Plans, 1917, 1956, Data and Documentation Office, Division of Facilities and Real Estate Service; Plans 1999, 2006, Office of Building Administrator, College Hall; Springer to Clarke, June 8, 1961, Philosophy, 1960–61, Box 55, College Dean's Records, UPA.

52. Ross email, April 15, 2004.

53. See Fontaine's letter to Penn's president about the institution's concern for the black West Philadelphia community: Fontaine to Harnwell, August 5, 1966, Philosophy 1966–1967, Box 77, College Dean's Records, UPA.

54. The picture was stolen at some point in 1967. In the late 1990s a restored plaque was moved to a less conspicuous place in College Hall. The plaque noted the establishment of a tiny scholarship in Wilson's name. See Wilson Alumni File, UPA; and William Mandel, "The Death of Pomp," *Pennsylvania Gazette* 69 (March 1971): 16–21.

55. Grunstra interview. Grunstra and his wife invited the Fontaines to their dinner parties.

56. See Guide to Courses, 1962–63, Folder: Daily Pennsylvanian, Box 58, College Dean's Records, UPA.

57. Interview with Murray Murphey on October 14, 2005; Grunstra interview. Some parts of the story can be followed in Philosophy 1960–61, Box 55, and Ad Hoc Committee, Chairman of the Dept. of Philosophy, Box 73, College Dean's Records; Dept. of Philosophy, 1960–65, Box 123, Presidents Papers; and Department Business, Harris documents, Fontaine Alumni File, UPA.

58. Jay Hullett email, September 28, 2004.

59. Harris documents, Fontaine Alumni File, UPA.

60. Fontaine to Davis, July 29, 1964, File 15, Box 1, AMSAC Papers, Moorland-Spingarn Research Center, Howard University.

61. Theodos to To Whom It May Concern, October 31, 1967, Appointment, Harris documents, Fontaine Alumni File, UPA.

62. Franklin, "The Dilemma of the American Negro Scholar," in Herbert Hill, ed., *Soon One Morning: New Writing by American Negroes, 1940–1962* (New York: Knopf, 1963), 60–76.

63. Ibid., 60–61.

64. From the essay by JAF in the *Pennsylvania Gazette* 66 (March 1968), in Fontaine Alumni File, UPA.

65. In Eric Erikson, *Childhood and Society,* 2nd ed. (New York: W. W. Norton, 1950, 1963), a popular analysis of social character, the author examines a type similar to Fontaine on 241–43; quote from Ross email, April 15, 2004.

66. Harris and Fontaine interviews.

67. Charles Kahn interview on November 29, 2006.

68. Funeral program in possession of Evelyn Fontaine Prattis.

69. Leonard Harris, conversation, November 8, 2006; Willa Belle Bullock to Dallet, July 18 [n.d., ca. 1980], Fontaine Alumni File, UPA.

70. Rolling Green's website, www.rollinggreenmemorial.com; park records for Fontaine, PGWH, 8, 16B, 1; telegram, Davis to Redding, Folder 42, Box 13, Redding Papers, 98.1, Brown University.

CONCLUSION

1. Alan Hart email, September 30, 2004.

2. Jay Hullett email, September 28, 2004.

3. Richard Schuldenfrei email, June 6, 2004.

4. *Graduate Studies Bulletin,* University of Pennsylvania, 1970–71, 1972–73, 1974–75; Minutes, September 30, 1969, Graduate Council Minutes, 1966–71, Graduate School, vol. 3, Archives of the University of Pennsylvania.

5. Fontaine, *Reflections on Segregation, Desegregation, Power and Morals* (Springfield, Ill.: Charles C. Thomas Publishers, 1967), 149.

BIBLIOGRAPHY OF THE WRITINGS OF WILLIAM FONTAINE

I have listed here all of the substantive professional writing that I believe Fontaine to have brought to some measure of completion. All the published work is discussed more fully in the biography; the unpublished work has not to my knowledge survived.

1939: *Fortune, matter and providence; a study of Ancius Severinus Boethius and Giordano Bruno.* Scotlandville, La., 50.

This is Fontaine's Ph.D. dissertation in philosophy from 1936. Pennsylvania's dissertations were regularly printed in limited paperback editions, but I do not know why this one was printed only at Southern University in 1939. The thesis contrasts the vision of Boethius to that of Bruno and argues that Bruno made Boethius's views consistent.

1939: "Philosophical Implications of the Biology of Dr. Ernest Just." *Journal of Negro History* 24: 281–90.

This essay interprets Just's speculations in biology in an attack on innate racial categories.

1940: "An Interpretation of Contemporary Negro Thought from the Standpoint of the Sociology of Knowledge." *Journal of Negro History* 25: 6–13.

This essay is a precursor to the article on "social determination" published in 1944.

1941: "Foreword." *Southern University Bulletin* 27 (March): v.

Fontaine introduces Southern's first research publication and claims objectivity for scholarly criticism.

1942: "The Mind and Thought of the Negro of the United States as Revealed in Imaginative Literature, 1876–1940." *Southern University Bulletin* 28 (March): 5–50.

A long, major, and significant essay that charts the dialectical evolution of African American thought and culture from Reconstruction to World War II.

1944: "Social Determination in the Writings of American Negro Scholars." *American Journal of Sociology* 49: 302–13.

Fontaine's most astute piece of writing turns the arguments of Marxist and pragmatist criticism against the environmentalism of African American sociology.

The piece has been reprinted in Leonard Harris, ed., *Philosophy Born of Struggle: Anthology of Afro-American Philosophy from 1917* (Dubuque, Iowa: Kendall/Hunt Publishing Company, 1983).

1948: "The Immediately Valuable in C. I. Lewis."

    From the title, this paper delivered to the Fullerton Philosophy Club at Bryn Mawr College would have discussed the complex of empirical and normative elements in Lewis's ethics.

1949: "The Paradox of Counterfactual Terminating Judgments." *Journal of Philosophy* 46: 416–20.

    The essay contrasts the view on counterfactuals of C. I. Lewis and Nelson Goodman.

1951: "Avoidability and the Contrary-to-Fact Conditional in C. I. Lewis and C. L. Stevenson." *Journal of Philosophy* 48: 783–88.

    The essay compares the two thinkers and argues that Stevenson has an unacknowledged debt to Lewis, whose views need to be argued for.

1952: "Functionalism in the Social Sciences."

    Fontaine delivered this lecture to the Fullerton Philosophy Club at Bryn Mawr College.

1953: "Bias in Social Science."

    This essay is listed in Fontaine's biography for the *Présence Africaine* Sorbonne Conference in 1956 as published in a volume entitled *Introduction to Social Science* (1953), but I have found no such title with an essay by him.

1956: "Of the Language and Paradoxes of Ruth Benedict's Patterns of Culture."

    This essay was submitted to the *Journal of Philosophy* in August 1956 but was never published. An educated guess tells me that it was a close relation to Fontaine's 1958 essay in *Philosophy of Science*.

1956: "Segregation and Desegregation in the United States: A Philosophical Analysis." *Présence Africaine* 8–10: 154–73.

    This is an earlier but longer version of the ideas in his 1958 article on means and ends in *Philosophy of Science*.

1958: "The Means End Relation and Its Significance for Cross-Cultural Ethical Agreement." *Philosophy of Science* 25: 157–62.

    This essay makes use of C. L. Stevenson's emotive theory of ethics to suggest how social disputes may be resolved.

1958: Review of Don Shoemaker, ed., *With All Deliberate Speed,* in *Harvard Educational Review* 28: 253–55.

    In this review of a book on the *Brown* v. *Board of Education* decision, Fontaine is moderate and modest in his assessment.

1959: "Toward a Philosophy of the American Negro Literature." *Présence Africaine* 24–25: 164–76. French version: "Vers Une Philosophie de la Littérature Noire Américaine" in the French edition of *Présence Africaine* 24–25: 153–65.

    This essay draws on some of the analyses Fontaine had made earlier in "The Mind and Thought of the Negro" (1942).

1960–61: *Readings in Philosophy of the Social Science.*

      Although this book was listed in a faculty activity report of 1960 and a sabbatical application of 1961 (for fall 1961) as a book being coedited by Fontaine and Sidney Axinn, then of Temple University, it was never published.

1961: *The Political and Social Thought of Contemporary African Leaders.*

      This collection of papers to be edited by Fontaine was accepted for publication by the University of Pennsylvania Press in 1961 but never delivered. The papers were presented at a series of lectures Fontaine moderated under the auspices of the American Society for African Culture in 1961.

1962: "Philosophical Aspects of Contemporary African Social Thought." In *Pan-Africanism Reconsidered*, ed. American Society of African Culture. Berkeley: University of California Press.

      This descriptive piece, I believe, derives from Fontaine's participation in the lecture series noted in 1961 above.

1963: "African Socialism."

      This chapter was promised but not delivered for John A. Davis and James K. Baker, eds., *Southern Africa in Transition* (New York: Praeger, 1966), for the American Society for African Culture. Fontaine gave a talk on this subject at the conference out of which the book came, but I believe he became too ill to produce a paper for publication.

1967: *Reflections on Segregation, Desegregation, Power and Morals.* Springfield, Ill.: Charles C. Thomas Publishing Co.

      This book contains material from earlier essays, but I find its conceptual heart to be its application of his modified ethical relativism to segregation, and this application occurs in the last chapter.

1968: "The Negro Continuum from Dominant Wish to Collective Act." *African Forum* 3, no. 4; 4, no. 1 (spring/summer): 63–75.

      This essay is an abbreviated form of chapter 1 of *Reflections* but has its basis in Fontaine's long article for the 1942 *Southern University Bulletin.*

1968: "Josiah Royce and the American Race Problem." *Philosophy and Phenomenological Research* 29: 282–88.

      This essay forms part of chapter 3 of *Reflections*, and the book appeared well before the essay.

SOURCES AND ACKNOWLEDGMENTS

A number of scholars have assisted my efforts in African American history, among them Robert Engs and Mary Berry. In what to him was an offhand remark, Clem Harris roused me to write the book. In 1978–79 Leonard Harris, now of Purdue University, began his own research on Fontaine. Harris interviewed many people now dead, and photocopied material in the Philosophy Department at the University of Pennsylvania that was later destroyed. Copies of this latter material are now in the Archives of the University of Pennsylvania in the Fontaine Alumni File, designated in my notes as the Harris documents. In a lengthy conversation on November 8, 2006, and subsequently, Harris shared with me his notes on his interviews, his recollections of his work on Fontaine, and his expertise. In addition to citing the now-archived material, I have also noted my irregular conversation with Harris, and I thank him very much for his assistance. In addition, I owe the greatest debt to my colleague Barbara Savage.

I asked many people to recall for me what they remembered about Fontaine. Most agreed—many eagerly and almost all with affection—to talk to me about him in interviews conducted in person, by phone, by email, or some combination thereof. Their names appear appropriately in the notes. I am especially grateful to members of the Fontaine family for their assistance in navigating the complexities of family history.

In my search to retrace Fontaine's steps, I spent time in a number of blind alleys. My Freedom of Information Act (FOIA) request to obtain any FBI files on Fontaine failed. I was also unable to find material on the man in the papers of Sidney Hook (Hoover Institution), Langston Hughes (Lincoln University), Thurgood Marshall (Library of Congress), Morgan State University, Ira De A. Reid (Haverford College), and Juanita Kidd Stout (Library of Congress). Attempted oral histories (interviews) that were unproductive included Robert Ackerman, James De Priest, William Gray III, Hilary Putnam, John Robison, Israel Scheffler, and James Spady.

The job of archivists and librarians is to find material for scholars, and I have usually spent little time in thanking them. But on this project they were invaluable in unearthing the resources: the Inter-Library Loan and Document Delivery staffs at the University of Pennsylvania; and archivists at the following colleges and universities: Buffalo, Fisk, Harvard, Howard, Lincoln, Morgan, Pennsylvania, and Southern. Special thanks go to Beth Howse at Fisk; Susan Pevar at Lincoln; Mark Lloyd and his staff at Pennsylvania, including first Amey Hutchins and then Nancy Miller; and Angela Proctor at Southern.

For reading drafts of the manuscript, I would like to thank Elizabeth Block, Paul Coates, Leonard Harris, Joel Isaac, Richard King, Leo Ribuffo, Barbara Savage, and, most of all, Kathy Peiss.

Last, but not least, I would like to thank the University of Pennsylvania and its one-time provost, Peter Conn, for the support of the institution, and the University of Pennsylvania Press for its commitment to the project.

While I have tried to mine every bit of information about Fontaine, I am convinced that there must be more, and I would welcome communication from anyone who has recollections or knowledge of written materials.

INDEX

Africa: and diplomacy, 107–9; Fontaine studies, 66, 109–15; and Garvey, 34, 108; and Harlem Renaissance, 34, 61; role of at Lincoln, 12–13, 20; at University of Pennsylvania, 113–15
African American culture, 18, 31–32, 61–62, 70, 112, 120
African American elite, 47, 98–100, 112, 119
African American history, 135; ignored in the white academy, 19; studied by Fontaine, 21, 28–35, 60–62, 122
African American Registry, 118
African Forum, 111
American Colonization Society, 12
American Council of Learned Societies, 64, 66
American creed, racism involved in, 3, 9, 28, 33, 35, 81, 129–30, 132
American Philosophical Association, 1–2, 75
American Society of African Culture, 111–12, 114
Analysis of Knowledge and Valuation, 27
analytic philosophy, 27, 77, 88
Army Reader, 73, 74
Ashmun Institute, 12
Association for the Study of Negro Life and History, 52
Atlanta University, 30, 52
"Avoidability and the Contrary-to-Fact Conditional," 89
Ayer, A. J., 1–2, 87
Azikiwe, Nnamdi, 16, 18, 19, 20, 109, 112, 113, 119

"Back to Africa," 34, 108
Baldwin, James, 109
Ballard, Mary Elizabeth, 6

Baton Rouge, 39, 41, 43, 44, 48
Beard, Charles, 97
Beauvoir, Simone de, 97
Benedict, Ruth, 97
Berlin, Isaiah, 97
Bethel Court, 5–6
Black Power, 118, 121
Black Skin, White Masks, 110
Boethius, 35–36
Bond, Horace Mann, 21, 109, 110; compared to Fontaine, 45, 126; in Louisiana, 43; writes to army, 75
Booker T. Washington School, 7
Boyer, Mary Elizabeth, 6–7
Brooke, Edward, 101
Brown v. Board of Education, 96, 102
Bruno, Giordano, 35–36
Bullock, Sam, 134
Bunche, Ralph, 65

Calverton, V. F., 16
Carter, Robert, 20, 112, 119
Catholics, 23, 80
Central Intelligence Agency, 111
Césaire, Aimé, 110, 112
Chester, 5–6, 8–12, 48–49, 86
Chester High School, 7–8
Chestnutt, Charles, 61
Chicago School (sociology), 65
Church of the Advocate, 99–100
civil rights, 28–29, 79–80, 96, 101–3, 116
Clark, Felton, 44–46, 48, 50, 52, 63, 84
Clark, Josiah, 44–45, 49
Clarke, Francis, 22–23, 35, 80, 85, 105
classical education, 12–14
Cohen, Morris, 97
Cold War, 79–80, 100–101, 107–9

College Hall, 85, 86, 117, 130

Communism, 20–21, 50–51, 79–80, 90, 107–9

Communist Party–USA, 51–52, 100, 108

Companion to African-American Philosophy, 123

conceptual pragmatism, 27

Conference on African Socialism, 112

Congress of Industrial Organizations, 71

Congress of Negro Writers and Intellectuals, 109–11, 112

"Conservation of Races," 30–31

Consolation of Philosophy, 36

"Construction of the Good," 55

Cook, Mercer, 109

counterfactual conditionals, 76–77, 89

Crisis, 30, 109

Critique of Pure Reason, 85

Crozier Theological Seminary, 86

Cullen, Countee, 33, 61

cultural pluralism, 53, 77

Cuney, Waring, 61

Daily Pennsylvanian, 102

Davis, Allison, 30, 65, 83

Davis, John, 109–11

Delaware County, 5–6

Dewey, John: Fontaine on, 55–58, 67; role in the history of philosophy, 23–24, 26, 84; and Stevenson, 87–89

Dickey, John Miller, 12, 14

Diop, Cheikh, 112–13

double consciousness, 31–33, 128–29, 131–33

Drake, St. Clair, 112

Du Bois, W. E. B., 43–44, 61, 68, 86; career of, 25, 26, 29–31; on double consciousness, 31–33, 128–29, 131–33

Dunbar, Paul Lawrence: Fontaine's study of, 8, 29, 60; poem at Fontaine's funeral, 133–34

Dunhan, Barrows, 101

Ebony, 82

Eisenhower administration, 101, 102

Ellison, Ralph, 34

emotivism. See *Ethics and Language*

ethics. *See* meta-ethics

Ethics and Language, 87–88, 104

Fact, Fiction, and Forecast, 76

Fanon, Frantz, 110, 112

Farber, Marvin, 119, 122, 131

Fascism, 20–21, 49, 51

Fauset, Jessie, 61

Fetchit, Stepin, 42

Fisk University, 13, 64–66

Fontaine, Belle, 91, 93, 95, 124–25; marriage of, 46–48, 54, 77, 78, 98–100, 133; remarries, 134

Fontaine, Cornelia Wilson Smith, 6–7

Fontaine, Herman, 11

Fontaine, William Charles, 6, 7, 12

Fontaine, William Thomas: administrative work of, 45, 77–78, 95, 131; African interests of, 66, 109–15; and American Philosophical Association, 1–2, 75, 90; and American Society for African Culture, 112–13; anti-Communism of, 100, 102, 109–11, 113, 117; attends conferences, 1–2, 52, 75, 90, 109, 112; and Azikiwe, 16, 18, 19, 20, 109, 112, 113, 119; book of, 119–30; and Carter, 20, 112, 119; and Clarke, 22–23, 35, 105; and Clarks, 44–46, 48, 49, 52; compared to Bond, 43, 45, 126; compared to Franklin, 126–27, 131–32; conservatism of, 118; on counterfactuals, 89; crucial essays of, 59–63, 68–70, 84–85, 120, 124; cultural interests of, 11, 17–18, 29, 54–55, 59, 66, 122–23; death of, 133; dissertation of, 35–36, 161; on double consciousness and Du Bois, 30–33, 128–29, 131–33; elusiveness of, xi–xii; and Farber, 119, 122, 131; and Frazier, 69–70, 126; funeral of, 133–34; and Goodman, 1–2, 75, 78, 80, 119, 131; growing up in Chester, 5–12, 48–49, 86; and Harlem Renaissance, 33–34; housing of, 6, 99; and Johnson, 64–65, 126; and King, 86, 116, 117, 121–22, 156 n.23; and Ku Klux Klan, 9–10; at Lincoln University, 12, 16–19; linguistic ability of, 8, 17, 20, 24, 36; and Locke, 33–34, 53–55; on lynching, 48; marriage of, 46–49, 54, 77, 78, 98–100, 133; modified ethical relativism of, 103–5, 110, 120–21; at Morgan State, 1, 77, 78, 81; and Morrow, 80–81, 91–92, 113–14, 122; and Nkrumah, 20, 70, 71, 72, 109, 113; office of, 130; pan-Africanism of, 109–13; political views of, 10–11, 51–52, 100–101, 108–9, 113, 116–17; pragmatism of, 31–33, 55–59, 67–68; promotion of, 113–14; and Redding, 45, 47; religious views of, 7, 47, 60–61, 99–100, 120, 121–22; role of in black and white commu-

nities, 98–100, 119, 132–33; role of in department of philosophy, 81, 95–97, 113–14, 123–24, 130–31; on role of war in social change, 10, 71–72, 103, 120; scholarly reputation of, 105–6, 113–14; on social identity, 33, 59–63, 69–70, 81, 120, 123, 126, 150 n.6, 158 n.41; society founded in honor of, 136; at Southern University, 37–40, 45–46, 63, 97; spends summer at Chicago, 52, 65; spends summer at Harvard, 25, 27–28; sponsors blacks at Penn, 117–18; and Stassen, 101; and Stevenson, 86, 88–90, 103–5; studies at Fisk, 65; studies at University of Pennsylvania, 22–23, 24–25, 35, 64, 66, 77; as a teacher, 15, 20–21, 45, 95–97, 113, 130, 135–36; teaches at University of Pennsylvania, 78–81, 86, 130; teaches illiterates, 72–75, 86; tenure of, 105–6; tributes to, 133, 135–36; tuberculosis of, 90–94, 105–6, 124–25, 131, 133; two competing interests of, 28, 36–37; and white philosophy, 84–86, 114–15, 126; and Wideman, 117–18, 156 n.4; works in shipyard, 71; during World War I, 9; during World War II, 70–75, 84; writes for *Présence Africaine*, 112, 162
Fontaine Society, 136
Fortune, matter, and providence, 35–36, 161
Franklin, John Hope, 126–27, 131–32
Frazier, E. Franklin, 30, 69–70, 126
free-floating intelligentsia, 68, 77–78
Fry, Ed, 11

Garvey, Marcus, 34, 108, 113
Goodman, Kay, 77, 119
Goodman, Nelson, 80, 85, 86, 87, 119, 124; and Fontaine, 1–2, 75, 78, 130–31; views of, 75–78
graduate training, 21–22
Granger, Stewart, 96
Gray, William, 86, 98, 119, 122

Haggard, H. Rider, 96
Hampton Institute, 13
Harlem Renaissance, 16, 33–34, 108; Fontaine on, 61, 110
Harris, Abram, 83
Harris, Pamela, 98, 100,
Harvard University, 22, 25–28
Hawkins, Jean and Vivian, 47, 98
Hawkins, Willa Belle. *See* Fontaine, Belle
Hegel, G. F., 23–24, 56–59, 84–85

Heraclitus, 92
"Historical Development of the Mind of the American Negro," 66–68, 84, 120
historically black colleges and universities, 12, 16, 21, 37–39, 82–83, 141 n.32, 149 n.2
Holabird Signal Depot, 72–75
Holmes, Eugene, 100
Hook, Sidney, 97
Howard University, 13, 38
Hughes, Langston, 14–15, 17, 33, 61, 62
Humphrey, Hubert, 80
Hunt, Herman, 11–12
Hunt, Nettie, 11–12, 49, 86
Husik, Isaac, 22, 35

"Ideology and Utopia," 58, 60, 144 n.11
illiteracy, 72–75
"Immediately Valuable in C.I. Lewis," 88, 162
instrumentalism, 26
Inter-American Congress on Philosophy, 104
Invisible Man, 34
Ivy, James, 109
Ivy Club, 130

James, William, xii, 23–24, 25–27, 30, 32, 53
Jews, 2, 22, 64, 75, 78, 80, 90
Johnson, Charles, 64–65, 126
Johnson, George, 19, 21
Johnson, James Weldon, 61
Johnson administration, 116
Journal of Philosophy, 76, 88–89
JSTOR, 123

Kallen, Horace, 53
Kant, Immanuel, 23–24, 85
Kennedy administration, 102, 107, 116
King, Martin Luther, 86, 116, 117, 121–22, 156 n.23
King Solomon's Mines, 96
Ku Klux Klan, 23–24, 42

Language, Truth, and Logic, 87
Lecturer of the Year, 130
Lewis, C. I., 27–28, 30, 36, 75–76, 86, 87–88
liberal internationalism, 102, 108–9, 113
Lincolnian. See *Lincoln News*
Lincoln News, 17
Lincoln University, 12–19, 20–21, 28–29, 33, 34–35, 39
Lippmann, Walter, 26
"Little Dog," 62

Locke, Alain, 16, 25, 33–34, 53–55, 59, 83, 86
logic, 26–27, 76, 86
logical positivism. *See* positivism
Longism, 42–43
Louisiana, 41–42, 49–52
"Lover of Mankind, " 17
lynching, 42–43, 48
Lyrics of Lowly Life, 29

Mannheim, Karl, 57–58, 60, 67–68, 77–78, 97
Marrow of Tradition, 61
Marshall, Thurgood, 17
Marx, Karl, 56–57, 97, 102, 109–10
Mbiti, John, 112
McCarthy, Joseph, 90, 100
McClure, John, 10–11
McKay, Claude, 33, 61
Mead, George Herbert, 23, 55–58
Mead, Margaret, 97
"Means End Relation," 104
Merton, Robert, 68
meta-ethics, 28, 87, 104; Du Bois's version of, 32–33; Fontaine's early view of, 55–58, 67–68, 88; Fontaine's mature views of, 88, 103–5, 110, 120–21
Mind and the World-Order, 27
"Mind and Thought of the Negro of the United States," 59–63, 84–85, 124
"Modern Nausica," 17
modified ethical relativism, 103–5, 110, 120–21
Morgan State University, 1, 77, 78, 81
Morrill Acts, 37, 43
Morrow, Glenn, 2, 80–81, 85, 91–92, 113–14, 122
Mphahlele, Ezekiel,112

Nagel, Ernst, 97
National Association for the Advancement of Colored People, 30, 42, 50
Native Son, 34, 62
Négritude Movement, 110, 114
Negro intellectual, 137 n.5, 139 n.10
New Deal, 24, 49, 50–51, 62, 71, 79
New Negro, 33–34, 54, 59, 66; Fontaine on, 61–62
New Orleans, 41–42, 43, 45
New School for Social Research, 83
Nix, Robert, 98, 119, 123
Nkrumah, Kwame, 20, 70, 71, 72, 109, 113

O'Daniel, Therman, 17
Organization for an Open and Progressive Society, 121

pan-Africanism, 108–11
"Paradox of Counterfactual Terminating Judgments," 89
Park, Robert, 64–65
Peirce, Charles, 23, 36
Phenomenology of the Spirit, 58, 64
Philadelphia Negro, 31
Phillips, Walter, 119
philosophy: as a discipline, 25–27, 36–37, 83–84, 87–88; Fontaine on, 120, 121, 124, 126; Fontaine studies, 22–24, 83; professionalism in, 25–27, 83–84, 85, 87–88, 124, 126; training in, 25–27, 83–84; at the University of Pennsylvania, 22–25, 35, 64, 66, 77–81, 85, 86, 93–94, 105–6, 113–15, 117, 119, 123, 130–31. *See also* white philosophy
Philosophy and Phenomenological Research, 119
Pinchback, Pinckney, 43
Plekhanov, Georgi, 97
Plessy v. Ferguson, 42
Popper, Karl, 97
positivism, 86–88
Powell, Colin, 101
pragmatic analysis, 77
pragmatism, 32–34, 55–58
Présence Africaine, 110–12
Price-Mars, Jean, 112
Princeton Theological Seminary, 12, 15
Princeton University, 12, 14, 15
Private Pete, 73–74
"Problem of Counterfactual Conditionals," 76
professionalism, in philosophy, 25–27, 83–84, 85, 87–88, 124, 126
"Prospects of a Scientific Politics," 57

Quakers, 5, 14, 80
Quest for Certainty, 55
Quine, Willard, 77, 78

race knowledge, 28–29, 35, 54
race relations, as a social science field, 64–66, 68–70, 126–27
Random House, 122
Redding, Saunders, 45, 47
Reflections on Segregation, Desegregation, Power and Morals, 119–26, 128, 132–33

Rice, Condoleeza, 101
Robeson, Paul, 112
Robinson, Jackie, 80, 101
Rolling Green Memorial Park, 134
Roman thought, 23, 35–36
Roosevelt, Eleanor and Franklin. *See* New Deal
Rosenwald Fund, 64, 66, 83, 84

St. Daniels Church, 7
Saunders, John, 119
Schwenksville, 77, 78
Scotlandville, 39, 44
Sea View Hospital, 91–92
Senghor, Leopold, 110, 112
Singer, Edgar, 23–25, 35, 80, 86
Siriaque, 96
Sivera, Edward, 61
"Social Determination in the Writings of American Negro Scholars," 68–70, 124
social identity, 33, 55, 59–63, 69–70, 81, 120, 123, 126, 150 n.6, 158 n.41
social science, 64–66, 68–70, 96–97, 126–27
sociality, 56
Society of African and Afro-American Students, 118
Society of African Culture, 110–11
sociology of knowledge, 57–59
Souls of Black Folk, 31–32, 66
Southern Negro Youth Conference, 51, 52
Southern University, 39, 43–46, 63, 97
Southern University Bulletin, 63, 66, 84, 122
Special Training Unit (U.S. Army), 72–75
Spengler, Oswald, 97
Stassen, Harold, 101
Stein, Gertrude, 26
Stevenson, C. L., 86–90, 103–5
Stout, Juanita, 119
Structure of Appearance, 76
"Study of Qualities," 76
Sun Shipbuilding, 70–72
Survey of Symbolic Logic, 27
symbolic logic. *See* logic
system of higher education, 21–22, 37–39, 82–83. *See also* historically black colleges and universities

talented tenth, 30, 32, 39
Toomer, Jean, 61

Touré, Sékou, 112, 113
Toynbee, Arnold, 97
Tribune, 119
Truman administration, 79–80, 96, 100, 102
tuberculosis, 90–94, 105–6, 124–25, 131, 133, 150 n.19
Tuskegee Institute, 13

Union of the Marine and Shipbuilding Workers, 71
University of Chicago, 23–24, 53, 83
University of Pennsylvania: administration of, 93–94, 105–6; African studies at, 66, 70, 112; appoints Fontaine, 1, 78, 79, 80–88; and Du Bois, 31, 85; history of, 22; Philosophy Department of, 22–25, 35, 64, 66, 77–81, 85–86, 93–94, 105–6, 113–15, 117, 119, 123, 130–31; racial awareness of, 85, 114–15, 116–17; school of medicine of, 90; tenure criteria of, 106; trains Fontaine, 21–25, 35, 64, 66, 70

Valerio, meaning of, 8, 91
Van Vechten, Carl, 16
Vietnam, 117

Wachman, Marvin, 119
Walcott, Joe, 92
Washington, Booker T., 13, 30
Washington, Paul, 100
Watts Grammar School, 7
West End, 6–7, 9, 11–12
Western civilization, 24–25, 32–33, 127
Western Marxism, 109
"We Wear the Mask," 133–34
White, Morton, 1–2, 78
white philosophy, 84–86, 114–15, 126
"Why We Fight," 74
Wideman, John, 117–18, 156 n.4
Wilkins, Roy, 42
Williams, Eric, 112
Wilson, Albert, 130
Woodson, Carter, 30, 65
World War I, 9
World War II, 49–51, 79; illiteracy in, 72–75; and Louisiana, 49–52; and race relations, 70–72
Wretched of the Earth, 110
Wright, Richard, 34, 62, 109
wuzzlehead, 69, 146 n.16